MEXICAN AMERICAN BASEBALL IN EL PASO

El Paso del Norte, The Way North

"El Chuco", a magical vortex, the heartbeat of three cultures, two nations, and one people. The influence of El Paso resonates upon American culture like a heartbeat across the landscape. From the wave of Mexican immigration during the Revolution, to "El Gancho," the trains that would swoop into town and take Mexican workers into the West, Southwest, and Midwest, to work in the fields, factories, and stockyards, El Paso was the ancestral starting point for generations of thousands of families to come to America and thrive, and build their country.

But at home, Mexicanos became Americanos, and forged a new identity from the advent of the railroads in the late 1880s, through race riots and conflicts in the early part of the 20th century, until today. The emergence of Mexican Americans in El Paso is paralleled by a legacy of playing baseball, creating a new narrative in the history of the Grand Ol' Game.

From Salvador Velásquez, the Willie Mays of Texas baseball, to Dudley Field, where *mariachis* in baseball uniforms would serenade the crowd before the game, they played baseball. From the old dusty streets and dirt lots of Segundo Barrio, to the lush field in Austin where the 1949 Bowie Bears overcame adversity to become Texas state champions, they played baseball.

El Paso's "*pachucho*" identity is now and forever seared within the memory of team cookouts at Ascarate Park and post-game meals at Chico's Tacos; with communities coming together in precious leisure time to eat, laugh, socialize, gossip, celebrate, and enjoy the game of baseball. They erased the border between the US and Mexico to play baseball, crossing it often to play against teams from Juarez, Chihuahua, and other areas; to play together on teams all over the region and Texas. They had more than language and culture in common, they played baseball.

In neighborhood pick-up games, semi-pro leagues, union teams, women's softball tournaments, in schools, churchyards and youth centers, in the Mexican leagues, in the minor leagues and eventually the Major Leagues, the Mexican Americanos of El Paso, "El Chuco," played baseball.

—Tomás Benítez is a writer from East LA with roots in Chihuahua, Mexico, and El Paso, Texas.

Front Cover: Six members of the El Paso Texans minor-league team play music at Dudley Field in 1951. Music was a huge part of El Paso culture in the early 1950s. "People sang as they worked, and many couldn't work unless there was a radio playing," local author Gloria López-Stafford wrote. (Courtesy El Paso Chihuahuas.)

Cover Background: This team of all-stars is from the Chihuahua State Baseball League, one of the top semipro leagues in Northern Mexico. The league was comprised of teams from Parral, Delicias, Ciudad Chihuahua, and Ciudad Juárez. The Juárez Indios won the league's pennant in 1944, the year this photograph was taken. (Courtesy Leopoldo Martínez family.)

Back Cover: This photograph of a team from Marfa, Texas, probably dates from the 1930s. The pile of cash sitting on top of the catcher's mitt likely represented the players' share of ticket sales from a big game. Semipro teams like this often drew huge crowds on holidays. (Courtesy Marfa Public Library.)

MEXICAN AMERICAN BASEBALL IN EL PASO

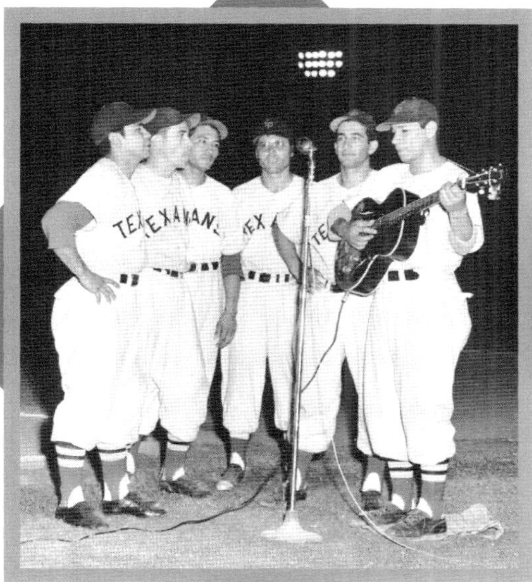

Richard A. Santillán, Eric Enders, Pete G. Flores, Donavan López, and Jorge Iber
Foreword by Ray Sánchez

ARCADIA PUBLISHING

ISBN 978-1-4671-2660-1

Published by Arcadia Publishing
Charleston, South Carolina

Printed in the United States of America

Library of Congress Control Number: 2017944957

For all general information, please contact Arcadia Publishing:
Telephone 843-853-2070
Fax 843-853-0044
E-mail sales@arcadiapublishing.com
For customer service and orders:
Toll-Free 1-888-313-2665

Visit us on the Internet at www.arcadiapublishing.com

El Paso is very close to my heart. My father, Carlos, and his family came through the city in 1931 from Tampico, Mexico, when he was nine years old, and eventually settled in East Los Angeles, where I was born. To all the California families originally from El Paso and Juárez who shared their wonderful baseball and softball photographs and remarkable stories. To my wife's extended families in El Paso: the Holguin, Beltran, Contreras, and Alva clans. Finally, I am spiritually beholden to my wife, Teresa, the heart and soul of my life and the merciful role model that I tirelessly strive to emulate each and every day.

—Richard

In memory of my father, Steve Enders, who taught me to love baseball and take pride in my Latino heritage, and for the immigrant ancestors on both sides of my family who labored in the cotton fields and the goldfields so I could be here today.

—Eric

To my wife, Martha, the love of my life for the past 65 years, and to my children Michael James, Kathryn Marie, Melinda Ann, Pete III, and Mary Elizabeth, who have made my life worthwhile. And to my friends on the Bowie High School 1949 championship team, you are gone but not forgotten. And for those who inspired me to write my novels *Guardians of the Gate*, *Harness the Mule*, and *On the Wings of an Angel*. Finally, to the Veterans Business Association and the Korean War Veterans Association Chapter No. 249 in El Paso, Texas.

—Pete

To my father, coach Pablo López, and to all the King Ranch players, fans, family members, and boosters. To my *tias* (aunts) Elsa Ruíz Gonzáles and Elda Ruíz Dawson, and to my mom, Enriqueta López. To my wife, Olivia Jaime, for her translation and patience with my research. To the wonderful institution of baseball: the more you contribute to the game, the more you receive from it. Last and most important, a great big shout to God for the many blessings he has bestowed on me throughout my life.

—Donavan

To my wonderful wife, Raquel, and our son Matthew. Thank you both for always being on my team.

—Jorge

CONTENTS

FOREWORD

Baseball was popular throughout the United States long before El Paso was established. The first recorded game in the nation, raw as it was, occurred in 1791. By the mid-1850s, there were games played throughout much of the country.

There is no documentation of the first baseball game ever played in El Paso, but it is almost certain that it came in the covered wagon era. *El Paso Herald-Post* sports editor Bob Ingram, who lived to the age of 93, once wrote: "There may have been many hostile Indians when wagon trains came to the western-most part of Texas in the mid to late 1800s, but when the wagon master shouted 'Circle your wagons' it's more likely he may have wanted to clear a space for a baseball game between the settlers and the pioneers."

People in El Paso and the immediate Southwest, including Mexican Americans, took to the game like fish to water. In fact, it became so popular that El Pasoans had a baseball field even before the city had a paved street.

One of the most prominent Mexican Americans in the early days of baseball in the El Paso region was Pete Leyva. Born in Presidio, Texas, in 1894, Leyva and his family moved to El Paso when he was a tyke. He was so good as a pitcher that he was the star of the El Paso professional team. Before that, he won what is perhaps the greatest semipro pitching duel ever held in El Paso—a 1-0 game over 16 innings with no relief at the old Rio Grande Park. That happened in 1919, after Leyva had returned to El Paso after serving in the Navy during World I.

Another prominent Mexican American figure in the early days of El Paso baseball was Leo Forti. He decided at an early age that he wanted to play baseball, but no team would take him on because he was so young. He went crying to his father, who suggested he form his own team. He took the advice to heart and not only formed a team but soon had a league of mostly Mexican American players that spanned from Arizona to Alpine, Texas.

I'm sure you're going to enjoy this book. Eric Enders, one of the coauthors, is a local baseball historian here in El Paso and has been a friend and fellow member with me on the El Paso Baseball Hall of Fame for many years. I can't think of a better group of people to record the history of Mexican American baseball in El Paso.

—Ray Sánchez
El Paso, Texas
December 2016

A local sportswriting legend, Ray Sánchez has been covering sports in El Paso since 1950, when he became the first Latino journalist hired by the *El Paso Herald-Post*. He has covered all aspects of El Paso baseball from Little League to pro ball. He was sports editor of the *Herald-Post* from 1981 to 1990 and is currently a columnist for El Paso Inc. He is the author of five books on sports history.

ACKNOWLEDGMENTS

This project to record the rich history of Mexican American baseball and softball in El Paso, Texas, is part of the remarkable work of the Latino Baseball History Project at California State University at San Bernardino (CSUSB). Supporters at CSUSB's John M. Pfau Library include Dean César Caballero and Sue Caballero, Jill Vassilakos-Long (head of archives and special collections), Iwona Contreras, Ericka Saucedo, Amina Romero, Carrie Lowe, Manny Veron, Brandy Montoya, Hayley Parke, John Baumann, and Stacy Magtedanz.

The authors are indebted to the players and families, including Frank Jacinto; Mary Alyce Riesgo Carrasco; Tony Ortega; Frankie Sandoval; Richie Campos; Alex Guzmán; Andrés, Andy, and Tony Nieto; Mark García; Tom Pérez Jr.; Nick Pérez; Teresa M. Santillán; Gene Chávez; Chris Docter; Juan Coronado; Patsy Hernández Castro; Ray Serra Jr.; Alicia Serra Stevens; Marcelino Saucedo; Charles and Ken Herrera; Fred Morales; Rubén Luna; Alexander Wolff; Al Barrios; Erin Curtis; John Echeveste; Al Padilla; Rose Marie Markus; Dianne Mejía-Sánchez; the Bowie baseball team of 1949; *Detroit News*; *Sports Illustrated*; Santa Monica Moose Lodge; St. Anne Catholic Church in Santa Monica; the Paul "Waxie" Hernández family; the David A. Vega Sr. family; the Baseball Reliquary; Whittier College; the Ethnic and Women's Studies Department at California State University at Pomona; La Plaza de Cultura y Artes; the Argentine American Legion Post 213; Mexican American Historical Society of the Midlands; the Southwest Chicago Project; the San Clemente Casa Romántica Cultural Center and Gardens; Las Señoras of Yesteryear; Alhambra Historical Society; the Peña family; King Ranch players, fans, members, and boosters; King Ranch Museum and Archives, archivist Lisa A. Neely and assistant archivist Jamene Toelkesfo; the Henrietta Memorial Center in Kingsville; South Texas Archives at James C. Jernigan Library of Texas A&M University–Kingsville; Brad Taylor, El Paso Chihuahuas; Bufe Morrison and Leo Caraveo, El Paso Baseball Hall of Fame; Shaylee Souza, Arizona State University Athletics; Nicole Glenn, J. Conrad Dunagan Library, University of Texas of the Permian Basin; Jim Paul, Hospice El Paso; Ester Sánchez, Marfa Public Library; Kathy Jennings-Brown, Midland Centennial Library; Robbin Barnes, Milwaukee Brewers; Michael Zagaris and Debbie Gallas, Oakland A's; Drew Bonney, University of El Paso Athletics; Larry Hernández, El Paso Bandits; Cecilia Aros Hunter; Prof. Leslie Gene Hunter; Prof. Harry R. Huebel; Robert Ayarzagoritia; Raúl De La Paz; Benny Sánchez; Lupita Borrego; Daniel Cuellar; Rolando Bazan; Rosie González Collin; Annela Solíz-Narayanan; Justin Hardmen; Cynthia Cervantez; Alonzo Chapa; Margarito Bañales Jr.; Mike Barrueta; Tom Carrillo; Gilbert De la Rosa; Dana Eisenga; Mark Enders; Rubén Félix; Jaime Frausto; Steve Kaplowitz; Raúl Real y Vásquez; Juan Rodríguez; Salvador Rodríguez Sr.; Ray Sáenz; Gabriel Saucedo; Don Wilson; Frank Palma; Isabel Ramírez; Michael D. Innis-Jiménez; and José F. García.

We wholeheartedly thank once again our in-house editor, Elisa Grajeda-Urmston, for her tremendous passion and tireless professional support, and give our never-ending approval and recognition to our technical consultant, Monse Segura. Finally, the Latino Baseball History Project and its lead author, Richard A. Santillán, extend our endless gratitude to Arcadia Publishing, Jim Kempert, and especially to our longtime editor and champion, and now compadre, Jeff Ruetsche, for his kindred spirit with the Mexican American baseball and softball communities of this country.

INTRODUCTION

The history of Mexican American baseball in El Paso is a long and storied one. But every story has a hero, and in this case, those heroes are the members of the 1949 Bowie High School team. The Bears came from the Segundo Barrio, a neighborhood poor in wealth but rich in character. They played their home games literally a stone's throw away from Mexico. Upon arriving in Austin for the state championship tournament, they were forced to sleep on Army cots in the basement of the Texas Longhorns' football stadium because no hotel was willing to house a team of Mexican American kids. Defiant in the face of bigotry, the plucky Bears captured the first state championship ever won by an El Paso high school.

The history of Mexican American baseball in El Paso teems with memorable personalities. Salvador Velásquez was a legendary prodigy who might have become the first Willie Mays if Major-League scouts had bothered to pay attention to Mexican American kids growing up on the border in the 1920s. Ray Sánchez became the *El Paso Herald-Post*'s first Latino journalist in 1950 and overcame prejudice to spend the next seven decades chronicling the exploits of the area's greatest ballplayers. Leo Forti started as a mediocre teenage player and grew into the visionary behind El Paso's greatest semipro teams. Teodoro Higuera's father prohibited him from playing baseball, but he nevertheless became a star with both the Juárez Indios and El Paso Diablos before reaching fame with the Milwaukee Brewers.

But more than anything, the story of Mexican American baseball in El Paso is the story of community: team cookouts at Ascarate Park; postgame meals at Chico's Tacos; *abuelas* making tamales for their grandkids to sell to raise money for baseball uniforms; Mexican American fans who created an atmosphere at Dudley Field so lively that the El Paso Diablos, for a time, became the most respected and imitated team in pro baseball. It is the story of a community that loves the game so much that it tore down its own city hall to build a baseball stadium. All these memories and more live on through the photographs in this book. We share them in the hopes that our readers will help make new memories in the years to come.

1

El Paso Community Baseball

The railroad arrived in El Paso in 1881, and organized community baseball arrived soon afterward. The El Paso Browns were founded in 1885 and were named after the color of their socks. They were organized by Juan S. Hart, publisher of the *El Paso Times*, who also played second base. Ironically, given their name, the Browns were an all-white team, but they played in what is now El Paso's Segundo Barrio. Their first makeshift ballpark was at the corner of Cotton and San Antonio Streets. "Baseball fever is all over town," the *El Paso Herald* declared.

In 1888, the Browns moved to the brand-new Sportsmen's Park. In 1908, a new park was built at Ninth Avenue and Florence Street. In 1919, the US military installed cannons at the ballpark site to fire into Mexico at Pancho Villa's troops, who were trying to recapture Juárez from the *federalistas*.

One of the early legends was Salvador Velásquez, a fleet-footed outfielder born in 1905 who played for decades. Many believed he would have been a Major-League star had he not lived so far away from all the scouts. Beto Méndez, another local legend, compared Velásquez to "Willie Mays, maybe better. He had all the potential."

For years, residents of the border region were labeled as either Mexican or American, as if it were impossible to be both. Around 1915, some El Pasoans began to think of themselves, for the first time, as Mexican American. That identity was forged through revolution and also through baseball. In 1916, a race riot broke out after Pancho Villa's troops massacred 18 Americans they captured in Mexico. In retaliation, El Paso's whites lashed out against their Mexican American neighbors, with a mob of 1,500 whites rampaging through the city and attacking every brown-skinned person they found. El Paso made headlines nationwide, and martial law was declared.

Five months later, racial tensions simmered again between Everybody's Team (which was all white) and the Walz Team, which a local newspaper described as "composed of Mexican players, though all were born in the United States and are American citizens." Racial slurs flew freely, and one fan pulled a gun on a Mexican American player during the game. Afterwards, a full-fledged brawl broke out, with rocks thrown at the Mexican players and the Anglo team's pitcher slashing the face of a Walz player with a broken bottle. The president of the league stopped the melee by pulling out a revolver and ordering everyone to go home.

The 1916 baseball riot was a tragedy, but it also marked the beginning of "Mexican American" as a distinct cultural identity among local ballplayers. In the century since then, Mexican Americans in El Paso have rooted fiercely for local high school teams like the 1949 Bowie Bears and 2009 Socorro Bulldogs, for semipro powerhouses like Forti's and the Fabens Merchants, and for youth teams that are part of the local fabric. Fortunately, many of these players were able to document their experiences in photographs. This chapter intends to tell their stories.

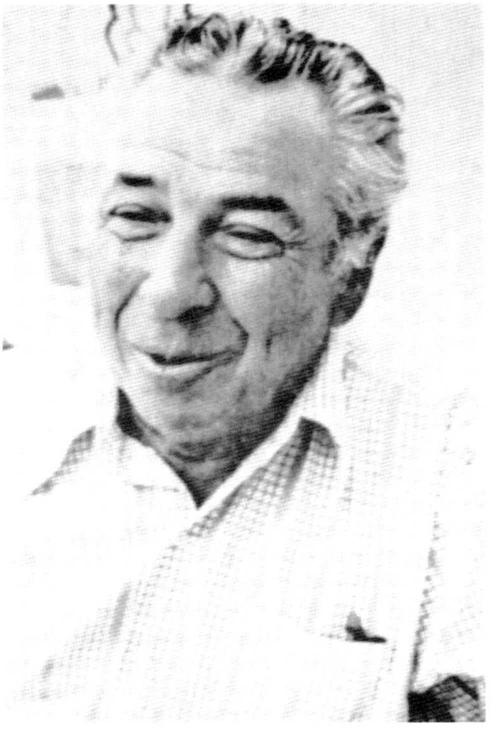

Lionel "Leo" Forti organized and managed Forti's, the legendary semipro team that dominated the baseball scene for decades. Venerable sportswriter Ray Sánchez called Forti "one of the most likeable, innovative, and unorthodox persons I ever met in my many years in sports." Forti recruited the region's best players, adopted innovative strategies on the field, and led his teams to 1,893 victories. He also sponsored local basketball teams, football teams, and boxers. Sánchez wrote, "He would play and run the teams and league himself. He and his teams found remarkable success in all of them, thanks to his determination and a brilliant mind." (Courtesy Bufe Morrison.)

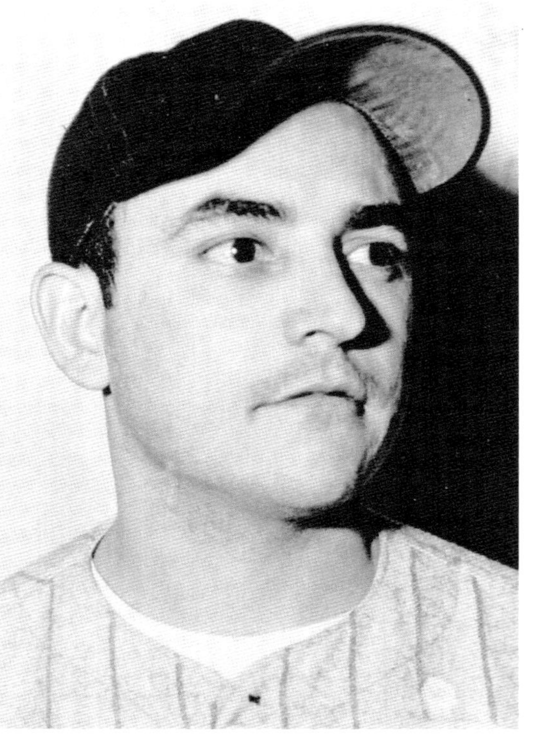

In 1946, shortstop Beto Portugal joined his older brother Pepe on the area's best semipro team, Forti's. Beto was part of the legendary Forti's infield of the 1940s and 1950s, a group including first baseman Manny Ayala, second baseman Kiki Meléndez, and third baseman Lolo Caldera. All four were elected to the El Paso Baseball Hall of Fame. A natural right-handed hitter, in 1948 he converted to batting left-handed and won the batting title in the El Paso City League the next year. He won eight local batting titles, three MVP awards, and five Gold Gloves. Beto Portugal was elected to the El Paso Baseball Hall of Fame in 1990. (Courtesy Bufe Morrison.)

Lolo Caldera was a legendary hitter in El Paso's semipro leagues for several decades. He started his career in 1937 but interrupted it to serve in World War II from 1942 to 1946. He played many years for Leo Forti's team, winning four MVP awards and two Gold Gloves at third base. Caldera played in several leagues, including the City League, International League, and Old Pro League, winning batting titles in each. He kept playing after undergoing heart surgery in 1980, remaining an active player in senior leagues into his 70s. Lolo Caldera was inducted into the El Paso Baseball Hall of Fame in 1993. (Courtesy Bufe Morrison.)

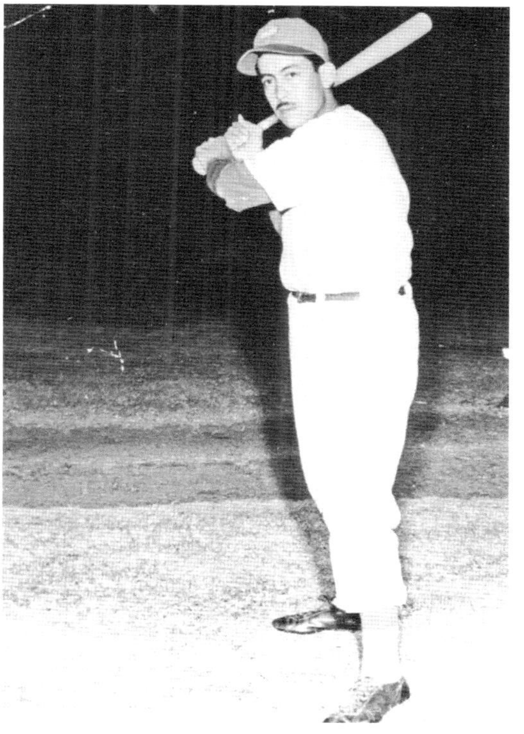

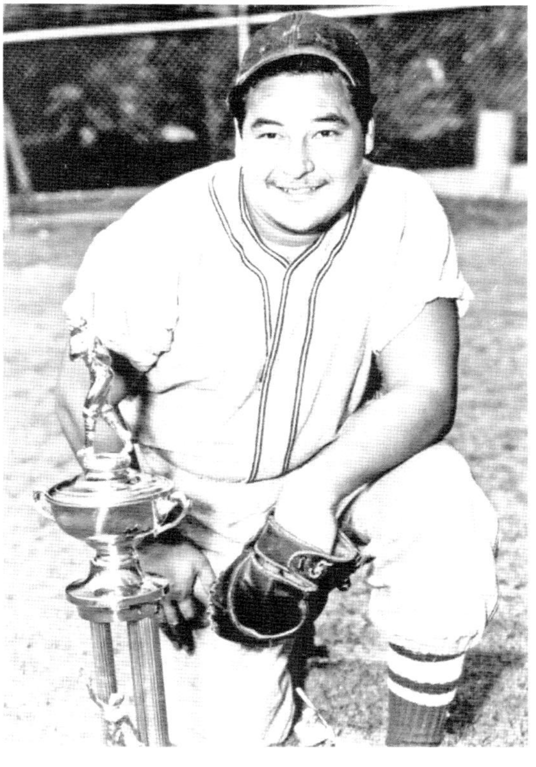

First baseman Manny Ayala was dubbed "the Babe Ruth of El Paso Sandlot Baseball" by *El Paso Herald-Post* writer Ray Sánchez. As a youngster in 1942, Ayala batted .391 for Bowie, an American Legion team from El Paso's Segundo Barrio that won the Texas state championship. Over 10 years in the 1940s and 1950s, Ayala batted .372 and won four batting titles, six home run titles, and three MVP awards in local semipro leagues. He was the semipro International League's career leader in home runs (133), runs (456), and hits (689). He also played pro ball briefly with the Juárez Indios. Ayala was elected to the El Paso Baseball Hall of Fame in 1990. (Courtesy Bufe Morrison.)

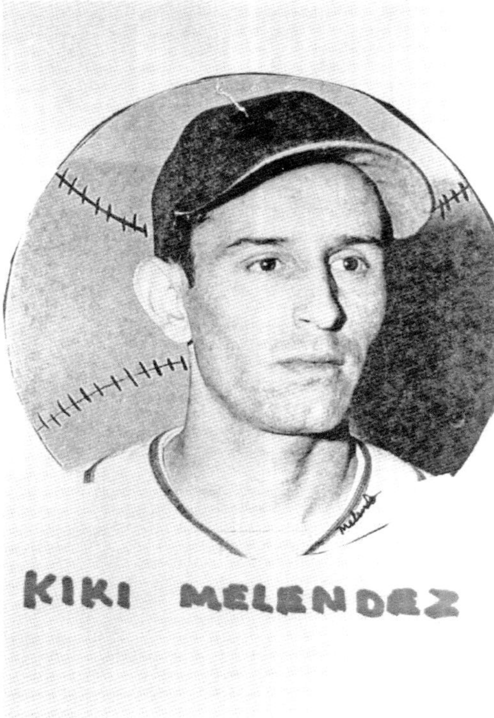

Enrique "Kiki" Meléndez was a mainstay of Borderland baseball throughout his 40-year career. Born in El Paso in 1928, he joined Forti's team in 1945 as a pitcher, second baseman, and third baseman. In 10 years with Forti's, legend holds that Meléndez won 90 percent of his games as a pitcher and hit .350. Over the following decades, he played in the Lower Valley, Upper Valley, City, Inter-State, and 40-60 Leagues and was named an all-star 19 times. He won eight batting titles and was his league's top pitcher 12 times. He was elected to the El Paso Baseball Hall of Fame in 1993; his son Jimmy was elected in 2001. (Courtesy Bufe Morrison.)

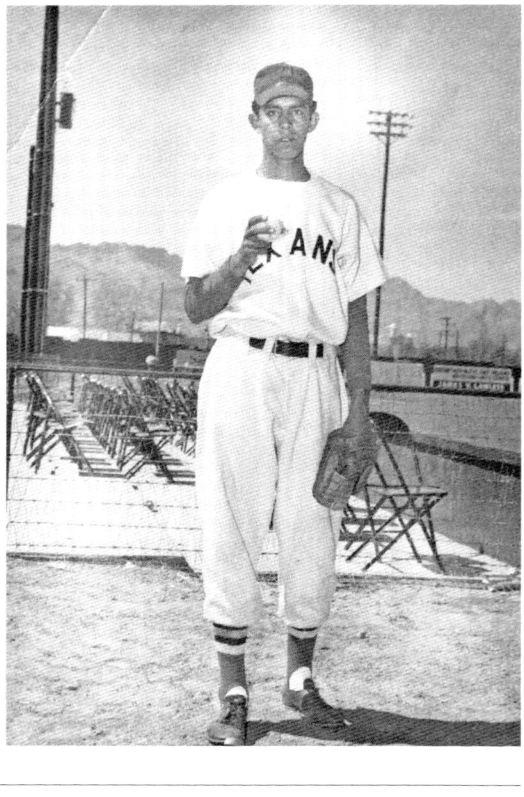

Hometown pitching sensation Rubén Porras poses at El Paso's Dudley Field in 1951. A tall, lanky curveball artist, Porras was signed by the El Paso Texans after a legendary high school career that included a state championship with the 1949 Bowie Bears. In his first pro season in 1951, Porras had 13 wins and eight losses. In 1952, he went 7-9 with a 5.18 ERA and then injured his arm while pitching in the Mexican Winter League. Porras served two years in the Army during the Korean War, and although he returned home safely, his lively arm was gone for good. He was inducted into the El Paso Baseball Hall of Fame in 1991. (Courtesy El Paso Chihuahuas.)

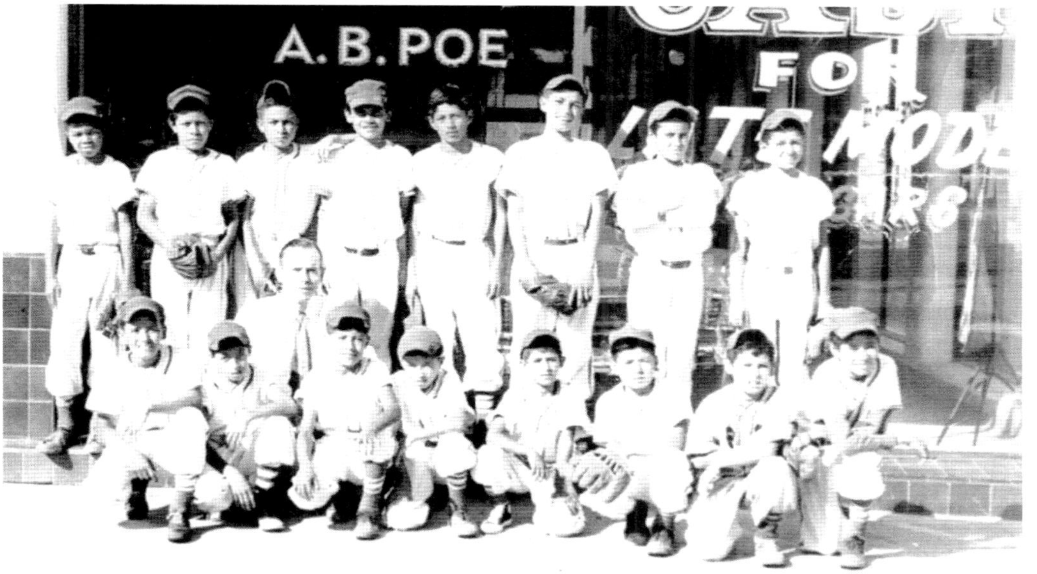

Little League and other youth baseball programs thrived in El Paso during the 1950s, as they did throughout much of America. The A.B. Poe auto dealership sponsored many youth baseball teams as well as adult teams in various semipro leagues. The c. 1951 team shown here included three Rodríguez brothers, Bob (first row, far left), Sal (first row, second from right), and Joe, who was often called "Lefty" (second row, third from right). (Courtesy Sal Rodríguez.)

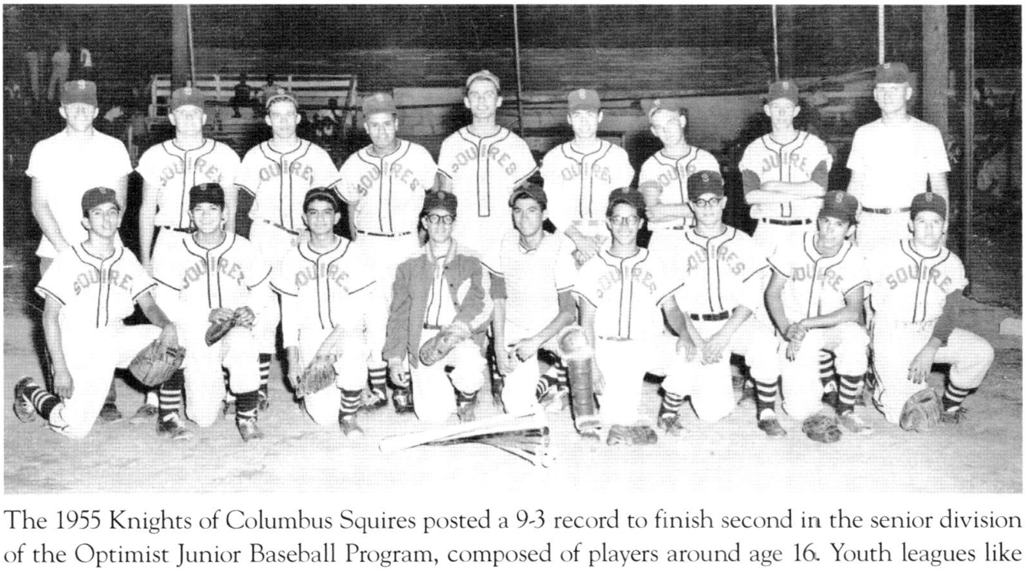

The 1955 Knights of Columbus Squires posted a 9-3 record to finish second in the senior division of the Optimist Junior Baseball Program, composed of players around age 16. Youth leagues like this thrived in El Paso during the 1950s, and line scores from their games were printed in the local newspapers. From left to right are (first row) Bob Anchondo, Héctor Madrid, Óscar Madrid, Agustín Blanco, ? Méndez, unidentified, Ron Perrotta, Joe Ochoterena, and Ruben Chávez; (second row) coach Ben Brooks, Bill Strain, Luís Villalobos, Chuy Valenzuela, Chuy Martínez, unidentified, Bufe Morrison, Bob Janes, and coach Gordon Coles. (Courtesy Bufe Morrison.)

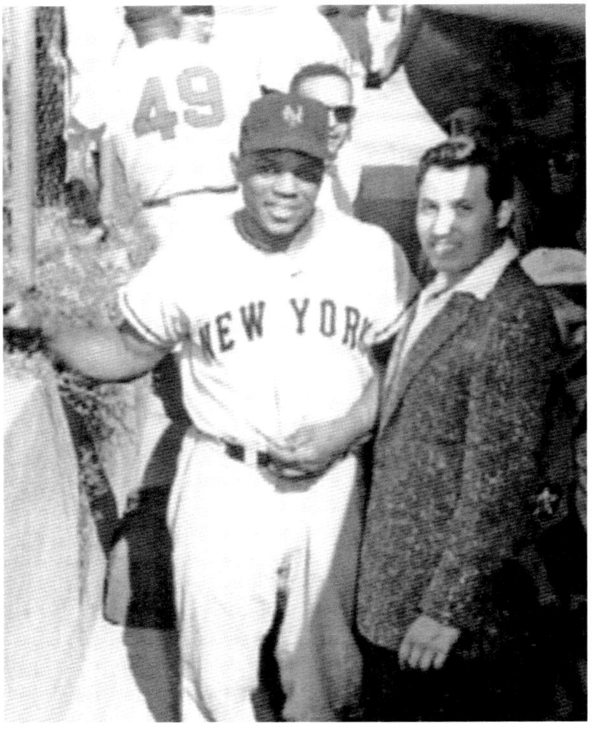

Legendary sportswriter Ray Sánchez poses in the Dudley Field dugout with Willie Mays on November 3, 1955. Sánchez has covered local sports in El Paso for 68 years, including 40 years at the *El Paso Herald-Post*, where he served as sports editor from 1981 to 1990. When the *Herald-Post* hired Sánchez in 1950, he became the paper's first Latino journalist. There were some complaints, but the editor, Ed Pooley, and the sports editor, Bob Ingram, stood by Sánchez. This photograph was taken at an exhibition game pitting a team of El Paso military all-stars against a squad of African American big leaguers including Mays, Hank Aaron, Ernie Banks, Larry Doby, and Don Newcombe. (Courtesy Steve Kaplowitz.)

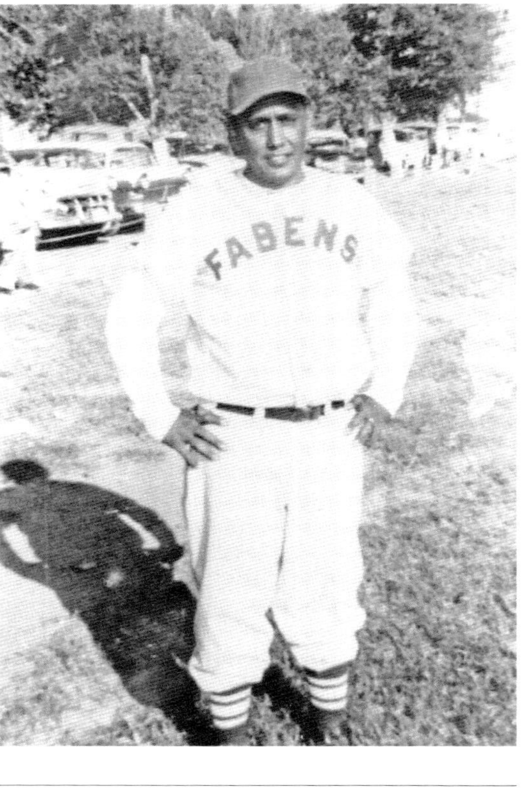

The Fabens Merchants represented the tiny cotton farming town of Fabens, Texas, whose population was over 90 percent Mexican American. Pictured is Alex Villalobos Jr., who played for Fabens High School in the mid-1940s and won two Battle Stars and a Purple Heart in the Korean War. In 1960, Villalobos took over as player-manager of the Fabens Baseball Team, renaming them the Fabens Merchants and joining the Lower Valley League, the most competitive amateur circuit in the El Paso area. Under Villalobos's management, the Merchants won six Lower Valley League pennants and never finished worse than second place. Villalobos was elected to the El Paso Baseball Hall of Fame in 1993. (Courtesy Bufe Morrison.)

In 1978, Hortencia "Stretch" López became the first female player elected to the El Paso Softball Hall of Fame. Born in El Paso in 1930, she began playing softball in the 1940s, with observers comparing her play at shortstop to a ballet artist. She later played for teams representing Ciudad Chihuahua and Ciudad Juárez. López was also an elite basketball player and track and field athlete. At the 1951 Pan American Games in Buenos Aires, she represented Mexico and won the gold medal in the javelin. Throughout the 1960s, she played both women's and men's softball on local teams sponsored by churches, oil companies, and auto dealerships, once leading her team to a 51-game winning streak. (Courtesy Bufe Morrison.)

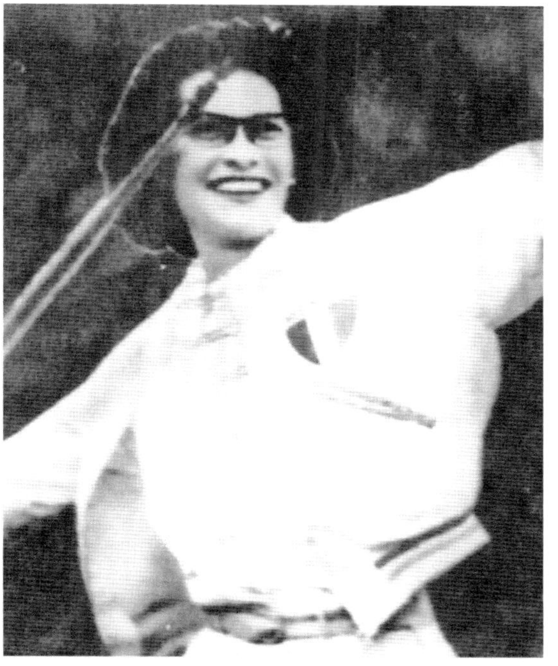

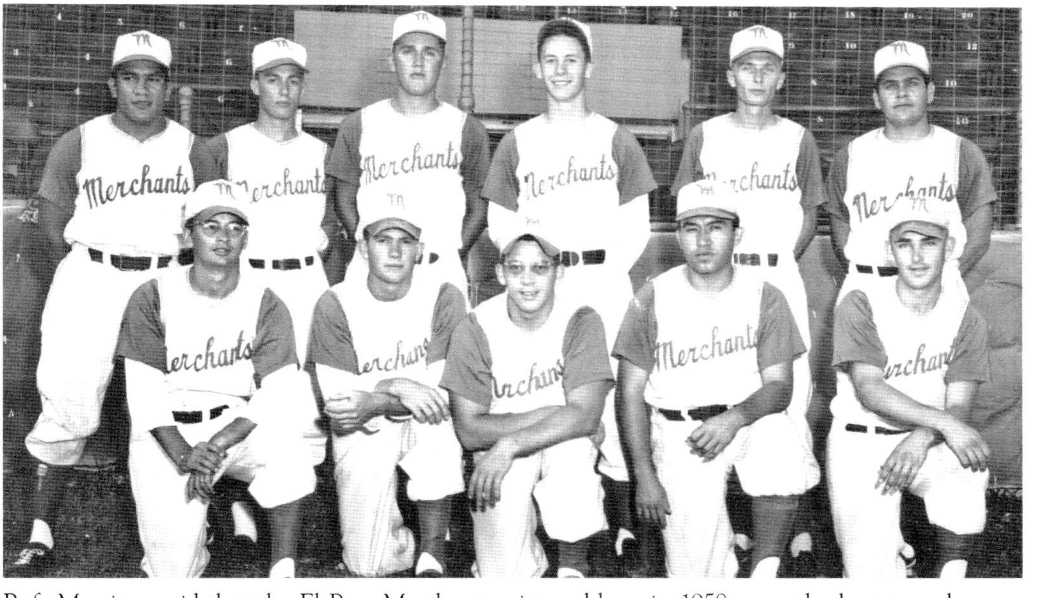

Bufe Morrison said that the El Paso Merchants, pictured here in 1958, were the best team he ever played on. The Merchants featured other local stars, including Bob Osborne, Jim Ochoa, Bobby Ochoa, and Joe Divis. Playing in the International League, a local youth circuit, they posted records of 48-11 in 1957 and 32-7 in 1958, finishing second in the Texas state National Baseball Congress (NBC) tournament the latter year. The International League drew large crowds at the local pro ballpark, Dudley Field, and the play was of such high caliber that its players were sometimes signed by Major-League teams. In 1958, this happened to catcher Tommy Arciniega. (Courtesy Bufe Morrison.)

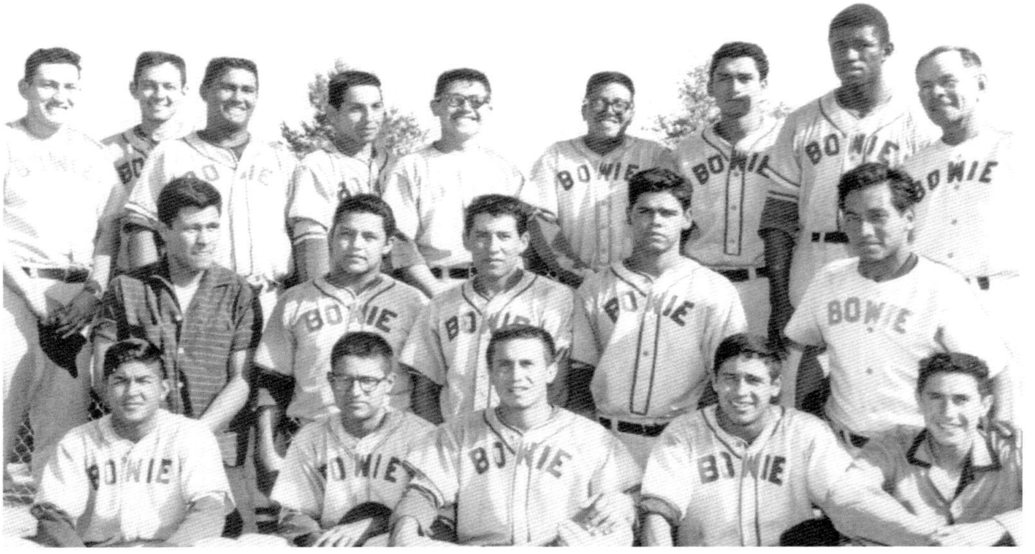

Bowie High School captured its fourth district championship in 1959, the final title in the career of legendary coach Nemo Herrera (third row, far right). The only non-Latino player, Nolan Richardson (third row, second from right), was all-district in baseball, football, and basketball. Richardson gave up a potential career in pro baseball to become a basketball coach, and in 1994 he coached the University of Arkansas to the NCAA championship. Other players included Margarito Bañales Jr. (first row, far left), Richard López (first row, third from left), Rafael Robles (second row, third from left), Robert Pérez (second row, fourth from left), Manuel Jaime (second row, fifth from left), and Luís Gaytan (second row, sixth from left). (Courtesy Margarito Bañales Jr.)

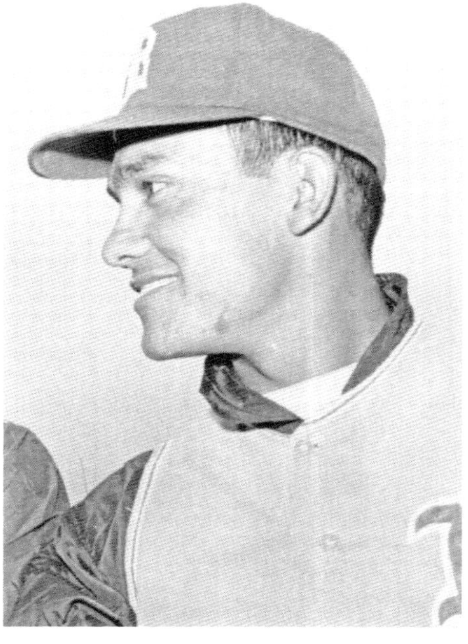

Raúl "Ruly" Medrano Sr. was one of the best pitchers in El Paso in the 1950s. Medrano starred in Optimist, Pony, and Babe Ruth Leagues before moving on to Ysleta High School, where he was a four-time all-district player and became the winningest pitcher in District 1-4A history. He pitched five years in the Kansas City A's farm system. Medrano's career was derailed by a shoulder injury, and he retired to coach his sons in youth baseball. Ruly Medrano Jr. was the head baseball coach at Eastwood High School for 14 years, and another son, Ryan Medrano, played in the Cincinnati and Seattle farm systems before becoming head coach at Eastwood in 2015. (Courtesy Bufe Morrison.)

From the 1950s through the 1990s, Mike Beltrán (right) was involved in virtually every kind of baseball played on the border. After a legendary Little League career, he pitched Ysleta High to a district championship in 1969. He moved on to Ranger Junior College and the University of Texas at El Paso (UTEP), where he was the ace starter. Beltrán pitched in Ciudad Juárez for five years, twice striking out 25 batters in a game. In 1972, he pitched for the Mexican national team in the World Cup. Beltrán spent time in the minor leagues from 1973 to 1982, including the Phillies farm system. In the 1990s, he led Del Valle High School to two district titles as head coach. He was elected to the El Paso Baseball Hall of Fame in 1991. (Courtesy Bufe Morrison.)

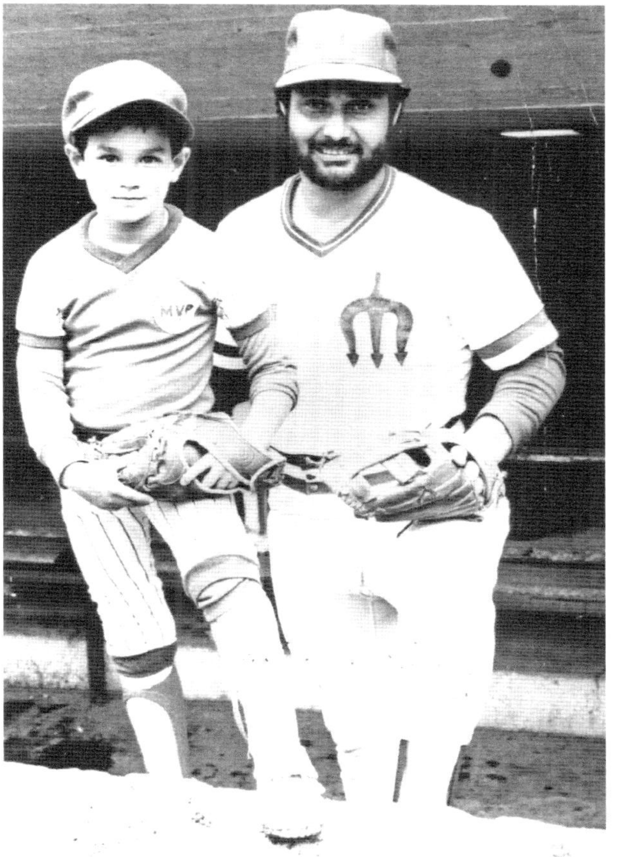

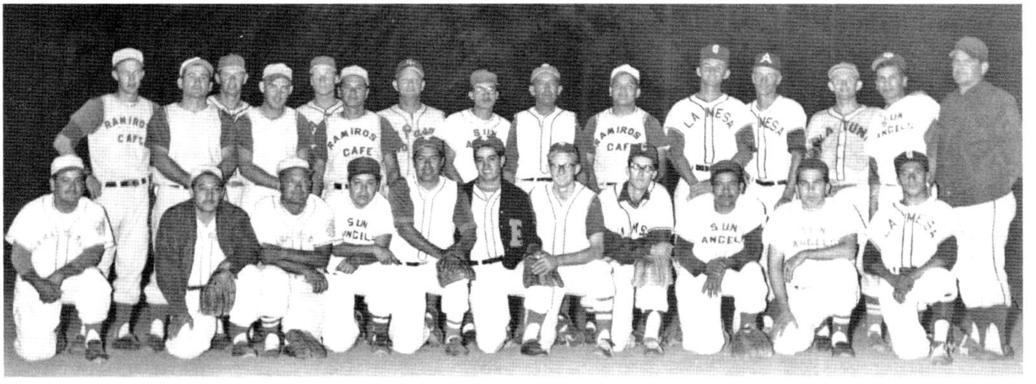

The El Paso City League was one of the strongest local semipro circuits during the 1950s and 1960s. City League All-Stars pose at the league's all-star game in Fabens during the early 1960s. The six teams in the league that year were Ramiro's Café, La Rana Verde, La Mesa, El Paso 40-60 Club, the La Tuna Feds, and the US Border Patrol. Ramiro's Café had eight players on the all-star team, including El Paso Baseball Hall of Fame members Lolo Caldera, Joe Hague, and Bufe Morrison (second row, fourth from left). Another hall-of-famer, 40-60 Club shortstop Jackie Harris, is seventh from left in the first row. (Courtesy Bufe Morrison.)

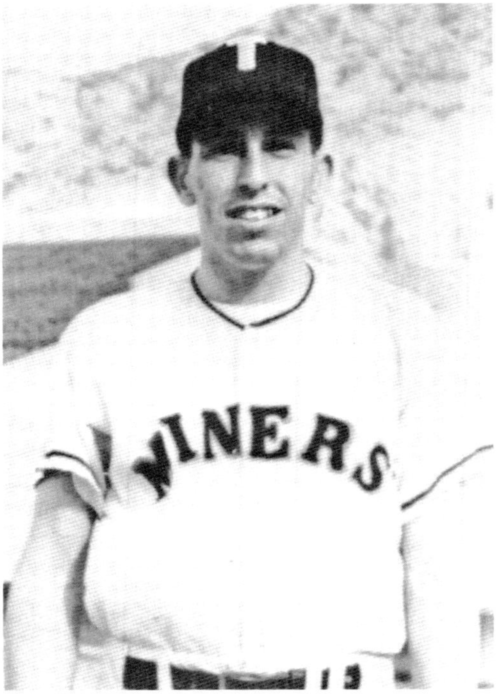

A star hurler in local semipro leagues for a quarter-century, Mike Barrueta posted a career record of 205 wins and 55 losses. After four stellar years at El Paso High School, he joined the pitching staff of the Texas Western Miners, posting a 23-7 record in college. During his decades in semipro ball, he won three awards as his league's best pitcher and was named MVP twice. Barrueta was inducted into the International Baseball Hall of Fame in 1986 and the El Paso Baseball Hall of Fame in 1992. His brother Ernie was also a noted local pitcher. In his later years, Mike Barrueta served as president of the El Paso Baseball Hall of Fame and as a scout for the Cincinnati Reds. (Courtesy Mike Barrueta.)

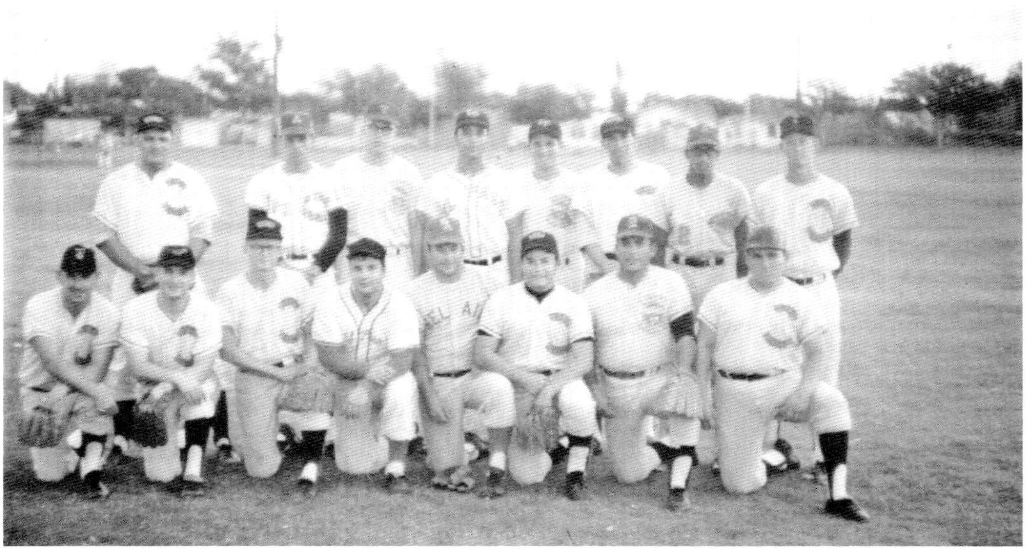

Tigua Auto Parts finished second in the 1968 City League standings, one game behind the Santa Rita Miners. At one point during the season, the Tigua club—nicknamed the Partmen—pitched four consecutive shutouts. Jackie Harris, a shortstop known for his stellar defense, won the league batting title at .481. From left to right are (first row) Bufe Morrison, Al Zinter, Jackie Harris, Vic Luera, Ron Forbes, Toby Tovar, Ruly Medrano Sr., and Ed Morales; (second row) Bob Kerr, Ernie Watts, Bob Arnold, Larry Stelly, Phil Ottone, Mike Barrueta, Andra Raboin, and Terry Witt. (Courtesy Bufe Morrison.)

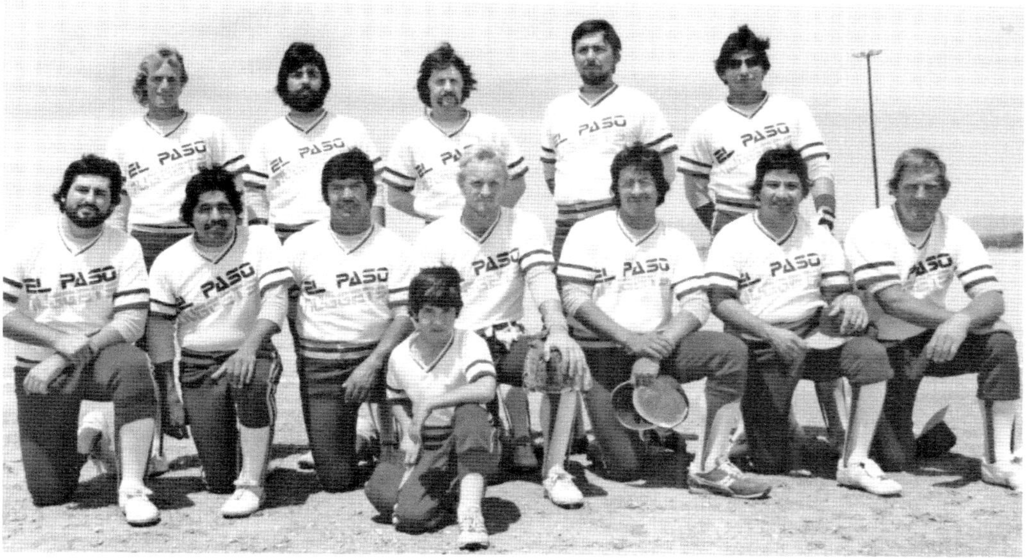

For several decades, the Lower Valley League was an ultra-competitive semipro circuit in the El Paso area. One of its teams, the El Paso Nuggets, is shown here during the late 1970s. From left to right are (first row) Jim Meléndez, Dave García, Eloy Alvarado, Burgo Gill, Rick Franco, Helo Rodríguez, and Bufe Morrison; (second row) Mark Rasmusson, Carlos Gamboa, Brad Kranz, Henry Burnadett, and Leroy Álvarez. Morrison, who made 15 local all-star teams and won seven MVP awards in his career, later helped found the El Paso Baseball Hall of Fame and the El Paso Softball Hall of Fame. (Courtesy Bufe Morrison.)

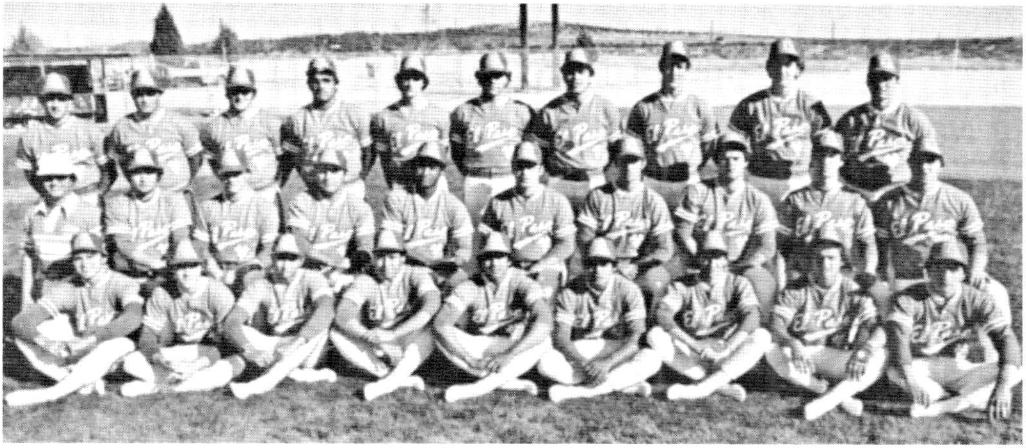

The baseball program at UTEP was founded in 1963 by former Major-Leaguer Andy Cohen. The 1981 squad pictured here was one of the last. From left to right are (first row) Rick Miller, Tony Thompson, Jorge Díaz, Óscar Romero, Rick Pérez, Art Flores, Sergio Baca, Danny Haygood, and Ricky Gámez; (second row) Robert Abdou, Rick West, Jeff King, Alex Brown, James Walker, Tom Thompson, Brent Hathaway, Russ Wortmann, Dain Hathaway, and Ed Wolfe; (third row) Ed Thayer, Bill Kinneberg, Jim Vance, Pico Córdova, Mike Maddux, Montie Wren, Mark Held, Warren Kastner, Mark Zimmerman, and James Lawler. (Courtesy Bufe Morrison.)

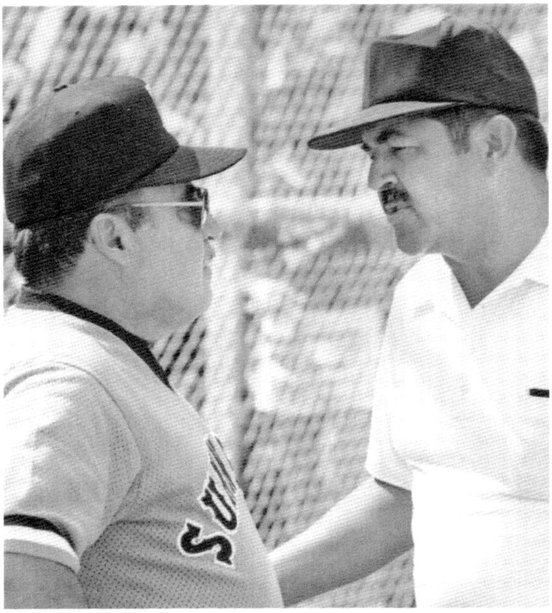

Math teacher Margarito Bañales Jr. (right) was a prominent umpire in El Paso for decades. After a playing career in which he helped Bowie High School win a district title in 1959, Bañales became an umpire in 1968. He taught algebra at Bel Air High School while also serving 29 years in the US Army Reserve and umpiring high school baseball and adult fast-pitch softball games at night. Bañales was elected to the International Softball Congress Hall of Fame in 2005. "His assertiveness and fairness has earned him the respect of coaches, players, administrators and softball fans everywhere he has umpired," his hall of fame citation read. (Courtesy Margarito Bañales Jr.)

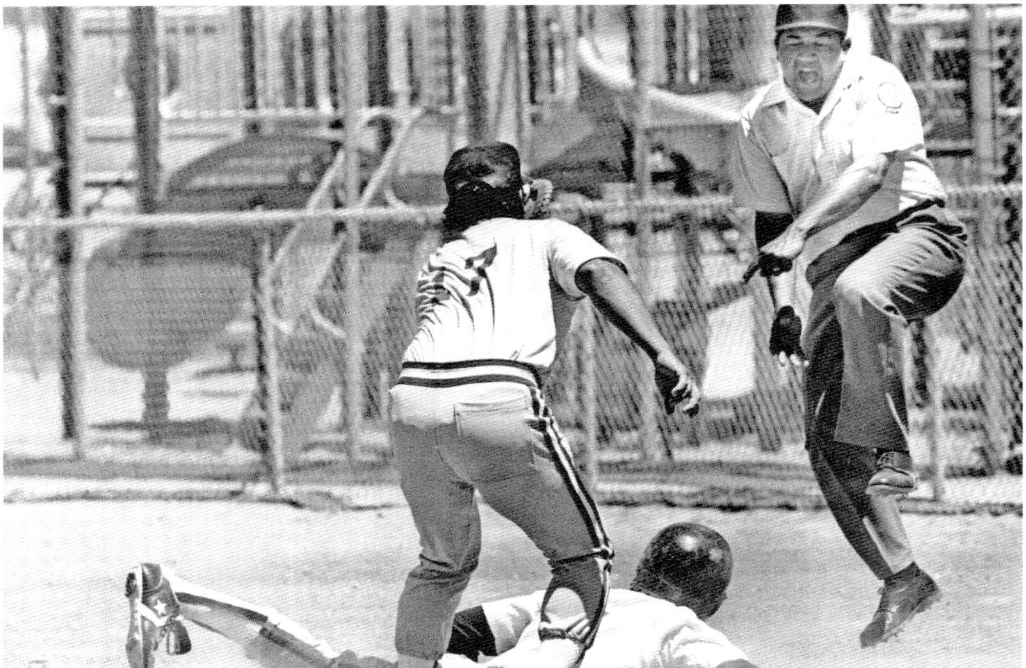

Longtime umpire Margarito Bañales Jr. is known for his colorful and expressive calls, as seen in this image by photographer Grace Sáenz for the *El Paso Times*. Bañales is seen calling out base runner Dave Capka of Las Cruces National Bank, who has just been tagged by Alamogordo third baseman Chris Sánchez. The game was part of the Latin American Fast-Pitch Softball Tournament, held in El Paso in 1990. (Courtesy Margarito Bañales Jr.)

More than a decade passed without college baseball in El Paso until El Paso Community College (EPCC) founded its program in 1996. In its first two decades, EPCC had 20 players drafted by Major-League teams. In 2002, head coach Ken Jácome guided EPCC to a 39-19 record and the National Junior College Athletic Association Region V championship. The team's offensive sparkplugs that year were Mark Enders (left) and Efrain Barraza, posing here after winning the regional title in Abilene. Enders, a product of Eastwood High School, batted .341 with 19 doubles and 25 stolen bases. Barraza, from Americas High School, batted .391 with 24 steals. (Courtesy Steve and Mark Enders.)

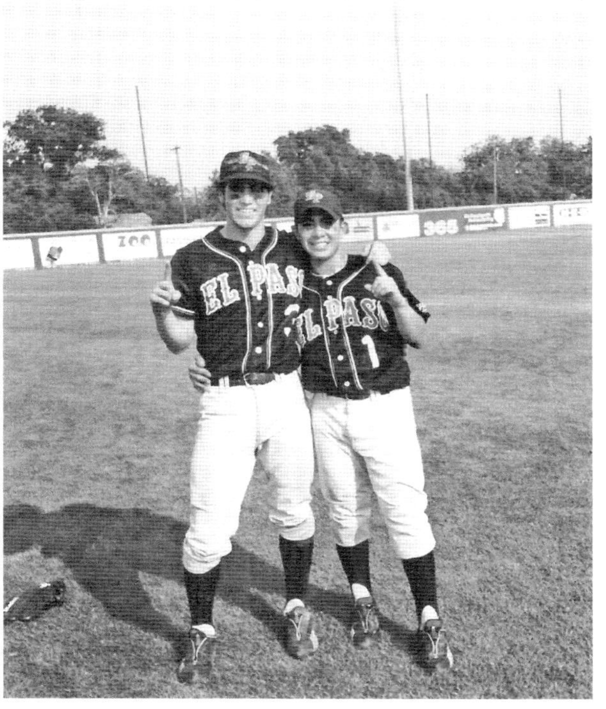

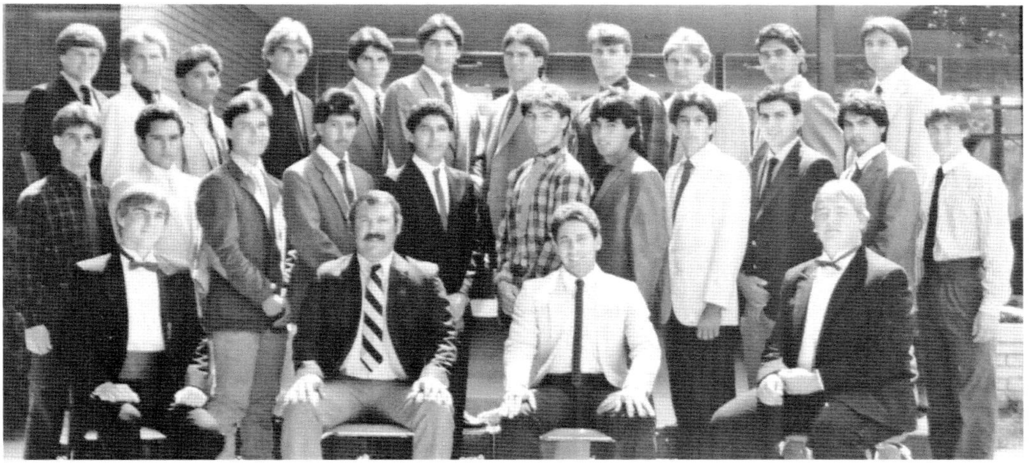

The 1986 Eastwood High School team won the 5-A area championship. The Troopers were led by left-hander Butch Henry and right-hander Frank Castillo. The two pitched a combined 20 years in the Major Leagues. Castillo and his father, Joe, are members of the El Paso Baseball Hall of Fame. From left to right are (first row) Sam ?, coach Ray Sáenz, assistant coach John Cázares, and unidentified; (second row) Mike Cataldi, Sal Payán, David Ortega, Rene ?, Victor Salazar, Larry Vucan, Manny Rivera, Richard Jones, Frank Castillo, Mano Escobar, and Jared Sáenz; (third row) unidentified, Mark Huttanus, Eddie Heredia, Butch Henry, Tony Sánchez, Ruly Medrano Jr., Eric Wagner, Matt Charske, Joe Yarbrough, Ernie Martínez, and Carl Aigner. (Courtesy Ray Sáenz.)

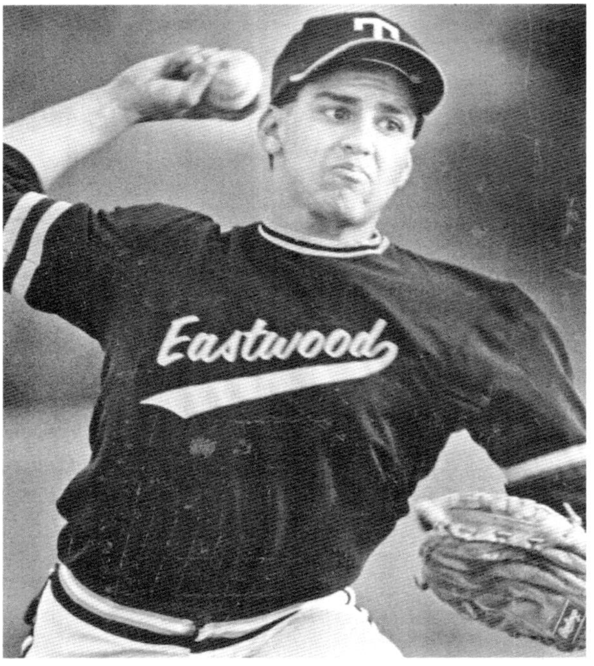

Eastwood High School graduate Frank Castillo had the longest Major-League career of any player born in El Paso. In his senior year with the Troopers in 1987, Castillo went 10-1 on the mound with a 0.79 ERA. During his 13-year career, he pitched for the Cubs, Red Sox, Rockies, Tigers, Blue Jays, and Marlins. His best game came on September 25, 1995, when he came within one out of pitching a no-hitter against St. Louis before giving up a triple and finishing with a one-hit shutout and 13 strikeouts. Castillo won a World Series ring with the 2004 Red Sox. He died tragically in a boating accident in Arizona in 2013. (Courtesy *El Paso Times*.)

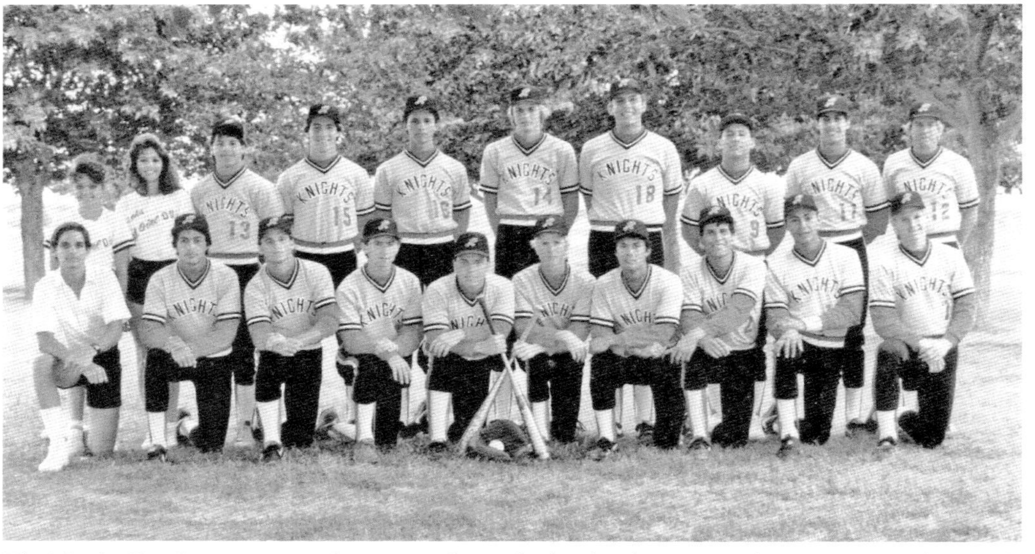

The Hanks Knights were one of two powerhouse high school teams in El Paso in 1986, along with the Eastwood Troopers. This Hanks 2-5A district championship team featured two future Major-Leaguers, Danny Pérez and Alan Zinter, as well as Cincinnati Reds draftee Darrin Glenn. Mike Williams was a two-time *El Paso Times* coach of the year. From left to right are (first row) Gerald Baskin, Ignacio Ramos, Jim Gant, Eric Brandenburger, James Estrada, John McClure, Thon Mayhugh, Danny Parada, Javiér Alvarado, and Darrin Glenn; (second row) manager Yvonne Aguilar, manager Christine Meléndez, Danny Pérez, Mike Eicher, Jai Keys, Jay Blackwell, John Harrist, David Pérez, Alan Zinter, and coach Mike Williams. (Courtesy Darrin Glenn.)

A gifted right-handed line-drive hitter, outfielder Danny Pérez starred at Hanks High School and Oklahoma State University before being drafted in 1992 by the Milwaukee Brewers. He spent parts of three seasons playing for the El Paso Diablos, then the Brewers' Double-A farm team. Pérez batted .325 overall as a Diablo and was called up to the majors for a cup of coffee in 1996. "The fact I was playing at Yankee Stadium didn't hit me right away," he told writer Ray Sánchez. "But as I was walking out into the stadium I noticed a bust of Babe Ruth. Then when I walked out and saw 50,000 people in the stands it hit me where I was." (Courtesy Milwaukee Brewers.)

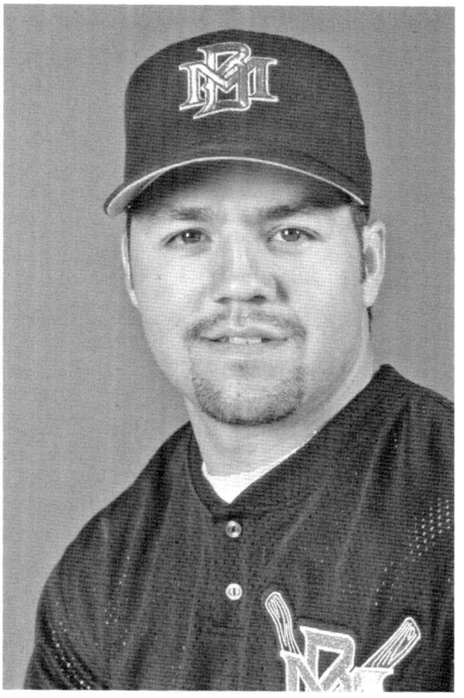

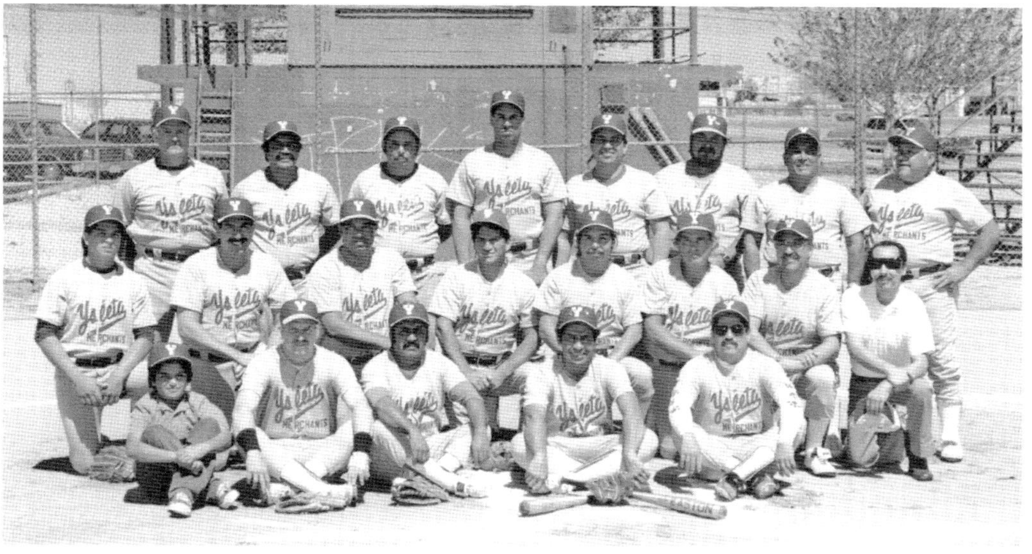

The Ysleta Merchants, a powerhouse for decades, won 23 consecutive games capturing the 1989 Lower Valley Old-Timers League championship (for players over age 40). The 1989 Merchants won the International 40-60 Tournament in Mexico. From left to right are (first row) unidentified batboy, Dave Patt, Manny Vásquez, Sonny Parra, and Roy Gonzáles; (second row) Lalo Bond, Mike Barrueta, Jessie Gonzáles, Lencho Cedillo, Lupe Barragán, Bufe Morrison, Sal Payán, and Tony Ruelas; (third row) Don Wilson, Henry Lascano, Robert Malfavor, Dan Martínez, Adam Salcido, Pablo "Moose" Camarillo, Chendo Cedillo, and Jesús "Bull" Rodríguez. (Courtesy Bufe Morrison.)

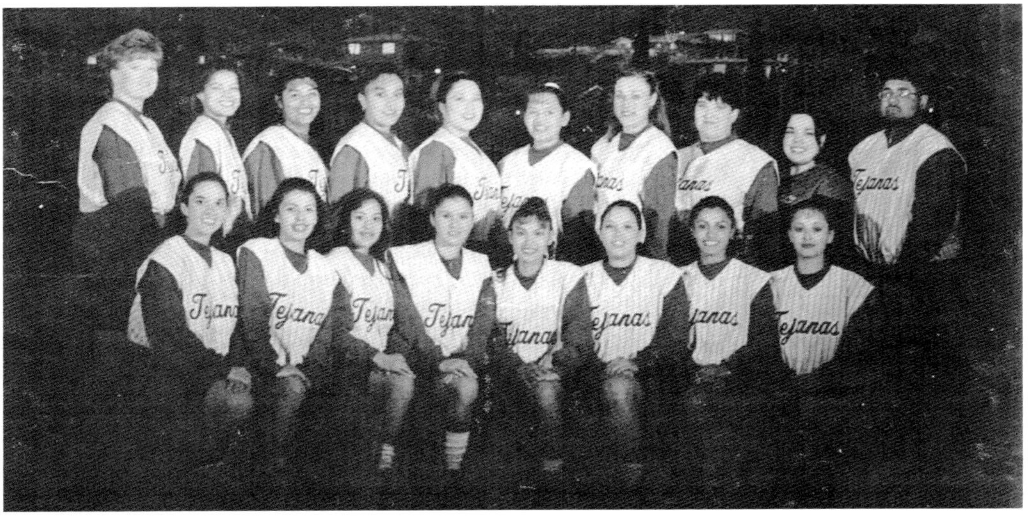

In 1997, El Paso Community College founded the first women's collegiate softball team in the city's history. The Tejanas' roster consisted entirely of players from local high schools, including Jennifer Cieslik, Claudia Jacques, Yvette Ramos, Kathy Rodríguez, and Veronica García from Andress High; Yvonne Contreras, Celina Estrada, and Annette Rodríguez from Bel Air; Ericka Colón, Roxanne Luna, and Jessica Baca from Hanks; Yvette Ruíz and Tina Caldera from Irvin; Diane Domínguez from Del Valle; Adriana Carbajal from Ysleta; and Edna García from San Elizario. The team was inducted into the El Paso Softball Hall of Fame in 2013. (Courtesy Bufe Morrison.)

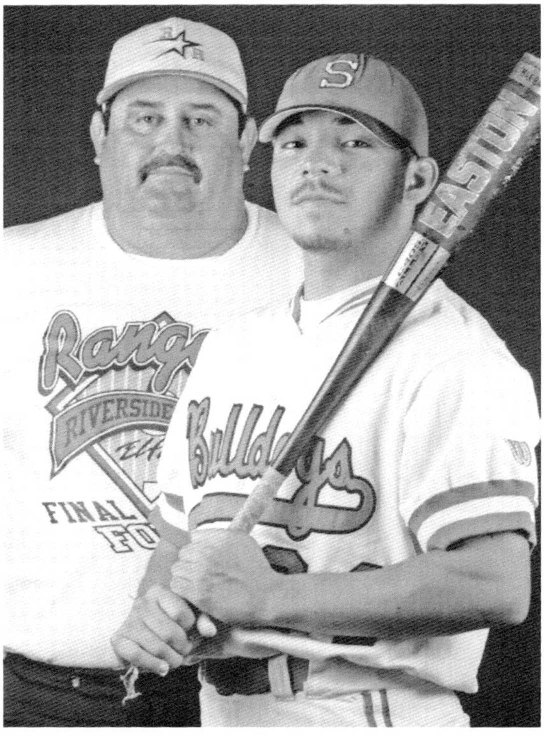

El Paso Times Player of the Year Omar Quintanilla (right) and Coach of the Year Jim Meléndez pose in 2000. In 32 years as coach of Riverside High School, Meléndez led the Rangers to 749 wins, 28 playoff appearances, eight area titles, and the final four of the state Class 4A tournament in 2000. He is the winningest coach in local high school history. Quintanilla, meanwhile, is the most notable player to come out of El Paso in the 21st century. He was an all-state player for the Socorro High School Bulldogs before being drafted in the first round by the Oakland Athletics in 2003. (Courtesy *El Paso Times.*)

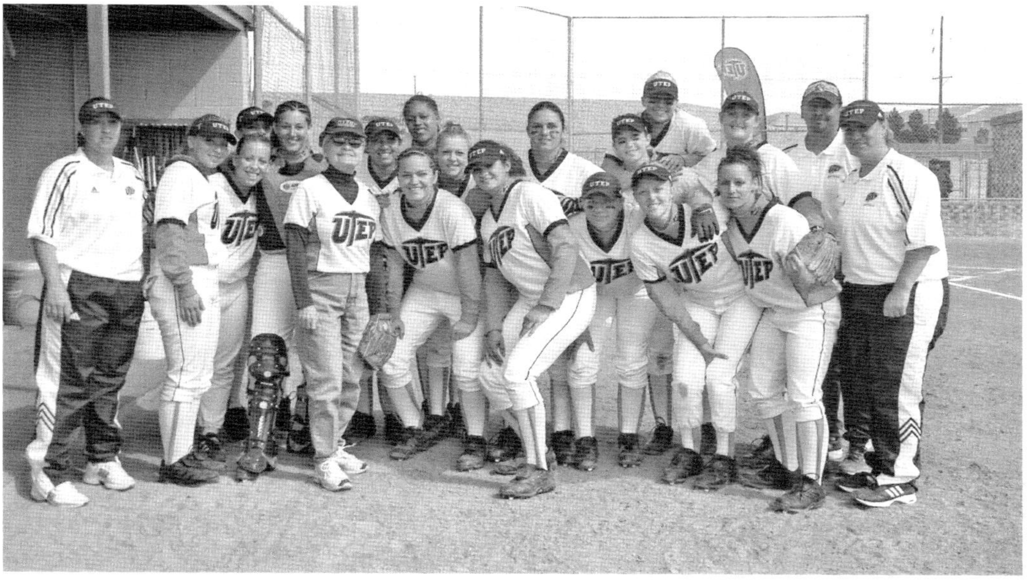

In 2004, UTEP founded its NCAA softball program and named the husband-and-wife team of James and Kathleen Rodríguez as the first head coaches. From left to right are Kathleen Rodríguez, Jennifer García, Gracie Borjas (top), Holly Cohen (bottom), Denise Emmons, UTEP president Dr. Diana Natalicio, Jawauna Davis, Veronica Flournoy (top), Malia Simmons (bottom), Karen Sjostrom, Renee DiPuccio, Deanna Camacho, Kristin Hardy, Lindsey Pridgen, Laura Joiner (top), Sierra Hannum (bottom), Megan Whiteaker (top), Cierra Cooper (bottom), James Rodríguez, and assistant coach Dana Lambert. (Courtesy UTEP Athletics.)

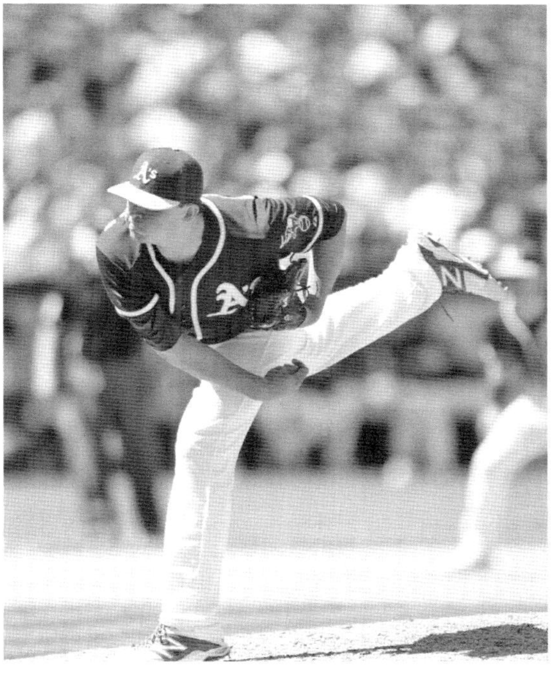

Through 2016, right-handed pitcher Fernando Rodríguez has pitched 216 career MLB games, more than all but two other El Paso natives (Frank Castillo and Armando Almanza). After graduating from Franklin High in 2002, Rodríguez struck out 40 batters in 24.2 innings at El Paso Community College, prompting the Anaheim Angels to draft him in the 18th round. Rodríguez made his Major-League debut in 2009 and retired the first batter he faced, Robinson Canó, on a groundout. His career was derailed in 2013 by Tommy John elbow surgery, but in 2015 and 2016, Rodríguez served as a key part of the Oakland A's bullpen. In 2017, he signed with the Chicago Cubs. (Courtesy Michael Zagaris/Oakland Athletics.)

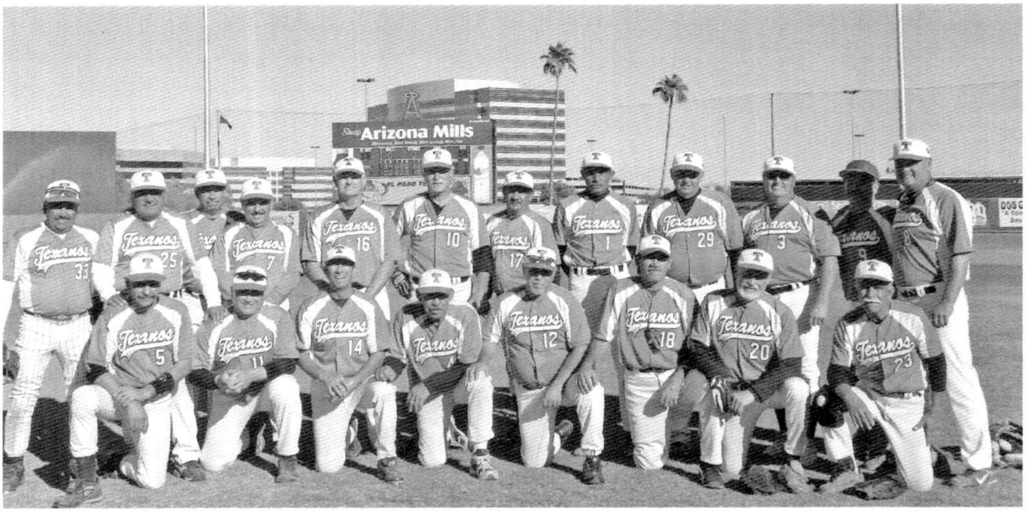

In 2011, the El Paso Texanos won the over-60 world championship, defeating a team from Tucson in the Men's Senior Baseball League World Series. The Texanos posted a 9-0 record in the tournament, which was held at Phoenix Municipal Stadium in Arizona. Team members are, from left to right, (first row) Beto Valles, Mike Barraza, Rudy Carrasco, Erasmo Figueroa, Jesús Martínez, Juan Zaragosa, Robert Padilla, and José Villa; (second row) Charlie Varela, Alfonso Parga, Pancho Favela, Jesús Muñoz, Don Wilson, Bill Juen, Héctor Zapata, Abel Encinas, Dave Weick, Mark Miller, Jesús Rodríguez, and John Paul. (Courtesy Don Wilson.)

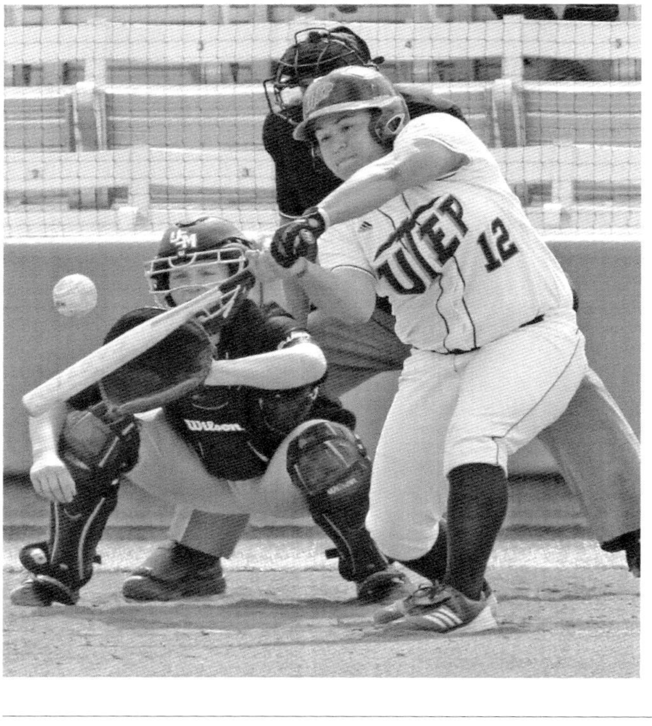

In 2012, UTEP Miners softball player Camilla Carrera led the nation with 32 home runs in just 57 games, the second-best season total in NCAA history (Laura Espinoza of Arizona hit 37 in 1995). Her rate of 0.60 home runs per game is the best of all time. The Tempe, Arizona, native also had a .447 batting average and a 1.199 slugging percentage—the latter the third-best mark in college softball history. "In our nine years of the program, she's the best hitter to come from UTEP," co–head coach Kathleen Rodríguez said. "She just put it together her senior year." (Courtesy UTEP Athletics.)

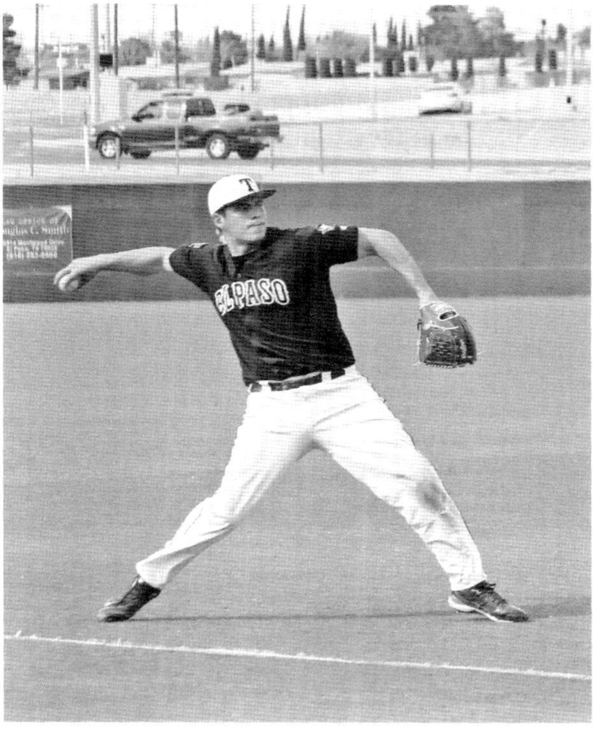

In 2014, EPCC third baseman Eudor García was a first-team Junior College All-American, batting .460 for the Tejanos with 14 home runs, 18 doubles, and 63 RBI in 51 games. After that season, the former Socorro High School star was drafted in the fourth round by the New York Mets, making him the highest draft pick in EPCC history. In 2015, he batted .296 for the Class A Savannah Sand Gnats, but his career was temporarily derailed by an 80-game suspension for performance-enhancing drugs. In 2016, García returned to bat .275 in the Class A South Atlantic League. (Courtesy Dana Eisenga.)

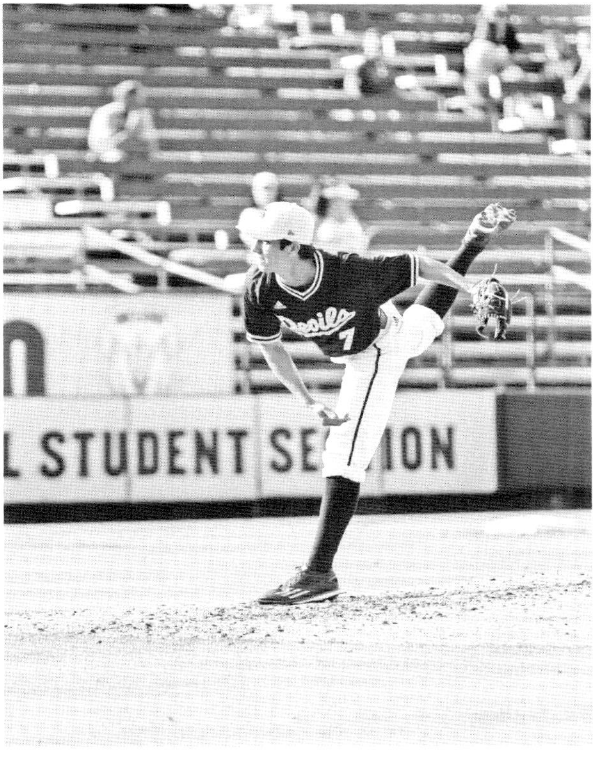

Right-hander Éder Erives was one of the best high school pitchers ever to come out of El Paso. Playing four years at Montwood High under coach Tom Carrillo, Erives twice won all-state honors. As a freshman in 2010, he pitched a no-hitter to clinch a playoff spot. During his senior year, he posted a 0.62 ERA, struck out 109 batters in 67 innings, and was named El Paso's "Mr. Baseball." At Arizona State University, he won the closer's job and was named honorable mention All-Pac 12 in 2016. "Erives' arm was indispensable this season," wrote ASU beat writer Dominic Cotroneo. "He pitched in more stressful innings than anyone and always gave the Devils the confidence they would need whenever he was on the mound." (Courtesy ASU Athletics.)

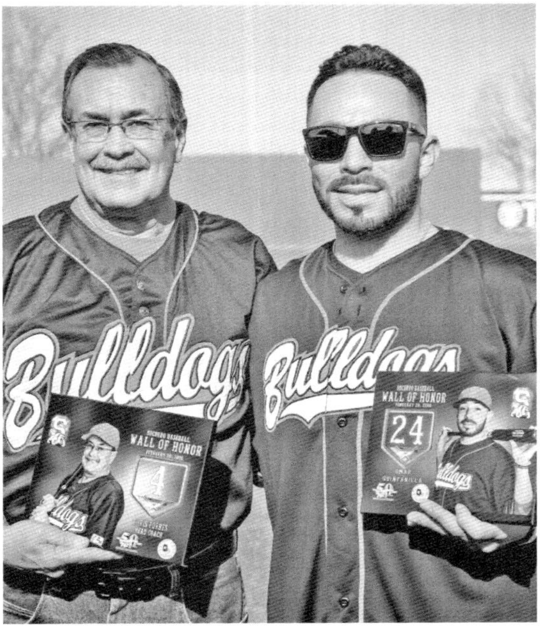

Former Socorro High School coach Jim Forbes (left) and shortstop Omar Quintanilla (right) were inducted into the Socorro Baseball Wall of Honor in 2016. Their numbers were retired and placed on the outfield wall. Forbes coached the Bulldogs for 25 years beginning in 1986, winning 577 games and 13 district titles. In 2009, he coached the Bulldogs to the state Class 5A championship, only the second local team (after the 1949 Bowie Bears) to win a state title. Quintanilla was a star for the Bulldogs in the early 2000s. As of 2016, he had played nine seasons in the Major Leagues with four different teams. His 402 career Major-League games are the most of any El Paso–born player. (Courtesy Andrés Acosta.)

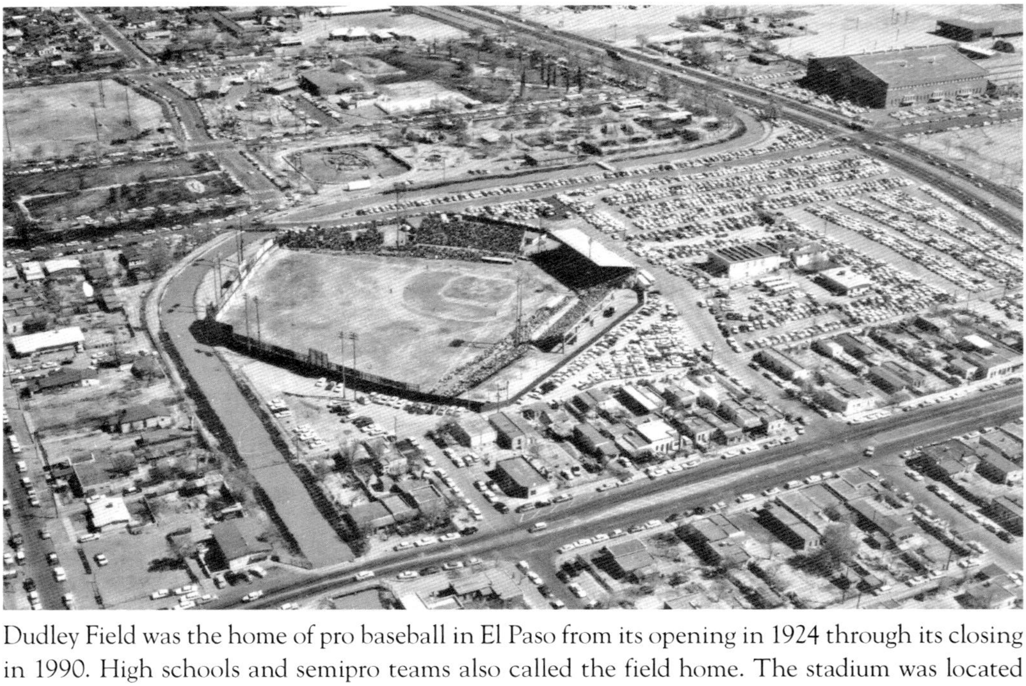

Dudley Field was the home of pro baseball in El Paso from its opening in 1924 through its closing in 1990. High schools and semipro teams also called the field home. The stadium was located on Alameda Avenue in South El Paso, neighbored by the El Paso County Coliseum and the landmark restaurant Chico's Tacos. It was jokingly called the "Dudley Dome" due to the lack of rainouts there. Joe DiMaggio, Mickey Mantle, Willie Mays, and Fernando Valenzuela are among the legends who played here. It was demolished in 2005, and the land is now part of the El Paso Zoo. (Courtesy El Paso Chihuahuas.)

2

Texans, Sun Kings, and Diablos

In El Paso, baseball players have often viewed the border as nothing more than an imaginary line, one that keeps moving. When the Segundo Barrio was settled by a farmer named Santiago Alvarado in 1834, it was still on the south side of the Río Grande. The river changed course in the 1850s, and the neighborhood, soon to be a hotbed of baseball, became part of the United States.

Baseball in Northern Mexico took off around the time of the Mexican Revolution. Many El Pasoans watched the war's battles from across the river, on the rooftops of multistory buildings like the Camino Real Hotel and the El Paso Laundry. Often, though, they found it boring. "There is more action to be seen in a big league baseball game than on the battlefield," an *El Paso Times* reporter complained. During the revolution, Francisco Villa slipped into and out of El Paso, eating his favorite dessert at the Elite Confectionary. The dish, a scoop of chocolate-covered vanilla ice cream, was called the "Elite Baseball."

In 1915, the new Mexican president tried to curry favor with his American political backers by promoting baseball in Northern Mexico. "[Venustiano] Carranza is going to encourage the American game of baseball in the Republic as a substitute for bullfights and other diversions along the border," the *New York Times* reported. Throughout the following century, teams from Juárez and Chihuahua would frequently cross the Río Grande to play in El Paso and vice versa.

Baseball in Northern Mexico ebbed and flowed based on the political situation. In 1926, two players, Manuel Almanza and Silvestre Santillanes, founded a baseball league for the state of Chihuahua, but in 1929, José Gonzalo Escobar, a general who had fought against Villa in the revolution, led La Renovedora, an armed uprising that gained widespread popularity in Northern Mexico. Due to the unrest, almost all baseball activity in Chihuahua was suspended. Throughout most of the 1900s, though, Mexican-born players continued to play on El Paso teams, El Pasoans played on teams throughout Mexico, and national identity often became blurred.

In 1946, for instance, the Mexican National League, an official part of the US minor leagues, included teams from Mexico City, Saltillo, Torreón, Chihuahua, and Ciudad Juárez—and a lone team from the United States, the El Paso Tejanos. The poorly financed league quickly went out of business, but it was emblematic of the degree to which baseball along the border is truly a two-nation sport.

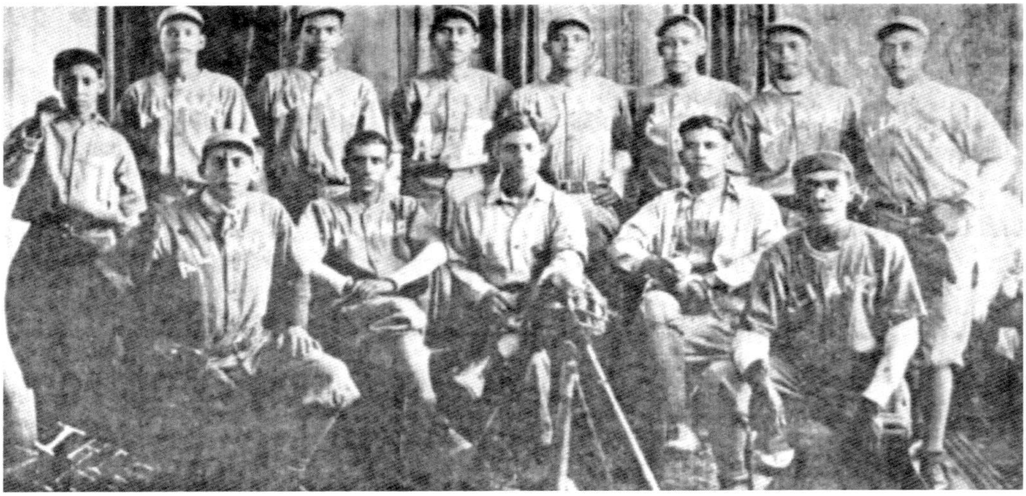

This photograph from 1922 or 1923 depicts the Alianza team from Chihuahua state, which played throughout Northern Mexico. From left to right are (first row) Herculano Labrado, Gonzalo Nolasco, Saturnino Cedillo, Arguijo Aguilar, and Epifanio Díaz; (second row) unidentified mascot, Ciriaco Mendoza, Leopoldo "El Texano" Parra, Daniel Frias, Mariano Flores, Salvador Durán, Juan Labrado, and ? Remedios. Ciriaco Mendoza was the father of shortstop Mario Mendoza, the Chihuahua City native who played shortstop for Pittsburgh in the 1970s and whose .215 batting average gave rise to the term "the Mendoza Line." (Courtesy Juan Rodríguez.)

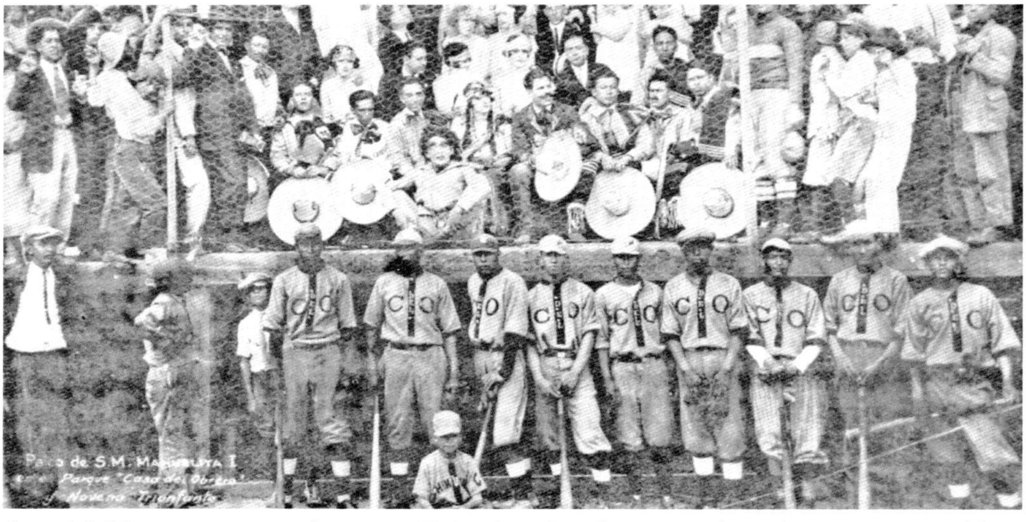

Casa del Obrero was a powerhouse in Chihuahua City from 1922 through 1930, sponsored by a socialist worker's organization. Teams were often sponsored by unions and political parties as a way of generating public support. Note the finely dressed fans behind the chicken wire fence, including Chihuahua's "Queen of Baseball," Manuelita. The fan in the black suit leaning against a post and holding a camera is Don Gilberto Tapia, editor of *El Heraldo de Chihuahua*. Players from left to right are Johnny García, Manuel Ojinaga, Adolfo Medellín, Alejandro Selís, José "Gordolobo" López, Trini Portillo, Esteban Nevárez, Lauro Barragán, and Horacio Ramírez.(Courtesy Juan Rodríguez.)

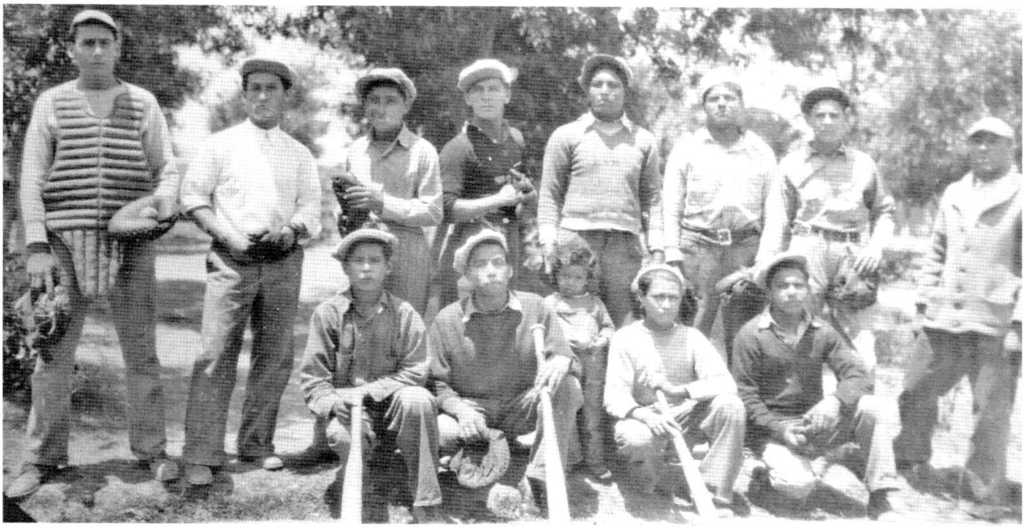

This informal sandlot team played in Chihuahua in the mid-to-late 1920s. The only identified player is Manuel Rodríguez, standing at far left, who was known in baseball circles as "La Gringa" or "Menonita" (Mennonite) because he spoke fluent English. Although he was the catcher on this team, Rodríguez would later go on to play first base for notable teams such as Chihuahua and Círculo Juvenil. (Courtesy Juan Rodríguez.)

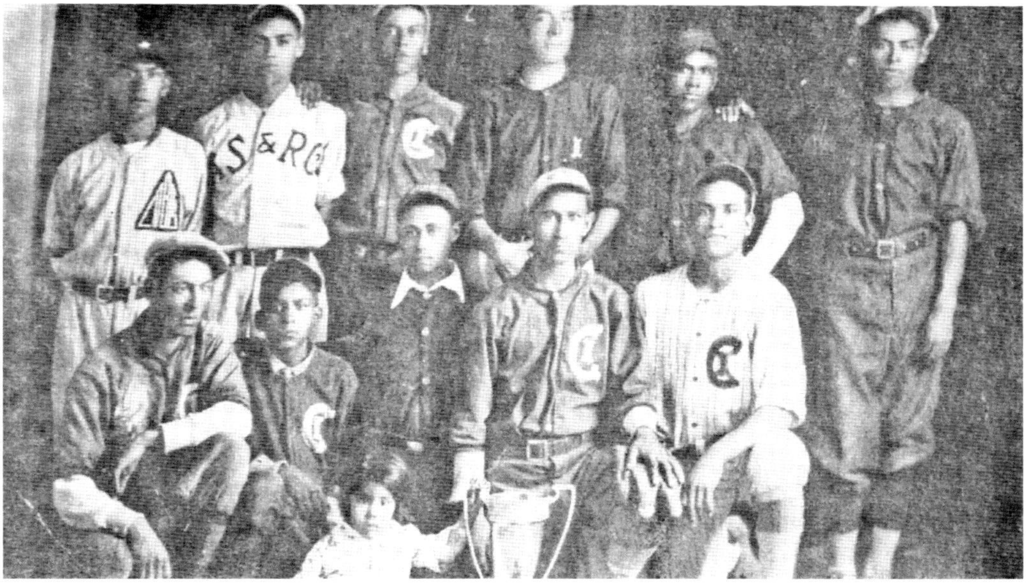

This 1929 photograph shows the Colonia Industrial team that played in Chihuahua state. While most players are wearing jerseys bearing Colonia Industrial's "CI" logo, at least one wears a uniform bearing the letters "AS&RCo," for the American Smelting and Refining Company, known today as ASARCO. Among the players pictured are Alberto Fraire, Luís Fraire, Victor Holguín, Genaro Castillo, and José Palomo (at far right). Luís Fraire, according to Mexican baseball historian Raúl Álvarez, had "the arm and the personality of a great pitcher." (Courtesy Juan Rodríguez.)

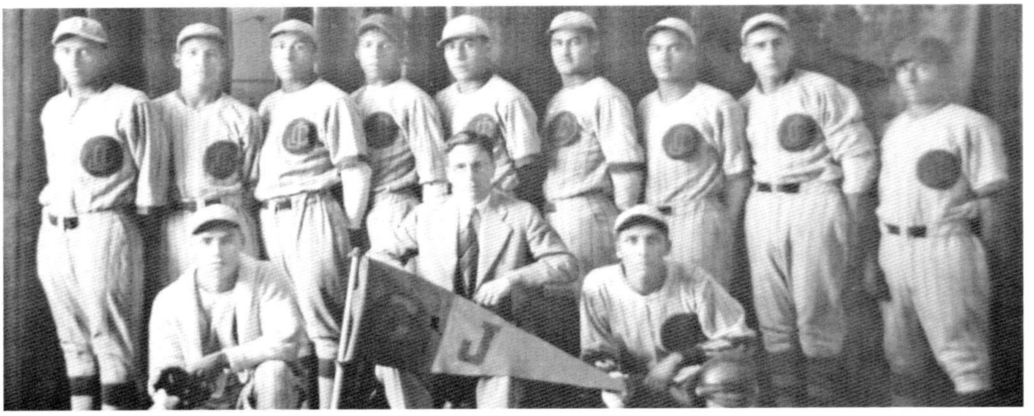

This team, Círculo Juvenil, won the national championship of Mexico in 1930. Círculo Juvenil was a youth center in Chihuahua founded in 1928 by Jesuit father Julio Vertiz that offered cultural programs and fielded teams in various sports. After winning the Chihuahua state title, Círculo Juvenil added players from Juárez and advanced to the national tournament, La Gran Competencia Nacional, which it also won. From left to right are (first row) Luís Fraire, Fr. Julio Vertiz (manager), and Agustín Palomares; (second row) Horacio Ramírez, Jesús Contreras, Luís "Cácaro" Ramírez, Memo Muela, Adolfo Medellín, Florentino Ruíz, Manuel "La Gringa" Rodríguez, Cosme Rodríguez, and unidentified. Jesús Contreras was the father of Mauro "El Mariachi" Contreras, who pitched for Juárez and other minor-league teams in the 1950s. (Courtesy Juan Rodríguez.)

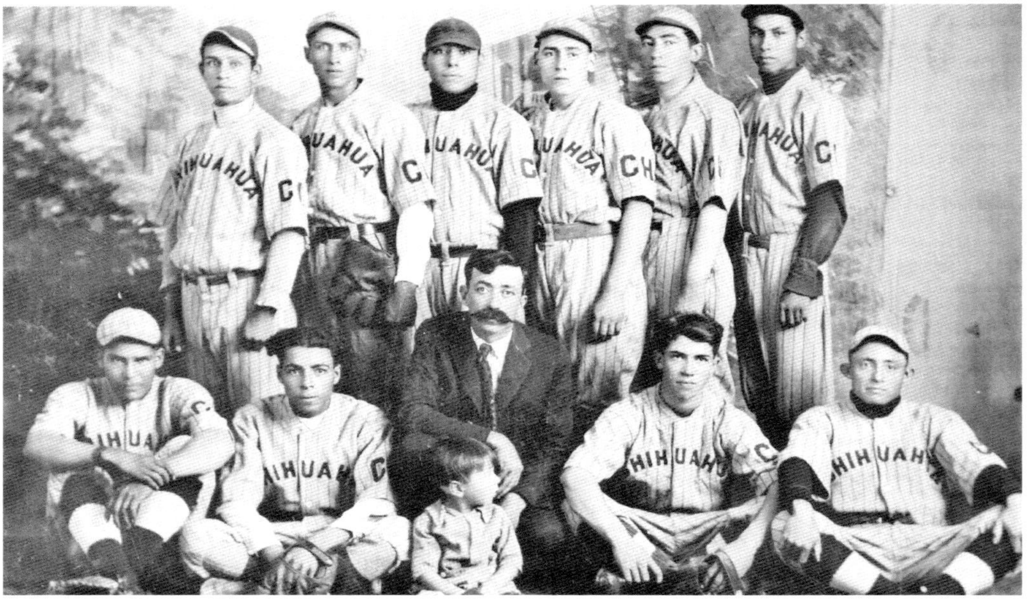

Little is known about this team, which represented Chihuahua City in the late 1920s or early 1930s. From left to right are (first row) José Jiménez, Alejandro Selís, manager José Carlos, Enrique "El Zapatero" Solis, and Trinidad "El Tamalero" Portillo; (second row) Juan "El Goose" García, José "Cuco" Rodríguez, Adolfo "Pequín" Medien, Manuel "La Gringa" Rodríguez, Manuel Acosta, and Benito Chávez. The young child sitting in front is probably the team mascot. (Courtesy Juan Rodríguez.)

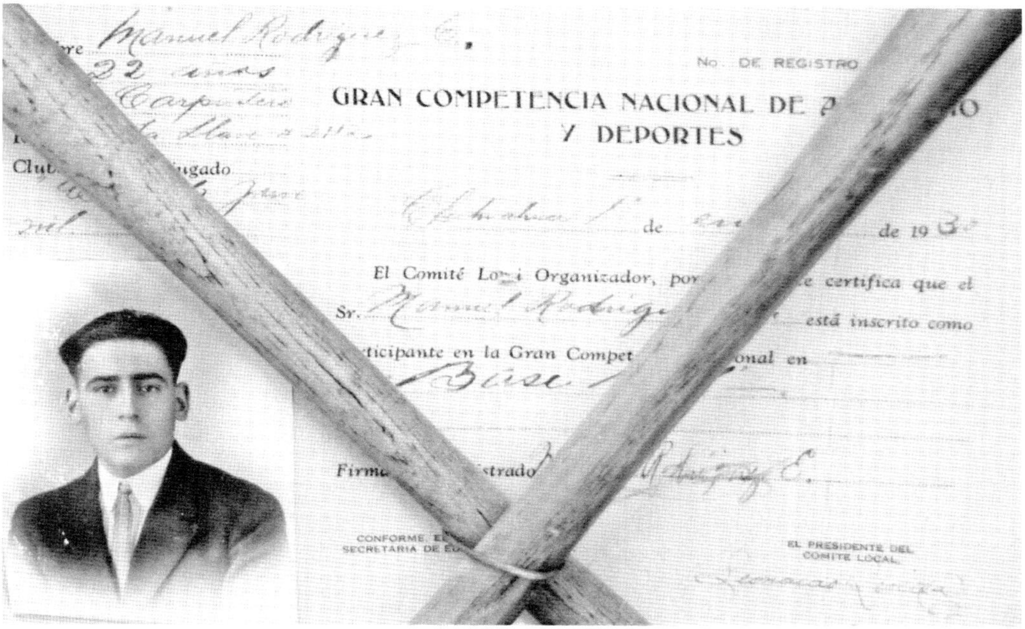

This certificate was issued to Manuel Rodríguez, first baseman for Círculo Juvenil, for participating in Mexico's national sports competition, La Gran Competencia Nacional de Atletico y Deportes, in 1930. Rodríguez was 22 years old and working as a carpenter. A native of Meoqui, Chihuahua, he moved with his father and brother to Hutchinson, Kansas, at 10 to escape the Mexican Revolution. Rodríguez returned to Mexico about seven years later, around 1924. His teammates in Chihuahua nicknamed him "La Gringa" because spending his teenage years in the United States had eroded his Spanish-speaking ability. (Courtesy Juan Rodríguez.)

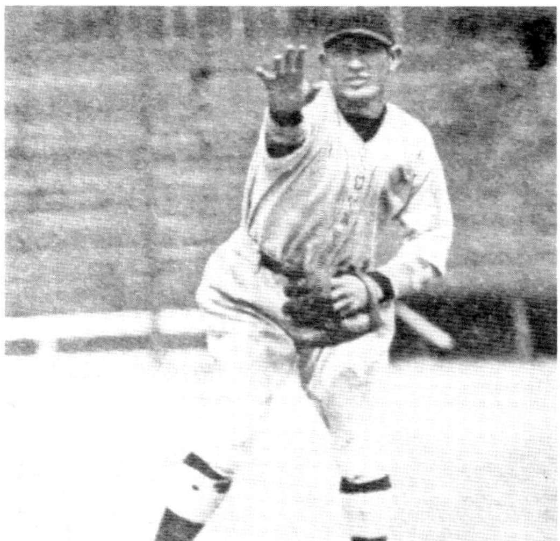

Right-handed pitcher Marcos Valdez Bugarini was born in 1906 in Julimes, a tiny village just north of Delicias in Chihuahua. In 1930, he joined Círculo Juvenil late in the season and helped them win the national championship. Bugarini, a curveball specialist, also pitched in El Paso and other locales in the outlaw Copper League in the mid-1920s. Later, he pitched for Monterrey and Veracruz of the Mexican League until the early 1940s. In a famous game on May 20, 1939, pitching for Monterrey, he defeated Las Aguilas and their Cuban ace, Martín Dihigo, 3-0. Bugarini was elected to the Mexican Baseball Hall of Fame in 1986. (Courtesy Juan Rodríguez.)

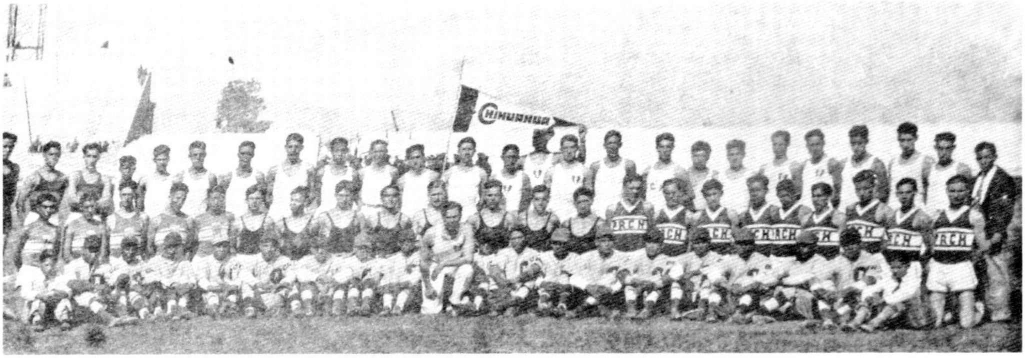

A delegation from Chihuahua attends the opening of the new Estadio de la Revolución in Torreón, Coahuila, in 1932. The accompanying festivities were part of a 25th-anniversary celebration for the city of Torreón, a ranching and textile center officially founded in 1907. The baseball players are sitting in the front row, and athletes from other sports are behind them. The man wearing white pants at front center is Leonardo "Nayo" Revilla, a basketball star and state legislator who was a key figure in building ballparks and gymnasiums throughout Chihuahua in the early 20th century. (Courtesy Juan Rodríguez.)

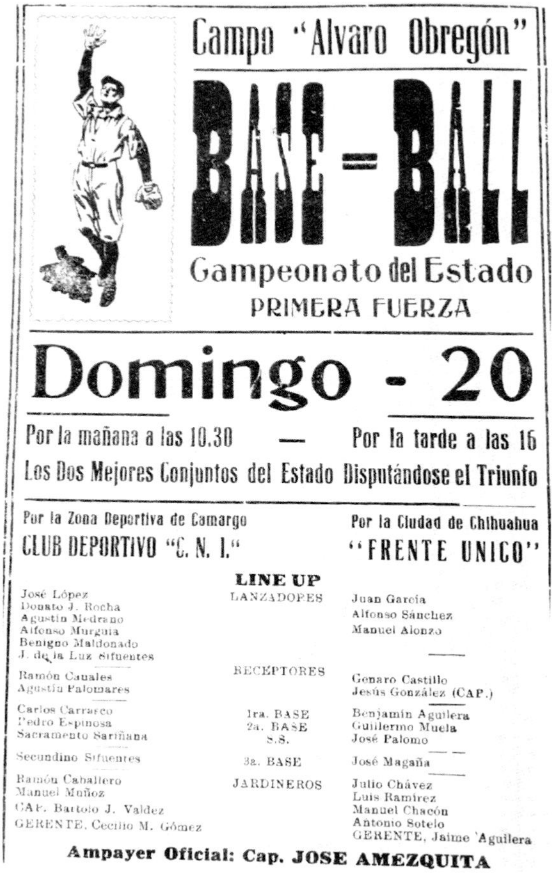

This 1933 poster advertises a Sunday doubleheader between "the two best teams in [Chihuahua] state," Frente Único and Club Deportivo. The first game was played at 10:30 a.m. and the nightcap at 4:00 p.m., avoiding the midday August heat. Frente Único, from Chihuahua City, represented El Frente Único de Ferrocariles, a railroad workers' union. Club Deportivo came from Camargo, an agricultural center on the Río Parral near Delicias. Club Deportivo was made up of engineers and hydrologists from the Comisión Nacional de Irrigación (CNI), a governmental irrigation agency. Club Deportivo boasted several renowned players, including Juárez native Chebo Hernández and Chihuahua City natives Ramón Caballero and Carlos Carrasco. (Courtesy Juan Rodríguez.)

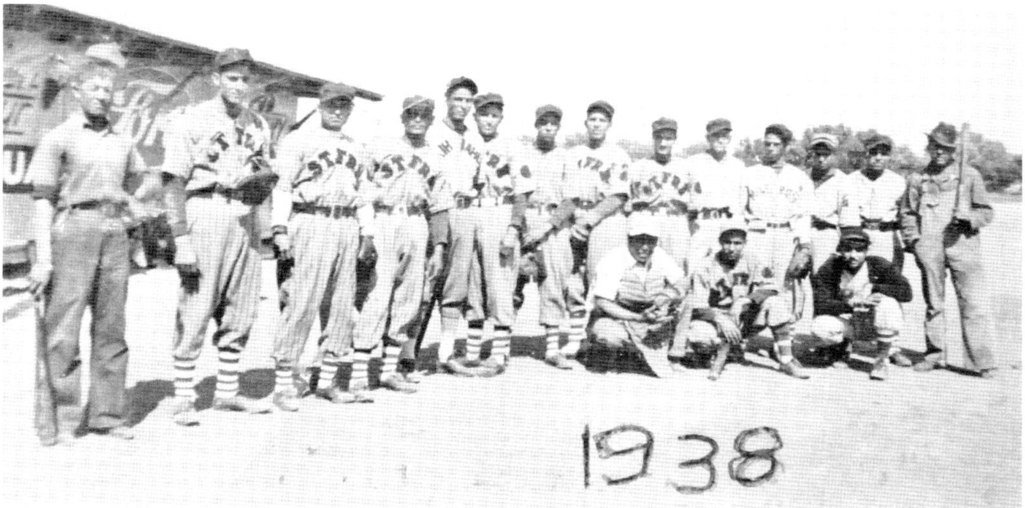

Mexican rail workers pose in Chihuahua state in 1938. The acronym STFRM stands for Sindicato de Trabajadores Ferrocarrileros de México, a union for railroad employees. In 1959, the STFRM staged one of the largest labor strikes in Mexican history, demanding higher wages and changes in the Mexican political system. The Mexican military and police crushed the strike on March 26, 1959. Their non-matching uniforms are notable. One player is wearing a Chihuahua uniform, another a Mineros de Parral jersey, and the player at far right is simply wearing farmer's overalls and a fedora. (Courtesy Leopoldo Martínez family.)

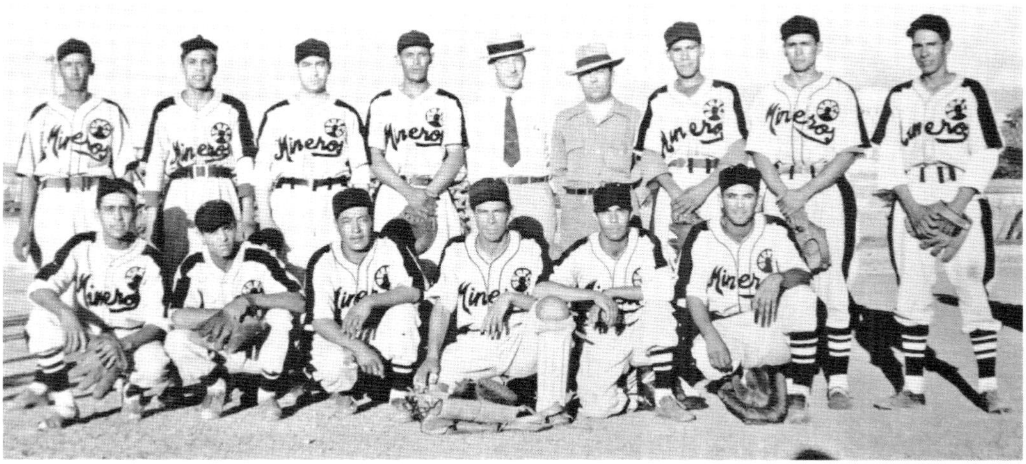

Los Mineros de Parral, sponsored by the American Smelting and Refining Company, were champions of the Chihuahua State Baseball League in 1943. Note the circular patches on the players' chests bearing the acronym ASARCO. The ASARCO refinery on the north bank of the Río Grande was a landmark in El Paso from 1910 through 2013, but the company mined most of its ore in Northern Mexico. "What was extraordinary about the history of ASARCO in México was how its executives transformed the wreckage of the Revolution . . . to the company's enormous advantage," wrote the historian Mark Wasserman. The only identified player in this photograph is Leopoldo Martínez, at far left in the first row. (Courtesy Leopoldo Martínez family.)

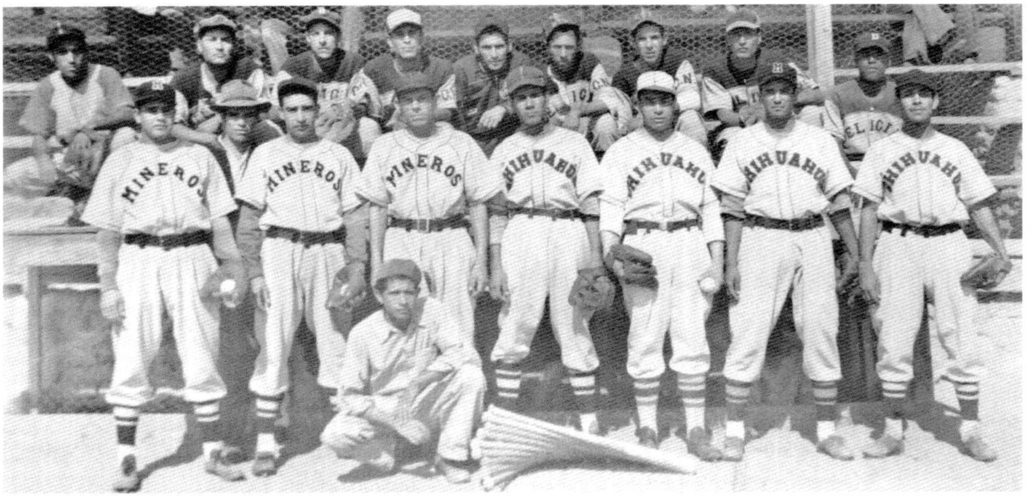

Chihuahua State Baseball League All-Stars pose in 1944. The league was comprised of teams from Chihuahua City, Parral, Delicias, and Juárez. The Delicias team was sponsored by the CNI. Until it was dissolved in 1947, the CNI was the Mexican government agency in charge of irrigation, waterworks, and other water-related issues. Note that the left-handed player for Chihuahua (third from right, first row) is wearing a right hander's glove on the wrong hand. Gloves for left-handers must have been difficult to find in Northern Mexico in the 1940s. (Courtesy Leopoldo Martínez family.)

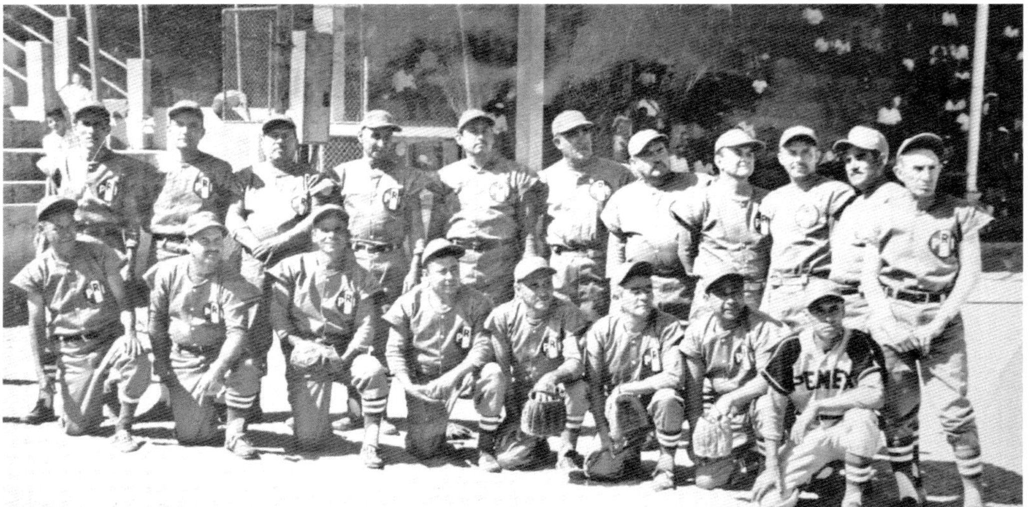

A team of older players poses in Chihuahua in the late 1940s. Their uniforms bear the logo of the Partido Revolucionario Institucional (PRI), the political party that held uninterrupted power in Mexico from 1929 through 2000. This photograph was taken after 1946, because that was the year the party changed its name from Partido Revolucionario Mexicano (PRM) to PRI. Note also that one of the players is wearing a jersey for Pemex, the state-owned petroleum company created by the Mexican government in 1938. (Courtesy Leopoldo Martínez family.)

Carmelo Hernández poses in his Juárez Indios uniform in the late 1940s. Hernández, an outfielder and second baseman, played for several minor-league and semipro teams in the border region, including the Gato Negro Bar team in Juárez. After retiring from baseball at 24 in 1950, he became chief electrician for Border Steel in El Paso, serving in that position for 30 years and raising seven children. (Courtesy John Hernández.)

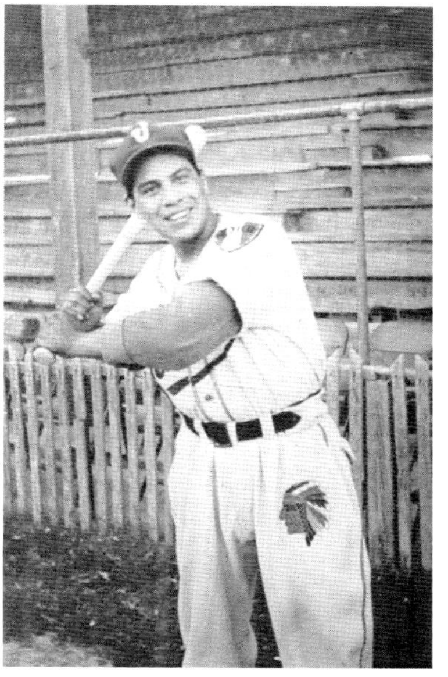

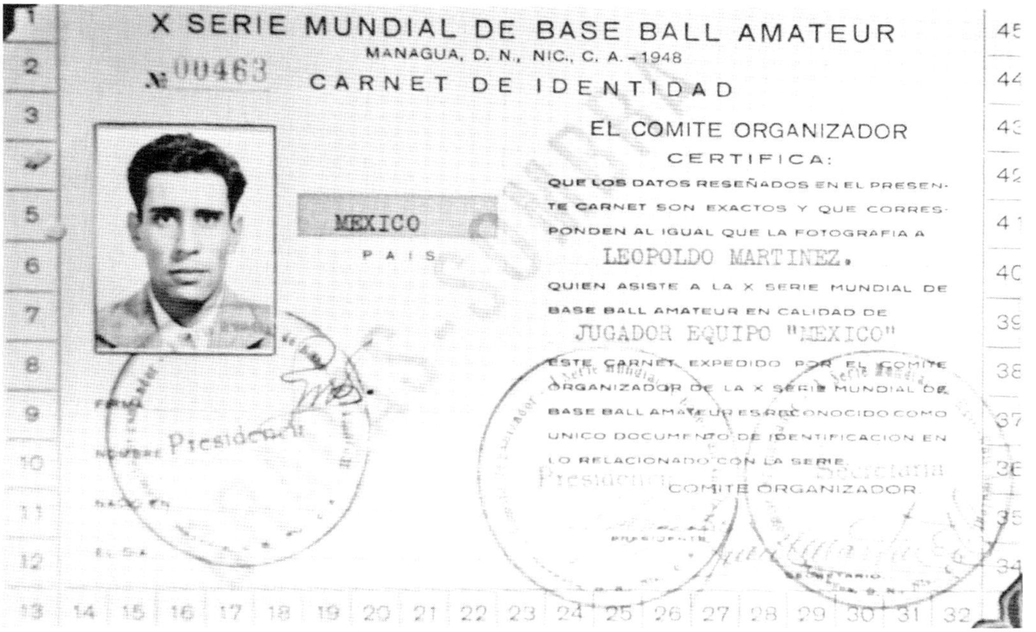

X SERIE MUNDIAL DE BASE BALL AMATEUR

MANAGUA, D. N., NIC., C. A. - 1948

№ 00463 CARNET DE IDENTIDAD

MEXICO

PAIS

EL COMITE ORGANIZADOR

CERTIFICA:

QUE LOS DATOS RESEÑADOS EN EL PRESENTE CARNET SON EXACTOS Y QUE CORRESPONDEN AL IGUAL QUE LA FOTOGRAFIA A

LEOPOLDO MARTINEZ.

QUIEN ASISTE A LA X SERIE MUNDIAL DE BASE BALL AMATEUR EN CALIDAD DE

JUGADOR EQUIPO "MEXICO"

ESTE CARNET EXPEDIDO POR EL COMITE ORGANIZADOR DE LA X SERIE MUNDIAL DE BASE BALL AMATEUR ES RECONOCIDO COMO UNICO DOCUMENTO DE IDENTIFICACION EN LO RELACIONADO CON LA SERIE.

COMITE ORGANIZADOR

Presidente

Secretario

This government identification card allowed Leopoldo Martínez to enter Nicaragua, where he competed in the 1948 Amateur Baseball World Series (also known as the Baseball World Cup) as a member of the Mexican national team. Mexico won five games and lost two in the competition but did not earn a medal. The Dominican Republic won the gold medal, Puerto Rico won silver, and Colombia took bronze. However, Mexican batter Miguel Corrales led the entire tournament in hits (12) and home runs (3). Martínez, a switch-hitting infielder, immigrated to El Paso shortly after this tournament and got a job with the Southern Pacific Railroad. (Courtesy Leopoldo Martínez family.)

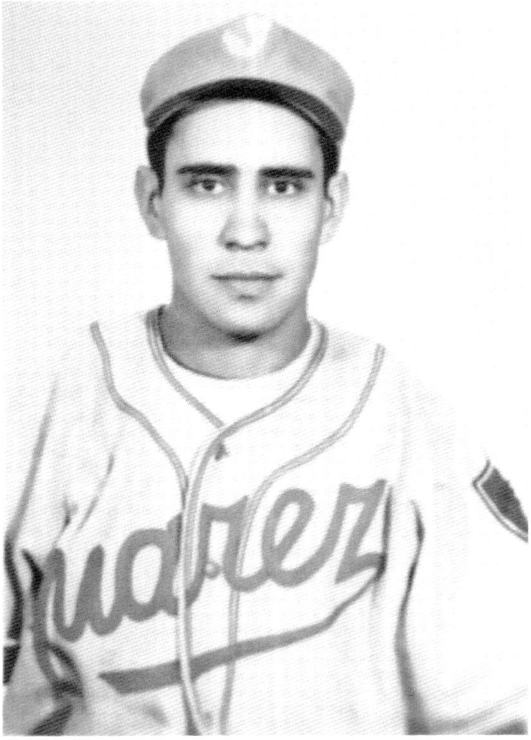

Infielder Leopoldo Martínez played for both the Juárez Indios and El Paso Texans in 1949, the year of this photograph. Born in Chihuahua in 1920, he played for teams in Texas, Mexico, and California from the 1930s through the 1960s. He eventually immigrated to the United States and settled in La Puente, California. "Though my dad never really talked about it, I know he faced lots of criticism as well as racial prejudice because he was of Mexican descent," his son, Ernie Martínez, told the *New York Times* in 2016. "He persevered by being the best player he could be and ignoring the prejudice. Baseball was a great equalizer for him. It did not matter what a player looked like. What mattered is how they played the game." (Courtesy Leopoldo Martínez family.)

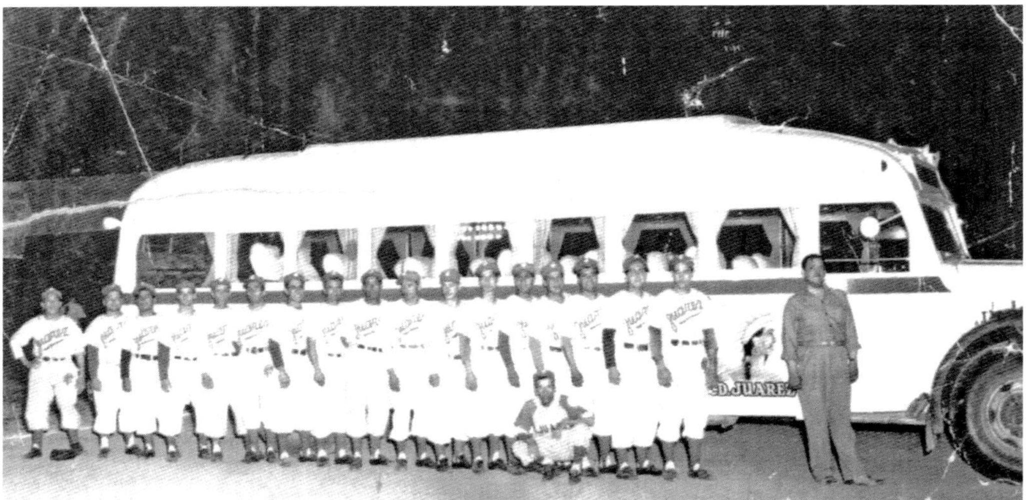

The Juárez Indios pose next to their team bus in the late 1940s or early 1950s. Road trips in the summer heat were one of the most difficult aspects of baseball in the desert Southwest. "The players and managers were put through severe endurance tests with long rattletrap bus jumps through desert country without air conditioning," local sportswriter Bob Osborne wrote in *From Browns to Diablos*. "The haul from Tijuana to El Paso and Juárez, and vice versa, was an especially torturous experience." (Courtesy John Hernández.)

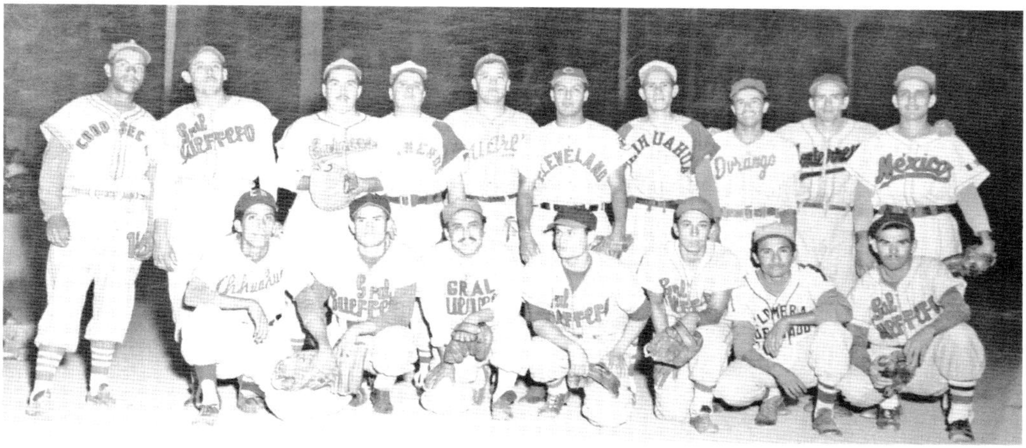

Cleveland Indians second baseman Roberto "Beto" Ávila poses in the 1950s with players from teams in Chihuahua, Durango, Juárez, Monterrey, and Parral, but most are wearing the uniform of General Guerrero, a small town in southeast Durango, perhaps an indication that this photograph was taken there. Ávila, wearing his Cleveland uniform, is fifth from right in the second row. A native of Veracruz, he was nicknamed "Bobby" by the American press but continued to be known as Beto in Mexico throughout his life. The only other identified player is infielder Leopoldo Martínez, at far right in the second row. (Courtesy Leopoldo Martínez family.)

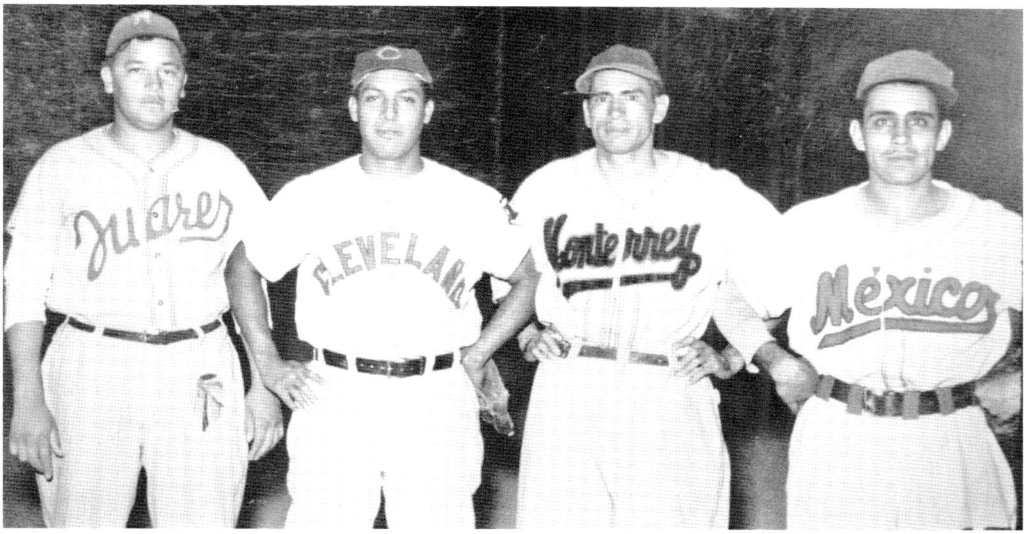

Roberto "Beto" Ávila (second from left) and Leopoldo Martínez (far right) pose with two unidentified players from Juárez and Monterrey in the early 1950s. Ávila began his career at 19 with the Pueblo Péricos and was reportedly the first player ever signed by the Major Leagues out of the Mexican League. He played for 11 years and won the 1954 batting title with an average of .341. "Everybody knows who Ávila was in Mexico," Fernando Valenzuela once said. "He was an inspiration for Mexican ballplayers to follow to the States and play in the Major Leagues." After his playing career, Ávila served as president of the Mexican League and mayor of Veracruz. (Courtesy Leopoldo Martínez family.)

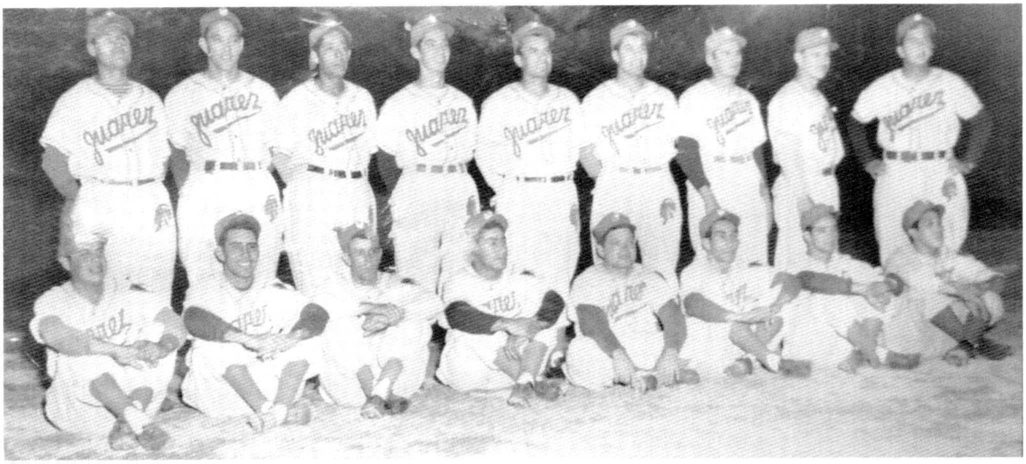

The Indios de Juárez pose in the late 1940s or early 1950s. Note the Indian headdress logo on their uniform pants, an unusual feature for baseball uniforms during this period. The Indios have been members of the Chihuahua State Baseball League since 1936 except for the period from 1973 through 1984 when they competed in the more advanced Mexican Baseball League. The Indios have won 11 Chihuahua State League pennants, most recently in 2000. The only identified player is Leopoldo Martínez, second from left in the first row. (Courtesy Leopoldo Martínez family.)

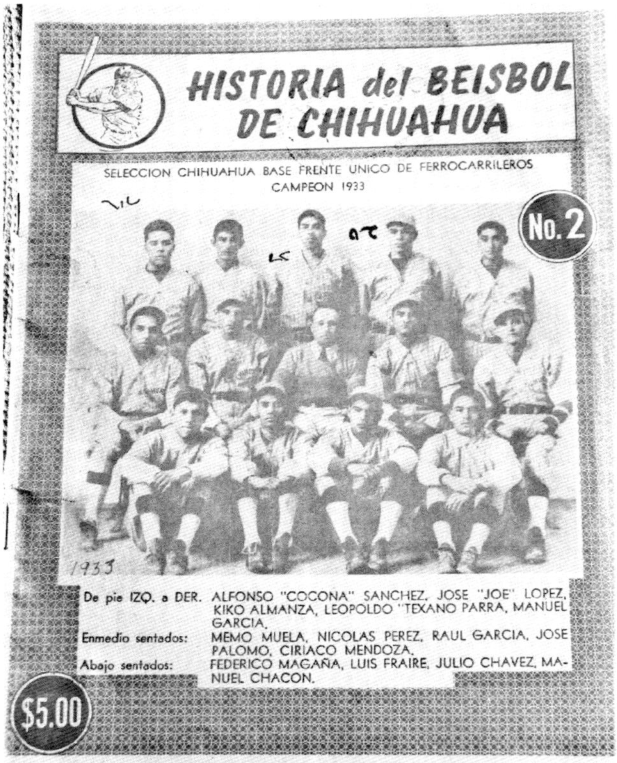

Historia del Béisbol de Chihuahua No. 2 was written by the renowned Chihuahua sportswriter and baseball historian Raúl Álvarez Herrera. It was probably published in the 1950s. This was volume two in a three-part series covering the history of baseball in Chihuahua and along the US–Mexico border. Álvarez was also a cofounder of the Tarahumara School of Baseball, a respected youth baseball program in Chihuahua. "Someone once said that Don Raúl was, in essence, a living encyclopedia, because he kept in his memory an innumerable amount of data, events, anecdotes and dates," *El Heraldo de Chihuahua* once wrote. Álvarez died in 2005. (Courtesy Juan Rodríguez.)

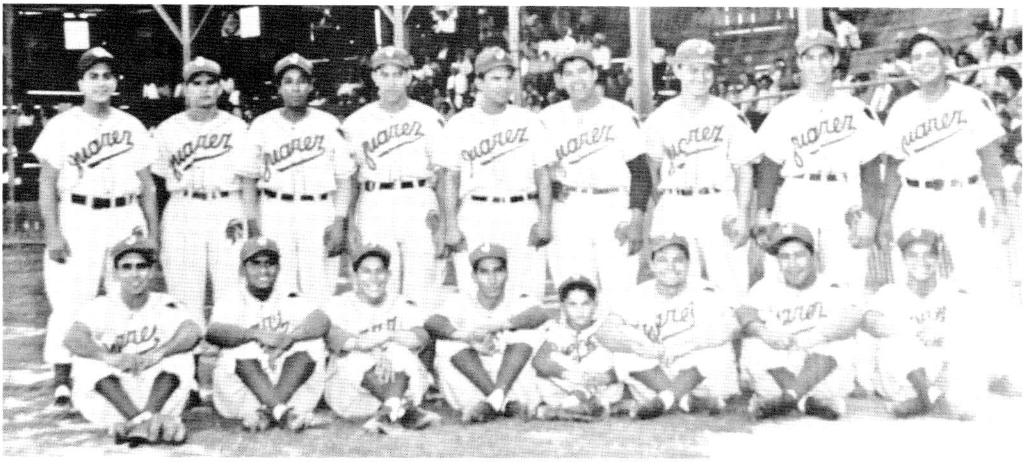

The Juárez Indios pose in the early 1950s, when their roster included Leopoldo Martínez (seated, far left) and Carmelo Hernández (standing, far right). The team name was reportedly chosen in honor of Benito Juárez, the beloved Mexican statesman who was born in a small village of indigenous Zapotecas. In his 1857 autobiography, Juárez described his parents as "Indians of the primitive race of the country." The wooden ballpark pictured here is probably Cerveceria Cruz Blanca Stadium, named after a local brewery. (Courtesy Leopoldo Martínez family.)

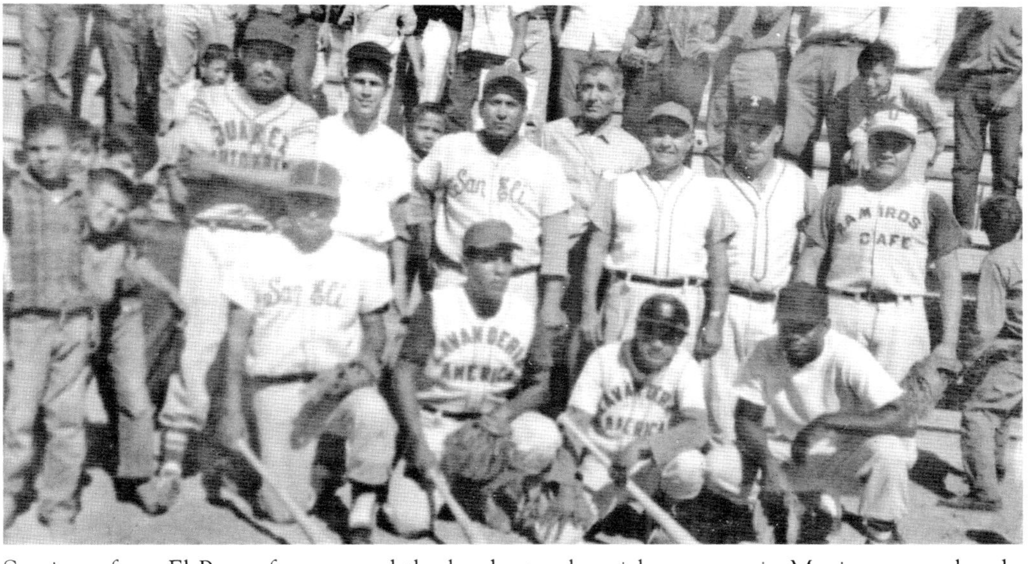

Semipros from El Paso often crossed the border to play pickup games in Mexico on weekends. This 1962 team in Delicias, Chihuahua, includes players borrowed from Ramiro's Café in the El Paso City League, supplemented with ringers from other area clubs. "We would go play three games—a single game on Saturday and a doubleheader on Sunday," said Bufe Morrison, a legendary semipro. "I traveled all over Mexico playing baseball. The people were real nice and loved the game." Players pictured include Joe Castillo (first row, far left), Hiawatha Draper (first row, far right) Chedo Cedillo (second row, third from left), Bufe Morrison (second row, sixth from left), and Toby Tovar (second row, far right). (Courtesy Bufe Morrison.)

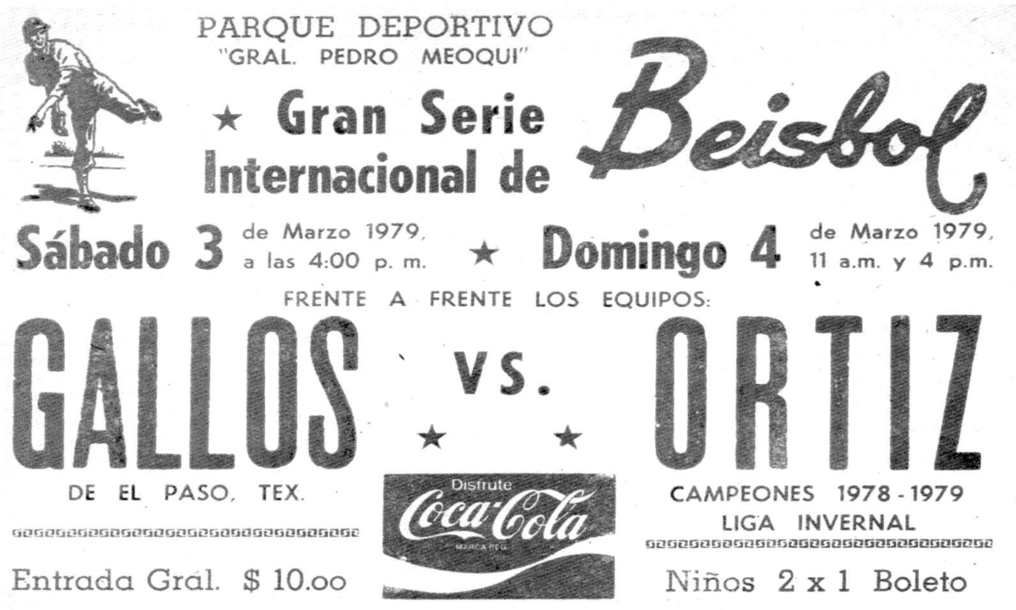

The Gran Serie Internacional de Béisbol annually pitted an American team from El Paso against a team from the Chihuahuan Winter League, one of the premier semipro leagues in Northern Mexico. This poster advertises the 1979 event, in which the El Paso Gallos faced Chihuahua, managed by Juan Ortiz. The games were played at Estadio General Pedro Meoqui in Delicias, an agricultural city in the Conchos River valley in northern Chihuahua. Estadio Meoqui was "one of the most beautiful in the region in its time" and a local landmark in Delicias, according to the local newspaper *El Pionero.* As of 2016, local citizens were petitioning the Mexican government to remodel the old wooden ballpark. (Courtesy Bufe Morrison.)

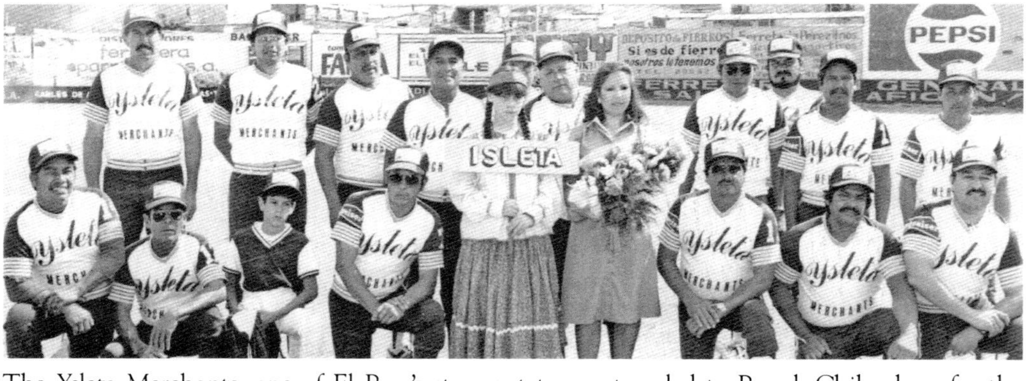

The Ysleta Merchants, one of El Paso's strongest teams, traveled to Parral, Chihuahua, for the International 40-60 Tournament in 1983. Parral, the headquarters of Mexico's silver mining industry, is best known as the town where Francisco "Pancho" Villa was assassinated in 1923. From left to right are (first row) Lalo Solís, Ponte Mestas, unidentified child, Agustín Cedillo, unidentified child, unidentified flower girl, Joe Cedillo, Henry Lescano, and Sal Payán; (second row) Mike Barrueta, Tony Ramos, Manuel Gallardo, Bufe Morrison, Jesús "Bull" Rodríguez, Bobby Camarillo, Pablo "Moose" Camarillo, Peter Zavala, and Armando Pedregón. (Courtesy Bufe Morrison.)

Teodoro Higuera grew up in Ejido Vallejo, a small town in Sinaloa, and spent his early 20s pitching in the El Paso–Juárez area. In 1977, he made 9,000 pesos per week pitching for a semipro team in Nuevo Casas Grandes, Chihuahua, southwest of El Paso. "My father didn't want me to play baseball, arguing that it was a drunken sport, since when games were finished on the ranches people started to drink," Higuera once said. Higuera won his father's blessing in 1979 and signed a pro contract with Juárez. After five seasons, the Indios sold Higuera's contract to the Milwaukee Brewers, who sent him directly to their Class AA team, the El Paso Diablos. Higuera was called up to the majors in 1985, posting two 20-win seasons before his career was derailed by a back injury. (Courtesy Milwaukee Brewers.)

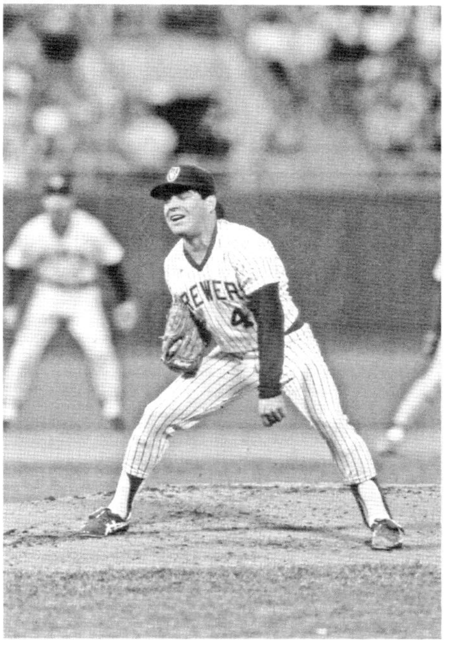

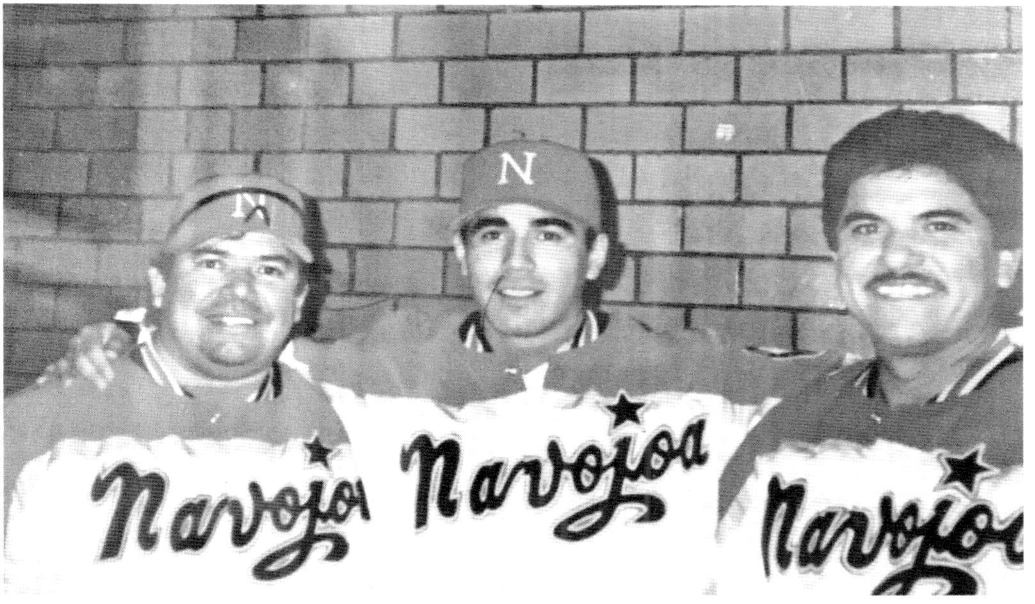

Left-handed reliever and El Paso native Rubén Félix (center) poses in 1994 with teammates Fernando Valenzuela (left) and Héctor "Caballo" Heredia on Los Mayos de Navojoa in the Mexican League. In 1988, playing for Socorro High School, Rubén Félix and his twin, Larry, were named District 2-5A co-MVPs. Both earned all-conference honors at New Mexico State University. In 1994, Rubén Félix went 6-0 with a 2.42 ERA for Corpus Christi in the Brewers farm system. He later coached with the Cleveland Indians and Baltimore Orioles. As of 2017, Rubén Félix is associate head softball coach at the University of Mississippi. (Courtesy Rubén Félix.)

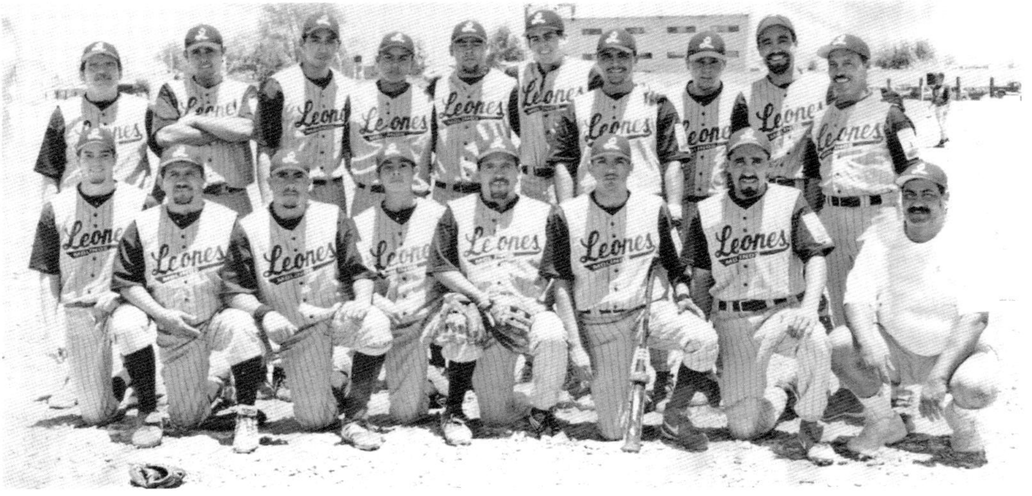

Los Leones de Ciudad Juárez was a summer team of veteran players from Mexico and collegiate players from El Paso brought in to play on weekends. Several players pictured here in 2001, including Efrain Barraza, Victor Colmenero Jr., Mark Enders, and Cody King, also played for EPCC in 2011. From left to right are (first row) Mark Enders, Alfredo Colmenero, Pete Guillén Jr., Efraín Barraza, Ángel Colmenero, Noe Rodríguez, Pepe Ceniceros, and Pete Guillén Sr.; (second row) Sal Márquez Sr., Sal Márquez Jr., Moy Martínez, Armando Ruíz, Victor Colmenero Jr., Cody King, Manuel Ibarra, Óscar Márquez, Charlie Ceniceros, and Victor Colmenero Sr. (Courtesy Mark Enders.)

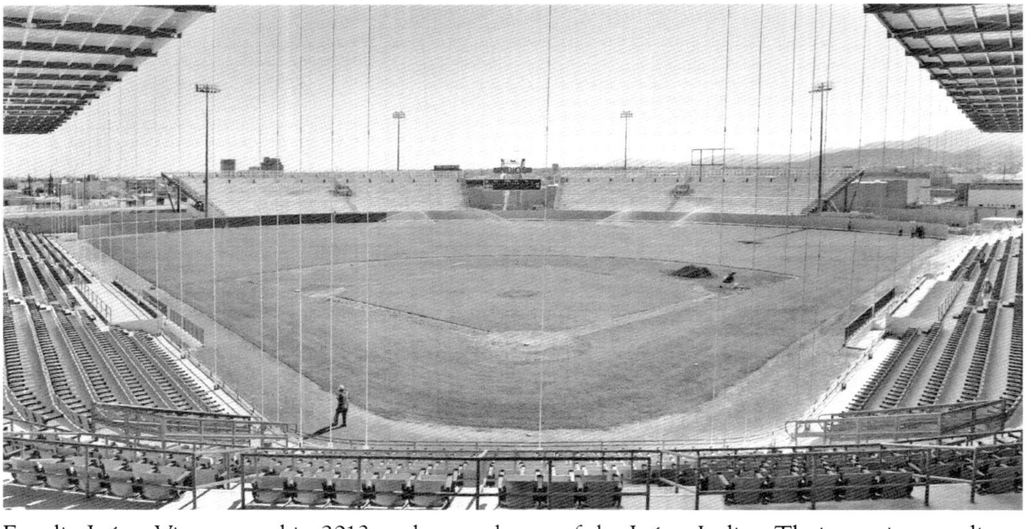

Estadio Juárez Vive opened in 2013 as the new home of the Juárez Indios. Their previous stadium, Estadio Carta Blanca, had been built four decades earlier when the team made its short-lived jump to the Triple-A Mexican League. The new stadium, with its optimistic name, signaled the dawn of a new era of hope in Ciudad Juárez. The 11,000-seat stadium features a state-of-the-art sound system and is seeking LEED green certification as a sustainable building. In 2017, the state sports institute, which operates the stadium, announced plans to sell the naming rights to an as-yet-unidentified corporate sponsor. (Courtesy Instituto Chihuahuense del Deporte y Cultura Física.)

3

Borderland Baseball

El Paso's first official minor-league team was the El Paso Mackmen, an all-white club that lasted just half a season in 1915 before folding. In the 1920s, El Paso was part of one of the most interesting leagues in baseball. The Copper League linked copper refining cities on both sides of the border. It was considered an "outlaw league" because it employed three Chicago Black Sox and other players banned from baseball for life. Commissioner Kenesaw Mountain Landis traveled to El Paso in an attempt to shut the Copper League down, but it continued to field integrated teams composed of Mexicans, Mexican Americans, whites, and banned Major-League players until it folded in 1927.

Affiliated ball returned in 1930 with the El Paso Texans, who played intermittently throughout the 1930s, with their league folding in 1932 and again in 1941. The Texans restarted after World War II under owner Pete Leyva, and between 1947 and 1957, El Paso's minor-league team employed more Mexican and Mexican American players than in any other period. Ownership changed hands seemingly every year, but general manager John Phelan provided continuity. Because the Texans were not affiliated with a specific Major-League team, Phelan had to acquire his own players, and signed many local stars and players from the Mexican League. In 1953, thirteen of the Texans' 20 players were Mexican or Mexican American, including former Bowie High School star Jimmy Ochoa.

In 1961, the El Paso Sun Kings debuted; they were community owned, a rarity in the sports world. The Sun Kings led the entire minor leagues in attendance in their debut season and later moved up to Double-A, the highest level El Paso had ever reached. To coincide with the move, the city spent $200,000 on concrete grandstands at Dudley Field, increasing its capacity to 7,200. The Sun Kings were eventually sold to Gene Autry and later the Los Angeles Dodgers, who moved the franchise to Connecticut in 1973.

A legendary franchise was born when Jim Paul bought the El Paso Diablos for $1,000 in 1975. With never-before-seen promotions like fireworks night and the San Diego Chicken, Paul remade the landscape of minor-league baseball in America. All of a sudden, everyone was copying El Paso. The Diablos were profiled in *Sports Illustrated* and were featured on the cover of *National Geographic*, and Paul tailored the lively ballpark experience to his largely Mexican American fan base. He made the team's logo a chile pepper, played Spanish-language music, introduced nachos to baseball, and sold $1 tamales at the concession stand. The Diablos thrived and moved into a new $6-million ballpark, Cohen Stadium, in 1991. Paul sold the Diablos in 1996, they moved to Missouri in 2004, and were replaced in 2014 by the El Paso Chihuahuas. El Paso's newest minor-league team is not only named after a neighboring Mexican state but is also, as of 2017, run by a Mexican-born co-owner (Alejandra de la Vega Foster) and a Mexican American field manager (Rod Barajas).

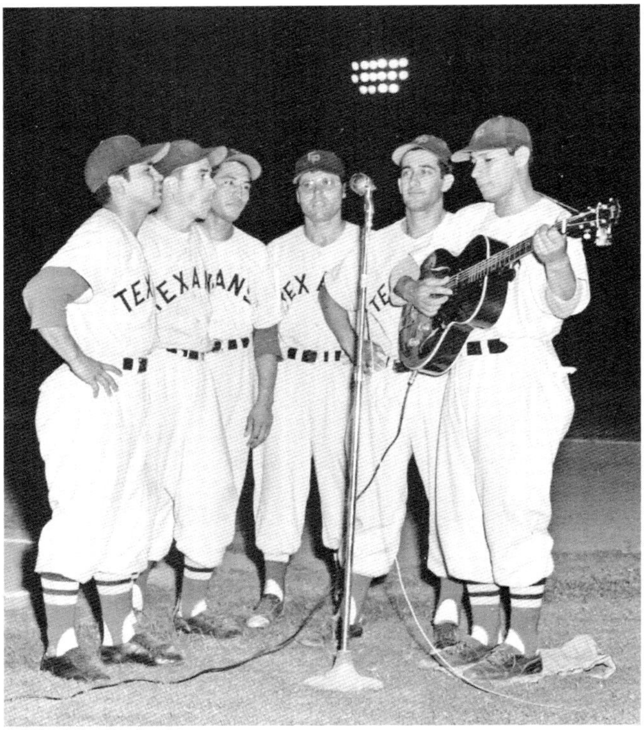

Six members of the 1951 El Paso Texans minor-league team play music at Dudley Field. The only identified player is infielder Héctor Mayer (second from right). Music was a huge part of El Paso culture in the 1950s, propelled by "border radio" stations located just across the Río Grande. Not bound by American broadcasting laws, they were sending signals of up to 500,000 watts hundreds of miles into the United States. "In those days everyone listened to the radio," local author Gloria López-Stafford wrote. "People sang as they worked and many couldn't work unless there was a radio playing." (Courtesy El Paso Chihuahuas.)

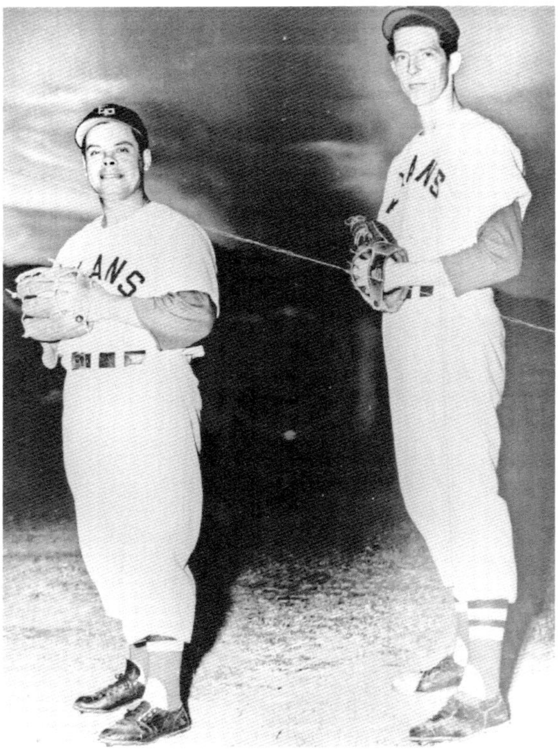

The two aces on the 1951 El Paso Texans were five-foot eight Gustavo "Chato" Bello (left) and six-foot four Bill Stites (right). The pair combined for 54 wins, with Stites posting a 29-9 win-loss record and Bello 25-13. They pitched an astonishing 651 innings. Stites was known for his poor attitude and hair-trigger temper, which enabled the Texans to acquire him from his previous team for only $25. Bello, meanwhile, was a native of Jalapa, Veracruz, who briefly pitched in the Brooklyn Dodgers farm system. He pitched in the border region for El Paso, Juárez, Bisbee, Douglas, Tampico, Saltillo, and Guanajuato, among other teams, from 1944 through 1961. (Courtesy El Paso Chihuahuas.)

El Paso Texans Delane "Dee" Noah (left) and Héctor Mayer are pictured in 1951. Mayer, a native of Nogales, Sonora, batted .271 in his third season with the Texans in 1951. The young shortstop was later sold to the St. Louis Cardinals for $4,000 plus five players. After rising as high as Triple-A Rochester, Mayer returned to his home country, playing for the Mexico City Reds from 1956 to 1961. The 1951 Texans played in the new Southwest International League, formed from a merger of the Arizona-Texas and Sunset Leagues. The league featured teams in Juárez, Phoenix, Las Vegas, and Tijuana, but lasted only a year, undone by the grueling travel. (Courtesy El Paso Chihuahuas.)

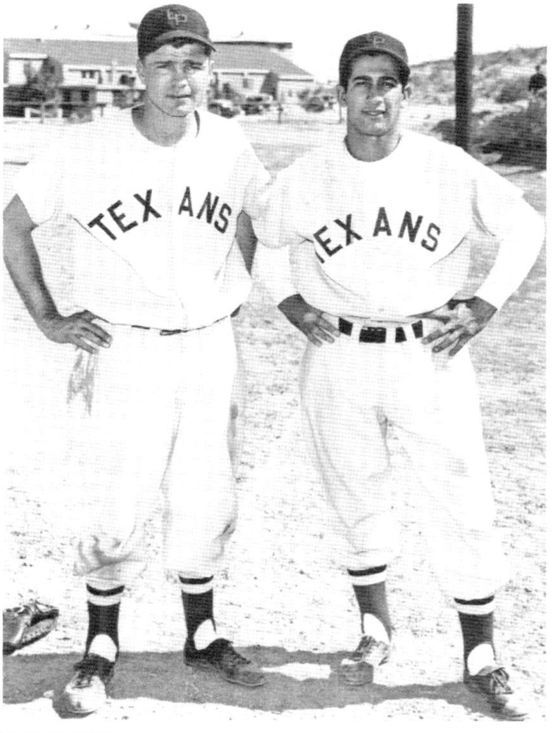

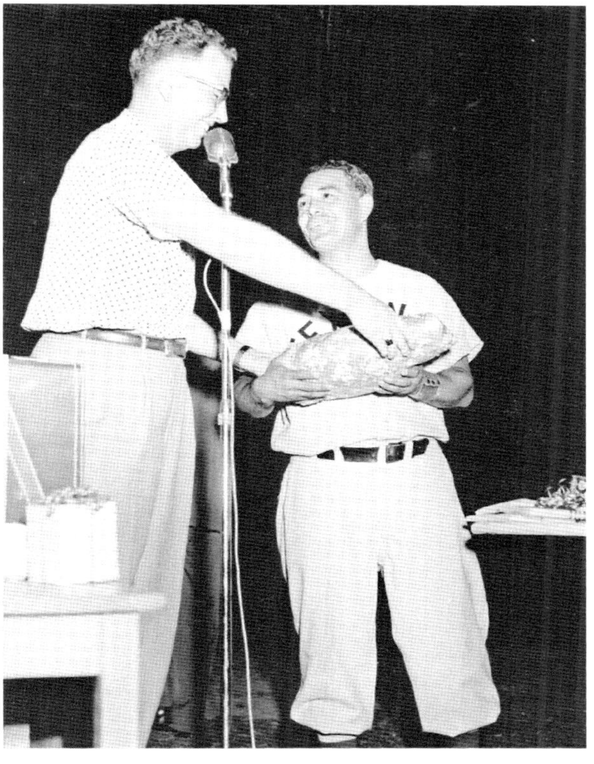

El Paso Texans general manager John Phelan presents a gift to Texans outfielder Ramón Vargas, who won the Southwest International League batting title with a .377 average in 1951. Vargas, 37 years old in this picture, spent two decades playing for minor-league and semipro teams in El Paso, Juárez, Tucson, Laredo, Nogales, and other borderland locales, rarely batting lower than .300. Phelan, a veteran newspaperman, first came to El Paso to be treated for burns suffered on the battlefield in World War II. In 1950, at age 29 and with no prior sports experience, Phelan quit his job at KTSM radio to become general manager of the Texans. One of his first moves was acquiring Vargas in a trade with the Juárez Indios. (Courtesy El Paso Chihuahuas.)

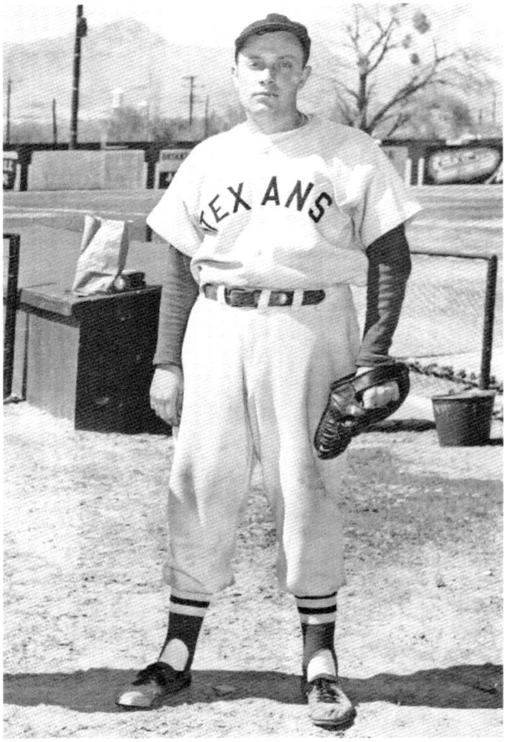

An unidentified El Paso Texan poses in 1951 at Dudley Field with the Franklin Mountains in the background. The Texans stayed in a dogfight for the Southwest International League pennant all season in 1951, entering the final day needing a win against Juárez at Dudley Field to clinch the second-half title. Alas, they lost. The season was a financial success, though, as the Texans attracted a franchise record 111,533 fans, not including the league all-star game, which drew an additional 7,344. In an unusual twist, the all-star game pitted the league's American-born players against its Mexican-born players. The Americans won 7-6. (Courtesy El Paso Chihuahuas.)

This image from a 1952 El Paso Texans program depicts Ventura Morales, a right-hitting outfielder from Hermosillo, Mexico, who was a mainstay in the Texans' lineup from 1950 through 1954. Playing in the hitters' paradise of Dudley Field, Morales knocked 20 or more homers three years in a row and batted .298 or better in each of his five seasons with El Paso. In the winter of 1949–1950, Morales was at the center of a dispute between the Texans and the Mexican League, both of whom claimed to have signed him. El Paso paid $1,300 to the Mexican League to settle the dispute and keep the player. (Courtesy El Paso Chihuahuas.)

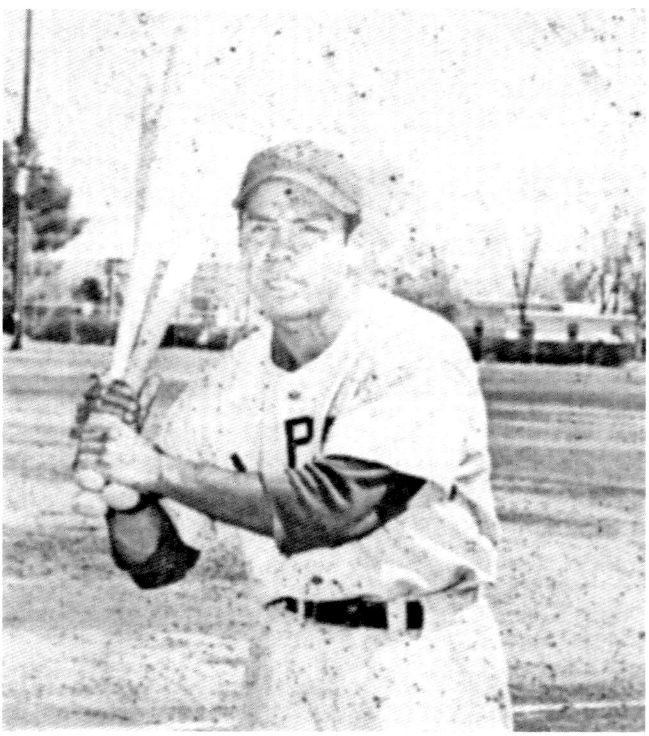

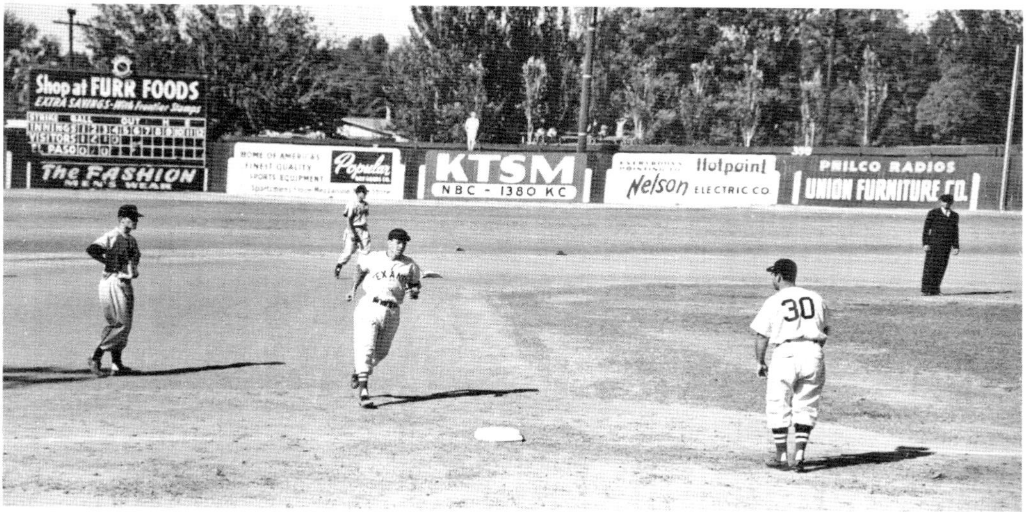

An unidentified El Paso Texan rounds the bases on a home run against the Bisbee-Douglas Copper Kings at Dudley Field sometime between 1949 and 1953. Note the unpadded, wooden outfield fence painted with advertisements for local businesses: KTSM Radio, Popular Dry Goods, Union Furniture, and Furr's Grocery Stores. Also notable is the presence of gloves on the playing field, indicating that this photograph was taken before 1954, when baseball passed a new rule prohibiting fielders from leaving their gloves on the playing field while their team was at bat. (Courtesy El Paso Chihuahuas.)

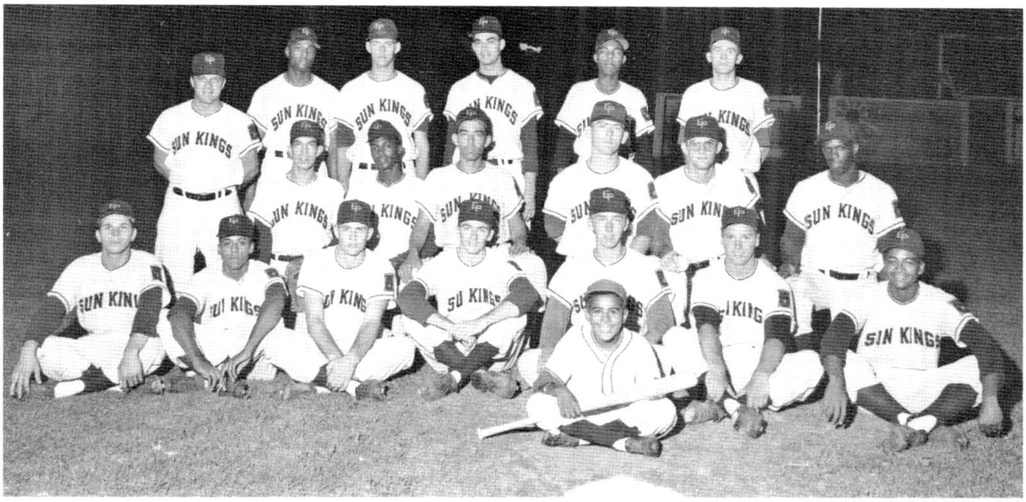

The El Paso Sun Kings pose for a team photograph during the franchise's debut season of 1961. The Sun Kings were owned and operated by the El Paso Sports Association, a local nonprofit group that included the Cohen brothers, Andy and Syd, as well as general manager John Phelan and chairman Dan Ponder, a former mayor of El Paso. This was the team's only season in the Class C Sophomore League; the following year, it moved up to Class AA. The 1961 roster included 12 Latino players, including Mexico natives Jesús Lechler and Héctor Holguín and Cuban star José Cardenal (first row, second from left). (Courtesy El Paso Chihuahuas.)

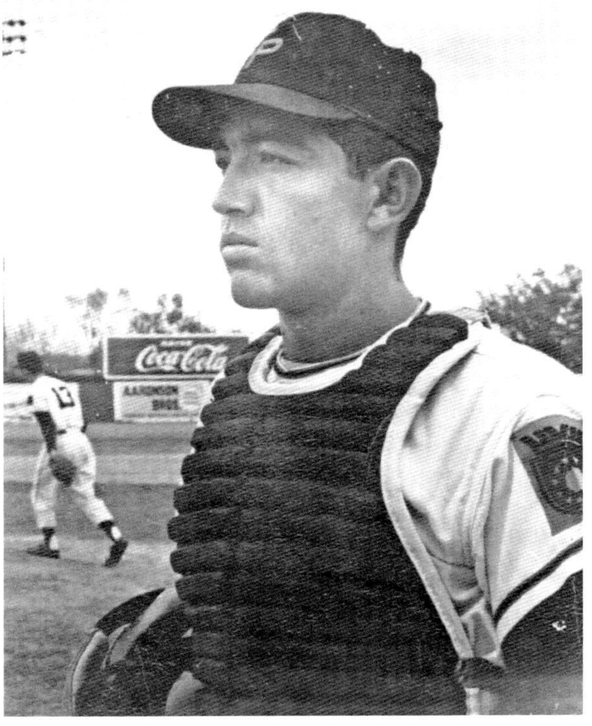

Jesús Lechler, a 21-year-old catching prospect, started his pro career with the El Paso Sun Kings in 1961. Lechler was originally from Piedras Negras, Coahuila, a border town just across the Río Grande from Eagle Pass, Texas. The Sun Kings were in their debut season in 1961, and as a Double-A franchise, they represented the highest level of pro baseball yet played in El Paso. Their parent team, the San Francisco Giants, was the Major-League leader in developing Latin American players, and having a farm team in largely Spanish-speaking El Paso was a boon to the organization. Latino stars such as Felipe Alou, José Cardenal, and Rigoberto "Tito" Fuentes played in El Paso during the 1960s. (Courtesy El Paso Chihuahuas.)

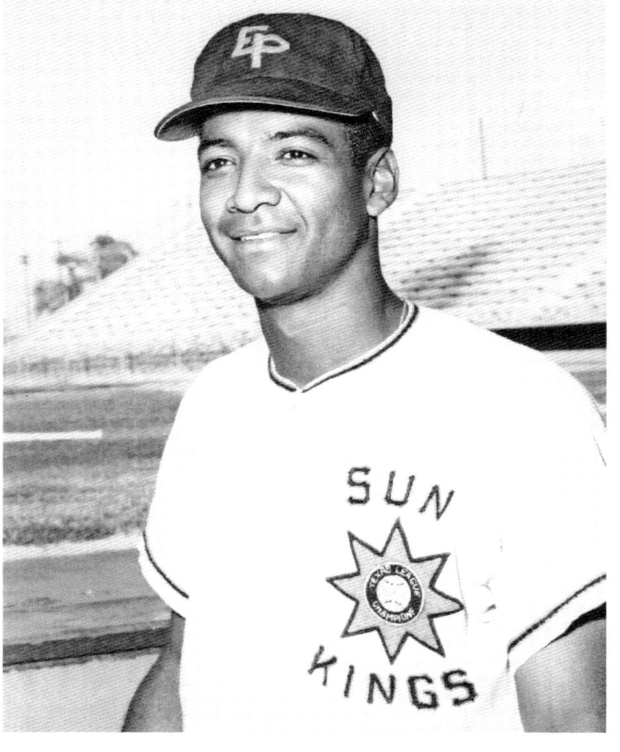

After signing Venezuelan third baseman Dámaso Blanco in 1961, the San Francisco Giants assigned the 19-year-old to their El Paso farm team in the hopes that playing in a Spanish-speaking community would ease his transition into American baseball. However, that backfired on one road trip when Blanco was not allowed to stay in the segregated hotel where the white players stayed. Blanco would play in the Giants' farm system for the next 14 years, making it to the Major Leagues for only 72 games in the early 1970s. "I was Willie McCovey's designated runner," he once said. "If Willie got a hit in the late innings, I ran for him." (Courtesy El Paso Chihuahuas.)

Right-handed reliever Minervino "Minnie" Rojas pitched for the El Paso Sun Kings in 1961 and 1962. The native of Villa Clara, Cuba, pitched poorly in El Paso, posting a 5.41 ERA over two seasons, but he was an immediate success upon being called up to the Major Leagues. He posted a 2.88 ERA as a rookie with the California Angels in 1966, and the following year, he led the American League in saves while receiving American League MVP votes. His career ended in tragedy in 1968, when his spine was severed in a hit-and-run car accident in Miami. The crash killed two of Rojas's three children and left him paralyzed for the rest of his life. (Courtesy El Paso Chihuahuas.)

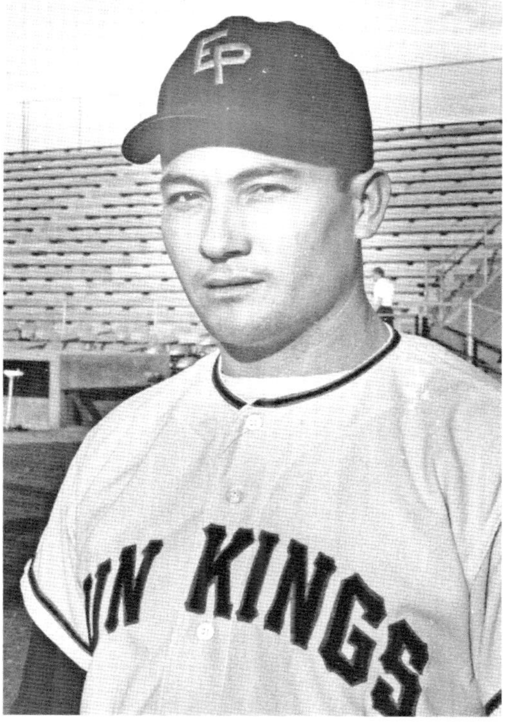

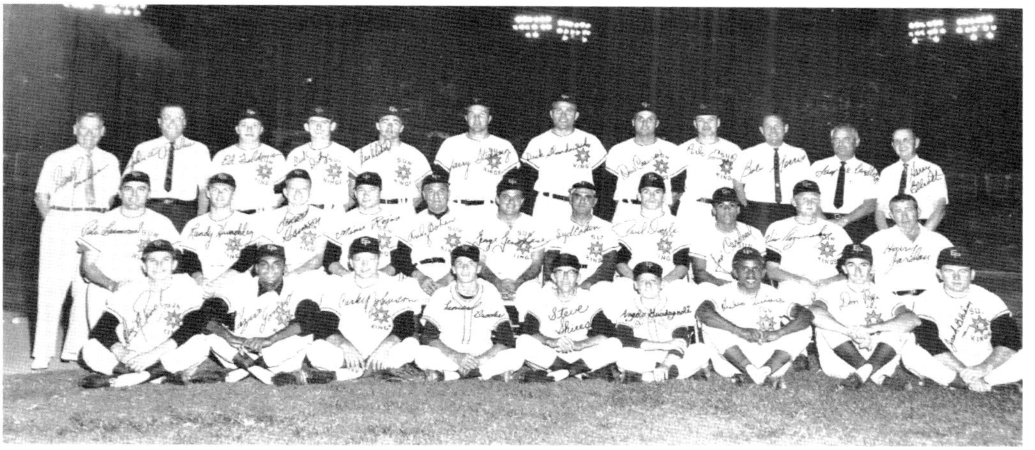

The 1963 El Paso Sun Kings are, from left to right, (first row) unidentified batboy, Lázaro Gómez, Corky Johnson, Leonard Brooks, batboy Steve Shires, batboy Angelo Guadagnoli, Julio Linares, Don Pope, and Jackie Blehm; (second row) Pete Carmona, Randy Hundley, Jerry Robinson, Minervino "Minnie" Rojas, vice president Andy Cohen, manager George Genovese, pitching coach Syd Cohen, Paul Doyle, José Cardenal, Vic Roznovsky, and trainer Harry Jordan; (third row) chairman Dan Ponder, team president John Phelan, Ed Feldman, Dick Dietz, Darrell "Dee" Weber, Larry "Moose" Stubing, Dick Slomkowski, Don Carlson, Arlo Engel, business manager Bob Morris, vice president Sam Pendleton, and concessions manager Harry Elliott. (Courtesy El Paso Chihuahuas.)

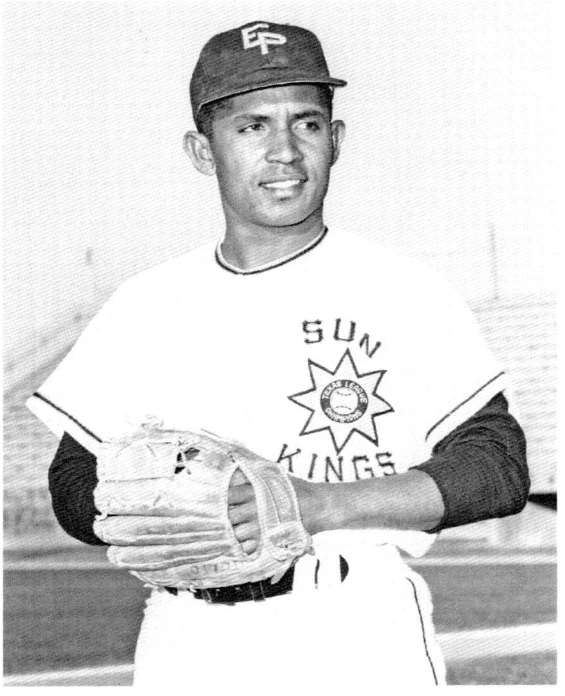

Infielder Julio Linares became one of the earliest Dominican players in the US minor leagues when he joined the San Francisco Giants' farm system in 1960. Linares played three years for the El Paso Sun Kings, manning second base in 1962, shortstop in 1963, and third base in 1964. He displayed decent hitting skills, batting .293 for his Sun Kings career. Despite playing 13 seasons at the Double-A and Triple-A levels, he was never able to make the jump to the Major Leagues. He finally made the majors in 1994 as a coach for the Houston Astros. As of 2016, he is the Astros' special advisor for Latin American player development. (Courtesy El Paso Chihuahuas.)

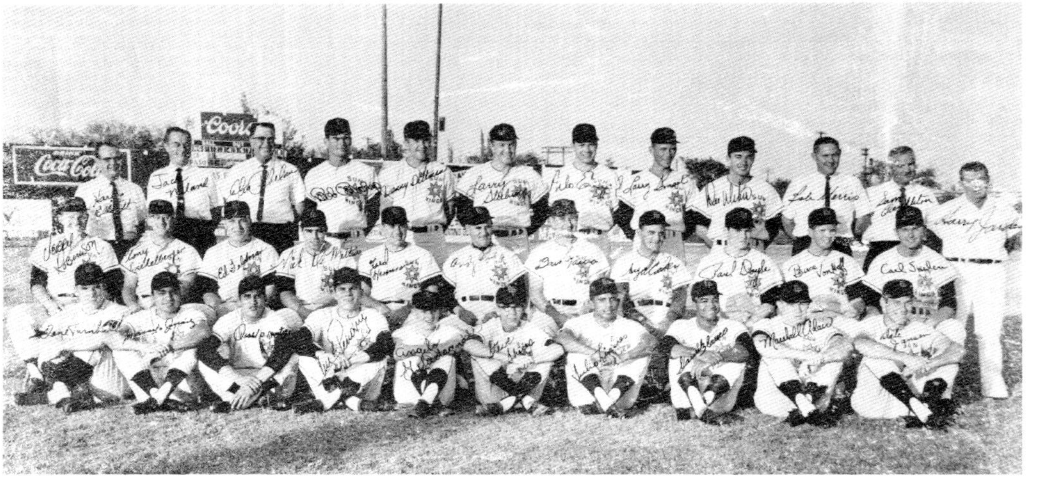

The 1964 El Paso Sun Kings are, from left to right, (first row) Dave Turnbull, Marcelo Juárez, ? Montoya, unidentified batboy, batboy Angelo Guadagnoli, batboy Steve Shires, Julio Linares, Dámaso Blanco, Marshall Adair, and Dale Jansen; (second row) Jerry Robinson, Tony Eichelberger, Ed Feldman, Nick De Mattea, Fred Herrmann, vice president Andy Cohen, manager Dave García, pitching coach Syd Cohen, Paul Doyle, Bruce Von Hoff, and Carl Shelen; (third row) concessions manager Harry Elliott, vice president Jack Niland, team president John Phelan, Bob Bishop, Denny Dittman, Larry "Moose" Stubing, Arlo Engel, Larry Smoot, Darrell "Dee" Weber, business manager Bob Morris, vice president Sam Pendleton, and trainer Harry Jordan. (Courtesy El Paso Chihuahuas.)

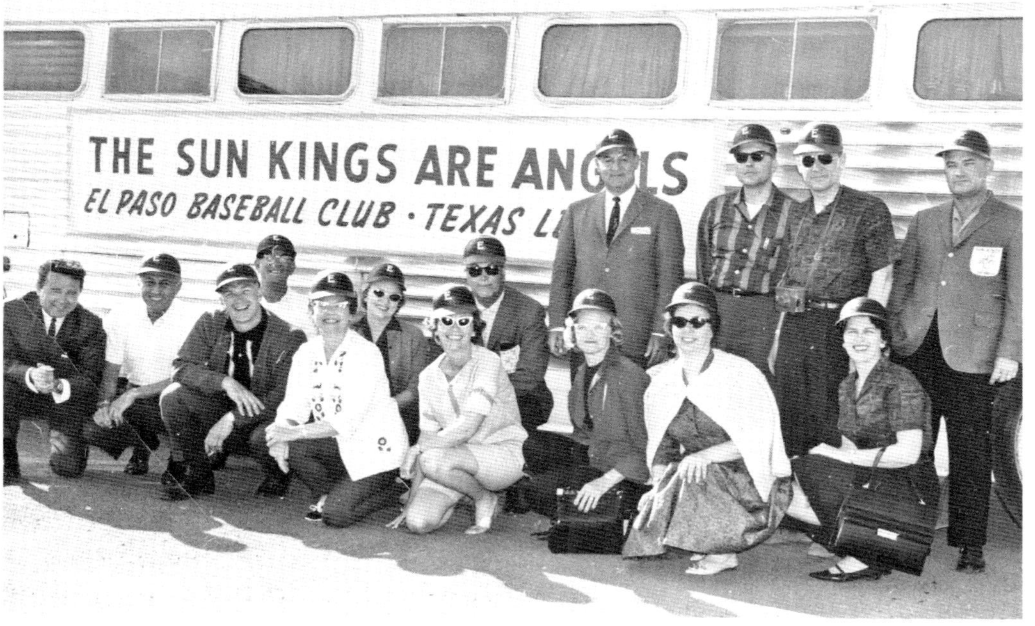

Executives and employees of the El Paso Sun Kings pose alongside the team bus sometime between 1965 and 1970, when the Sun Kings served as the California Angels' Double-A farm team. The legendary Cohen brothers were both former big-league players and renowned figures in El Paso baseball. Andy Cohen (standing, far left) played second base for the New York Giants, while Syd Cohen (standing, far right) pitched for the Washington Senators. Syd, with his dark complexion and fluency in Spanish, was able to pass as Mexican when the situation called for it. In 1931, he reportedly played on a team in Nogales, Sonora, under the alias "Pablo García." (Courtesy El Paso Chihuahuas.)

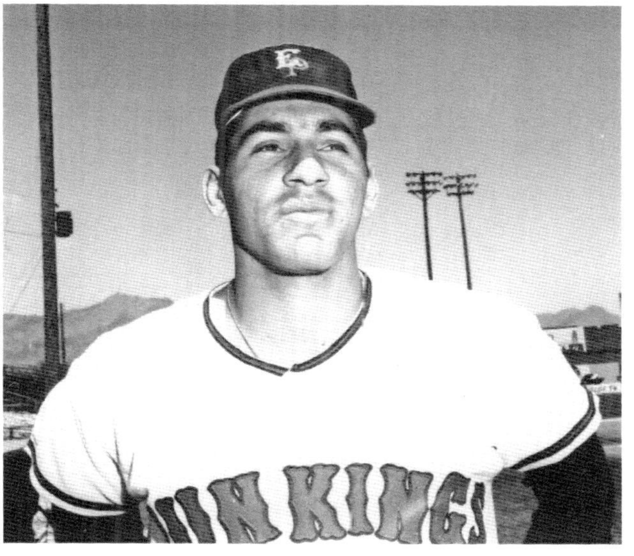

Felipe Leal, a native of Matamoros on the Texas-Mexico border, pitched for the El Paso Sun Kings in 1967. It was Leal's last stand in affiliated pro ball, as the 24-year-old posted an 8.47 ERA in the hitter's haven of El Paso and was swiftly released by the Angels organization. He spent the next 12 years pitching for teams throughout the Mexican League, including Chihuahua, Mexico City, Nuevo Laredo, Monterrey, Pueblo, Tampico, and Saltillo. (Courtesy El Paso Chihuahuas.)

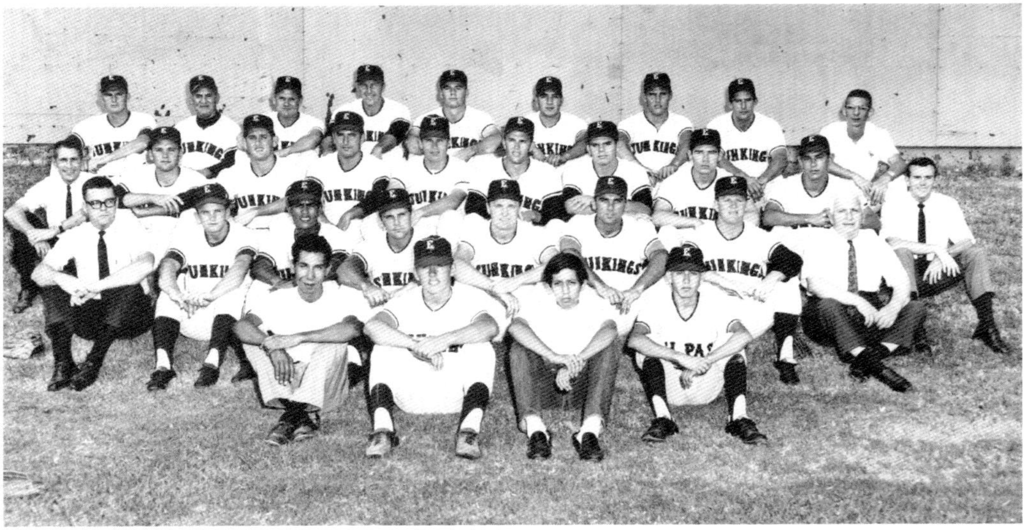

The 1967 El Paso Sun Kings went 73-67 and finished third in the Texas League. Their best player was third baseman Aurelio Rodríguez (third row, second from right), who would play 17 seasons in the Major Leagues and become recognized as one of the greatest defensive players of all time. Rodríguez, a native of Cananea, Sonora, on the Arizona-Mexico border, batted .327 with a .921 OPS. Other identified members include vice president Andy Cohen (fourth row, second from left), manager Rocky Bridges (fourth row, third from left), first baseman Moose Stubing (fourth row, fourth from left), and pitcher Andy Messersmith (third row, second from left). (Courtesy El Paso Chihuahuas.)

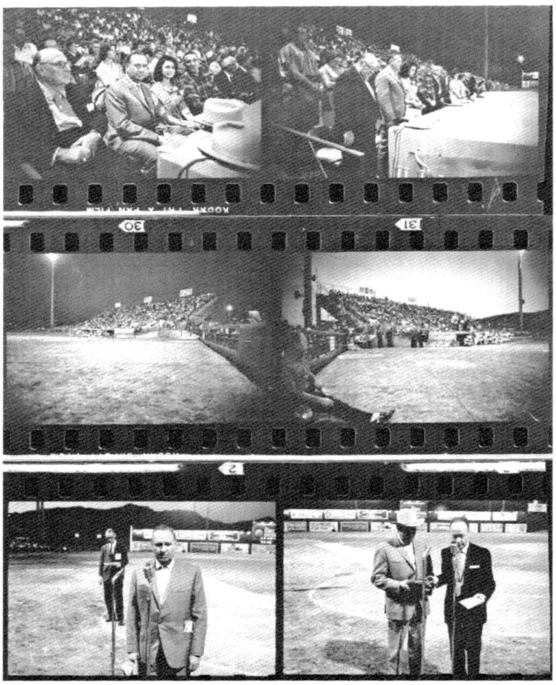

This contact sheet of 35-millimeter photographs provides a rare glimpse of the Dudley Field crowd at an El Paso Sun Kings game during the late 1960s. The stands were usually lively and festive, especially on nights like this when the Sun Kings hosted movie star Gene Autry, who owned the El Paso team and its parent club, the California Angels. The top two images show Autry, in a gray suit, sitting in the front row next to an unidentified "Miss Sun King." The bottom two images show Autry (with cowboy hat) speaking to the crowd while standing next to mayor Judson Williams. (Courtesy El Paso Chihuahuas.)

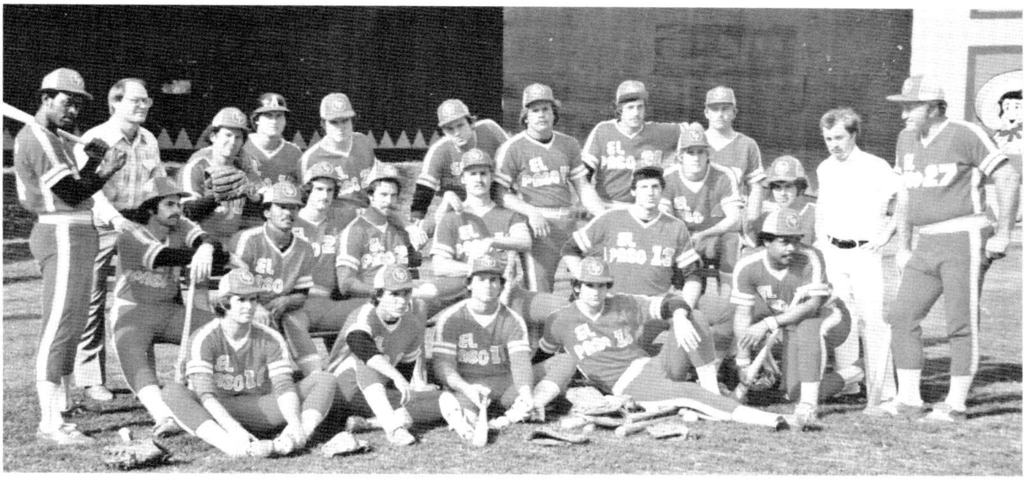

The Texas League champion El Paso Diablos are pictured next to Dudley Field's outfield fence in 1978. Orlando Ramírez (second row, second from left), the Colombian shortstop, batted .282. With inventive promotions like 10¢ hot dog night and the San Diego Chicken, the Diablos became minor-league baseball's most successful (and most often imitated) franchise. "If I had to pick one franchise that placed a premium on fun, that made every game a rollicking adventure, the El Paso Diablos were the winners, hands down," the journalist David Lamb wrote in *Stolen Season*, his classic book about minor league baseball. "No one else even came close." (Courtesy El Paso Chihuahuas.)

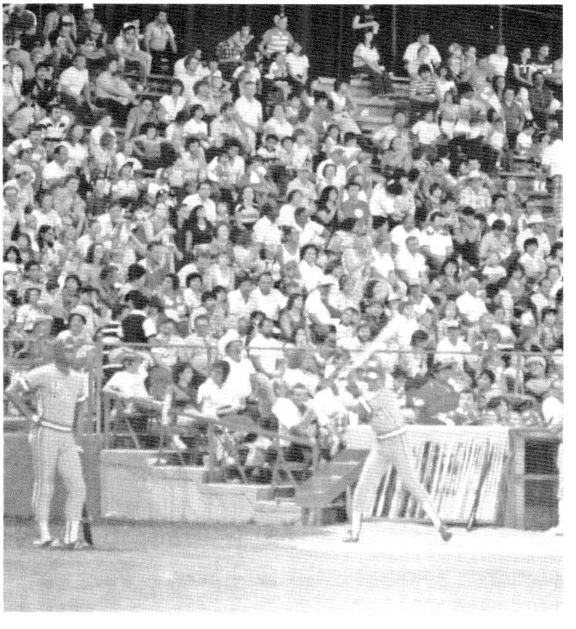

Fans at Dudley Field, most of them Mexican American, watch the El Paso Diablos in action in the early 1980s. "El Paso is a beer and nachos-for-breakfast kind of town, with a population that is 65 percent Hispanic, most earning the minimum wage on assembly lines and in apparel factories," David Lamb wrote in *Stolen Season*. One local tradition was that whenever a Diablos player hit a home run, he walked alongside the stands as appreciative fans filled his batting helmet with one-dollar bills. Players from Mexico and other Latin American countries often used this extra money to make long-distance calls home. (Courtesy El Paso Chihuahuas.)

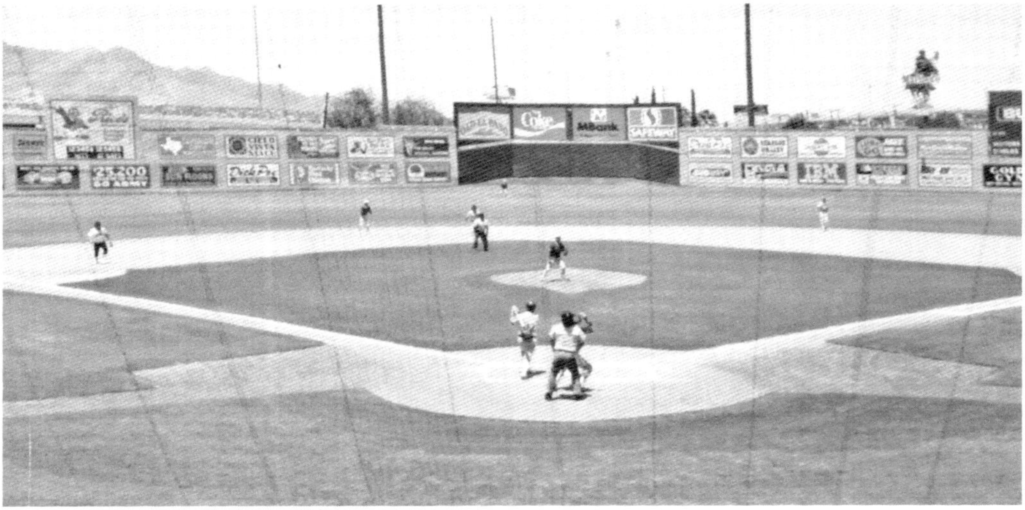

This photograph of Dudley Field was taken during the 1989 Texas League All-Star Game. In *Stolen Season*, David Lamb referred to the ballpark as "the wacky Dudley Dome, the very symbol of minor league baseball's second Golden Age." Dudley was home to every minor-league team that called El Paso home from 1924 through 1990. "In the heart of south El Paso, just a long home run from México and the waist-deep waters of the Río Grande," Lamb wrote, "The grandstands were built with adobe brick, and there was a small hill in center field that covered an irrigation ditch, resulting in marvelous battles between man and ball." (Courtesy El Paso Chihuahuas.)

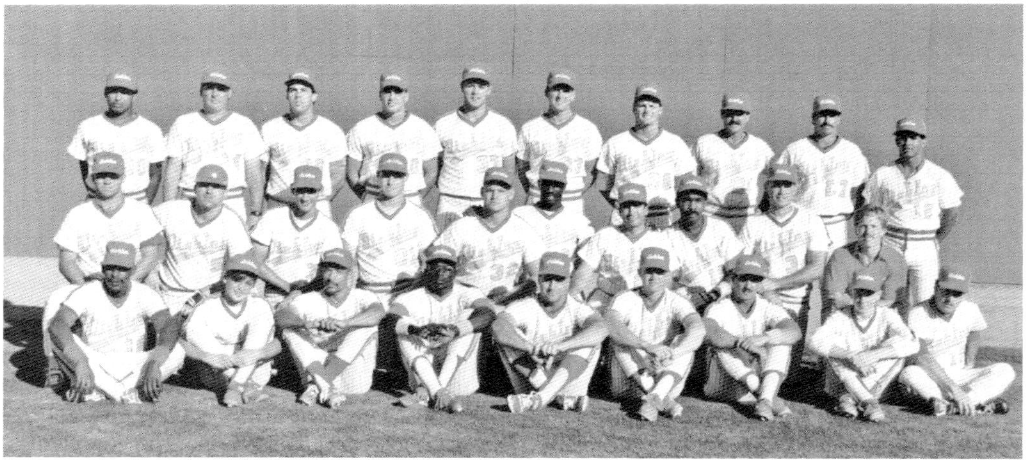

The El Paso Diablos pose on the day their new ballpark, Cohen Stadium, opened, June 13, 1990. For Spanish-speaking minor-league players, El Paso was a good place to be assigned, with familiar language and culture. This team was led by Dominican second baseman Sandy Guerrero (second row, third from left) and Puerto Rican shortstop Charlie Montoyo (first row, third from right). Left-handed pitcher Narciso Elvira was born in Veracruz, Mexico, and attended high school in Ciudad Juárez. Venezuelan infielder Jesús Alfaro (second row, third from right) became a legend in El Paso, playing five seasons for the Diablos and batting exactly .300 with 444 RBI. (Courtesy El Paso Chihuahuas.)

4

The 1949 Bowie Bears

The history of Bowie High School is one of the most intriguing stories in the city of El Paso. The poorest section of the city, the Segundo Barrio (the second ward or second neighborhood) produced some of the most prominent citizens of El Paso. Among them was Raymond Téllez, El Paso's first Mexican American mayor, who was later appointed ambassador to Mexico by Pres. John F. Kennedy; Nolan Richardson, famous basketball coach and member of the National Collegiate Basketball Hall of Fame; Olympic basketball players Kiko and J. Martínez; movie stars Joe Rentería and Rubén Moreno; photographer Alfonso Casa Sola; and artist Manuel Acosta. Javier Montes, class of 1948, set a Texas state record in the mile run of 4 minutes and 25 seconds. Javier later had a successful track career at Texas Western College, now the University of Texas at El Paso, and took part in the 1952 Olympic Games in Helsinki, Finland

But nothing contributes to the true meaning of history at Bowie High School more than the day in 1949 when a handful of young boys from the barrio became the first Texas high school baseball champions. The accomplishment of Bowie High School resulted from the leadership of an outstanding coach, Nemo Herrera, who molded a handful of players into a disciplined playing machine that achieved a victory that remained unchallenged in El Paso for more than 60 years.

This championship was a special event for these humble, dedicated young players whose hair has since turned gray. This legacy lives on for a group of young baseball players from El Paso's south side who ventured to Austin almost 70 years ago. Seventeen barrio boys traveled to a distant land, some for the first time out of El Paso, to play against all odds. Today, only three survive. They were the object of acute discrimination and were treated like second-class citizens. They remember the hurt, but they refused to allow it to stand in their way. They would rather talk about the games and what they achieved than the pain they suffered.

The surviving members of the 1949 team, now in their twilight years, still retain a strong sense of self-reliance and gratitude, but as time fades away, so does the memory of this great event and its members. The memories of the games and their departed fellow teammates still remain in their hearts. This is their extraordinary and heartfelt story.

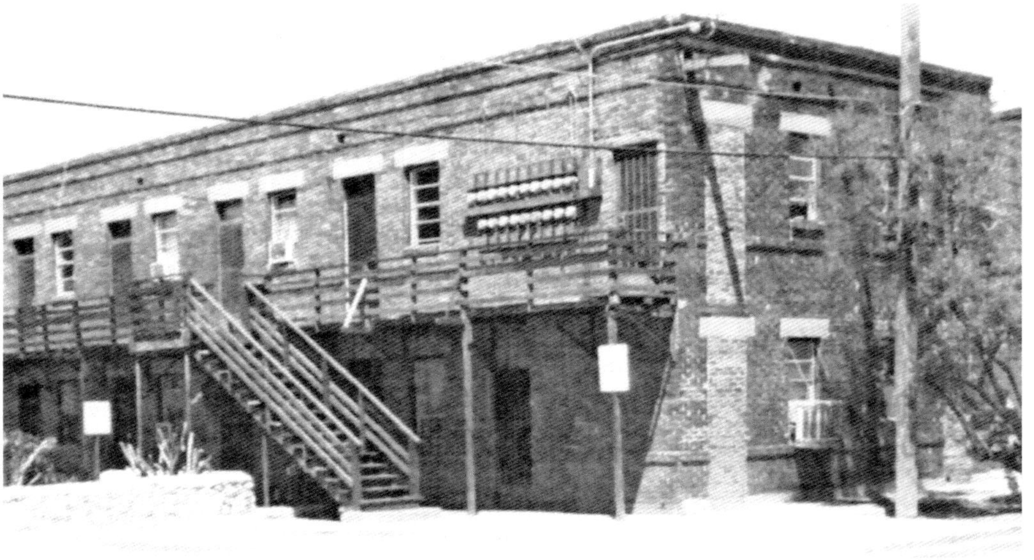

The Mexican Revolution of 1910 brought many refugees teeming into El Paso, Texas. The south side of El Paso had been an integral part of the city since the mid-1800s. It is one of the poorest sections in town. In the early 1900s, there were dirt roads and empty fields, and people lived in modest adobe homes called *jacales*. Later, as the railroad extended its tracks from El Paso to Los Angeles, California, most men in the neighborhood worked for the Southern Pacific Railroad. (Courtesy Pete G. Flores.)

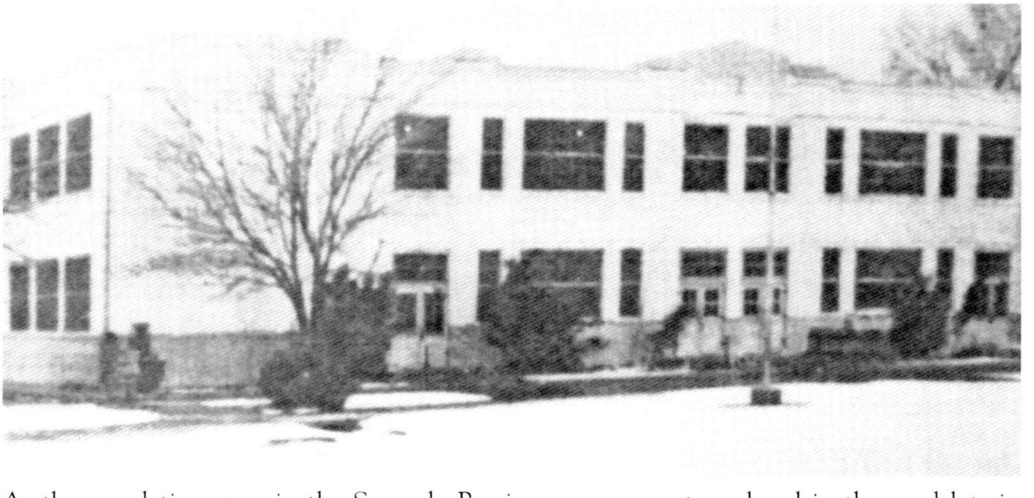

As the population grew in the Segundo Barrio, many youngsters played in the sand lots in the area. In 1888, the city established its first athletic field, Sportsmen's Park, on the corner of Florence and Fifth Streets. The first school in the area was opened by a man from Spain who named it Olivas Villanueva Aoy. It was originally a private school called Mexican Preparatory School. The black community started its own school, which was later renamed Frederick Douglass. In 1892, a second school, Alamo School, was opened due to overcrowding at Aoy. (Courtesy Pete G. Flores.)

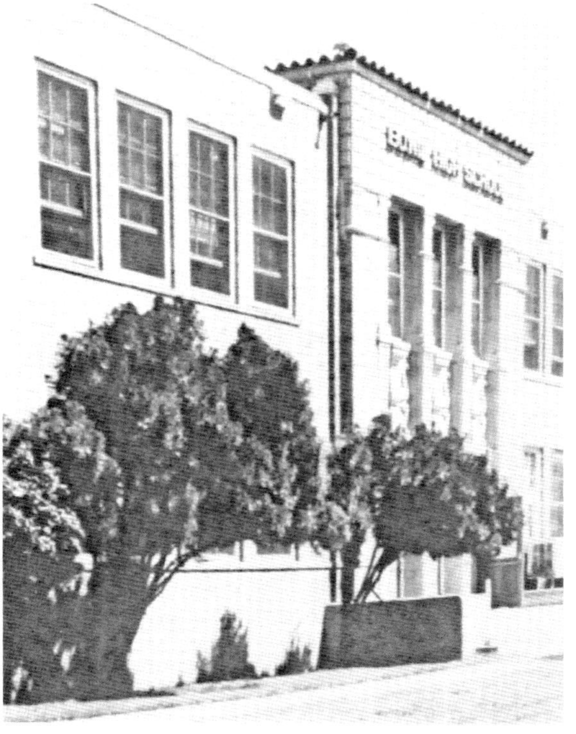

In 1927, Bowie Grammar School was converted into a high school. It became a home away from home for many students whose houses had no indoor plumbing or electricity. The school allowed the students to use the bath facilities. Young men from Segundo Barrio distinguished themselves in World War I, World War II, and Korea. Marcelino Serna was the most decorated Texas veteran in World War I. During World War II, former Bowie students served in the highly decorated 2nd Battalion, 141st Infantry Regiment, 36th Texas Infantry Division, Company E. Many lost their lives in Italy. Ambrocio Guillen was posthumously awarded the Congressional Medal of Honor for action in Korea. (Courtesy Pete G. Flores.)

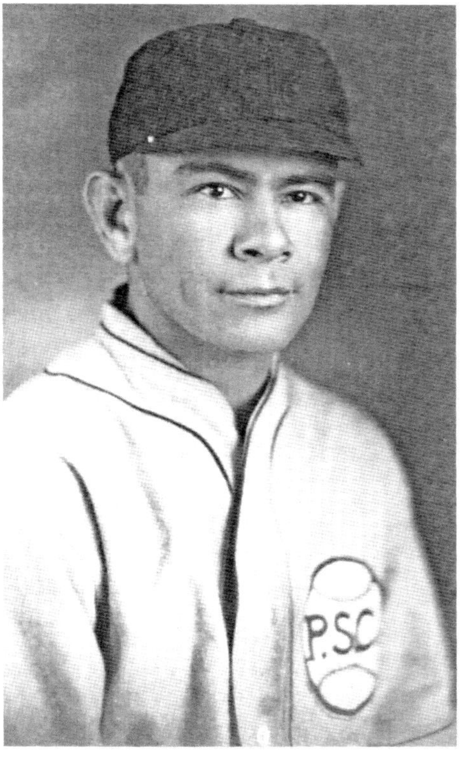

Coach William Carson Herrera, better known by his nickname "Nemo," assumed the role of educator, benefactor, counselor, truant officer, and parent to his schoolboys. He started in the late 1920s at Sidney Lanier High School in San Antonio, and coached winning teams at the school until 1945, when he moved to El Paso and assumed a similar role at Bowie High School. He retired from coaching in his 80s. He was often respectfully referred to as "El Viejo" (the old man) as a loving expression of patriarchal authority. La Bowie, as it was called, sent many young men into World War II with the all–Mexican American Company E of the Texas National Guard's 141st Infantry Regiment late in 1940. Nearly half of the soldiers had been Bowie Bears. Forty former Bowie students gave their lives in the war. (Courtesy Pete G. Flores.)

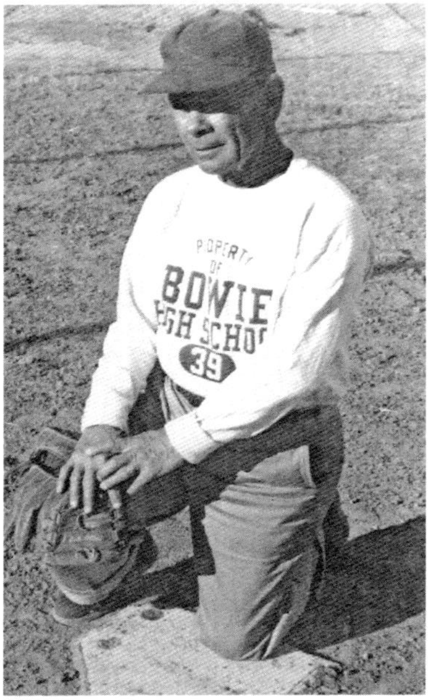

Coach Nemo Herrera was born in Brownsville, Texas, in 1900. His mother was Anglo and his father Mexican, having migrated to Brownsville from Tampico. Nemo attended Brackenridge High School in San Antonio. He played forward on the basketball team and second base for the Eagles baseball team. In 1921, Nemo attended Southwestern University in Georgetown, Texas, where he earned his degree. He also played semipro ball during the summers between 1919 and 1922. At Southwestern, he was the captain of the basketball team and lettered in baseball for three years. His baseball team won the Texas Interscholastic Athletic Association title. He played for the Galveston Sandcrabs of the Texas League and in the Mexican League in Tampico. One of his lifelong friends was Chicago White Sox immortal Ted Lyons. (Courtesy Pete G. Flores.)

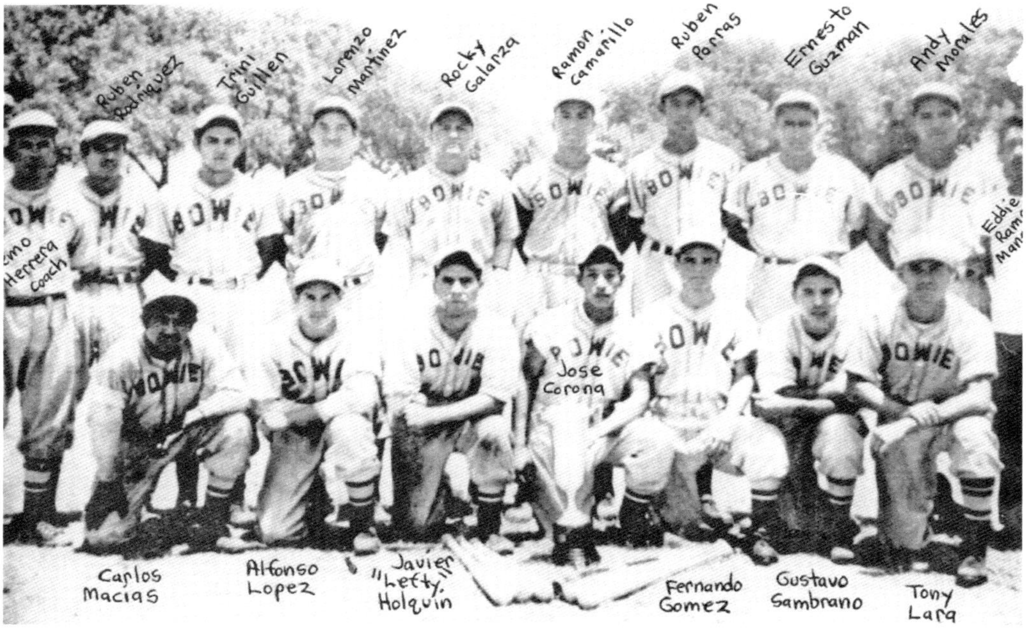

These are the 1949 state champion El Paso High School Bowie Bears. From left to right are (first row) Carlos Macías, Alfonso López, Javier Holguín, José Corona, Fernando Gómez, Gustavo Sambrano, and Antonio Lara; (second row) coach Nemo Herrera, Rubén Rodríguez, Trini Guillen, Lorenzo Martínez, José Galarza, Ramón Camarillo, Rubén Porras, Ernesto Guzmán, Andy Morales, and Eddie Ramos. Herrera had many sayings, including, "It's not who you are or where you're from, but rather it's who you become." Only Rodríguez, Morales, and López are still alive. (Courtesy Pete G. Flores.)

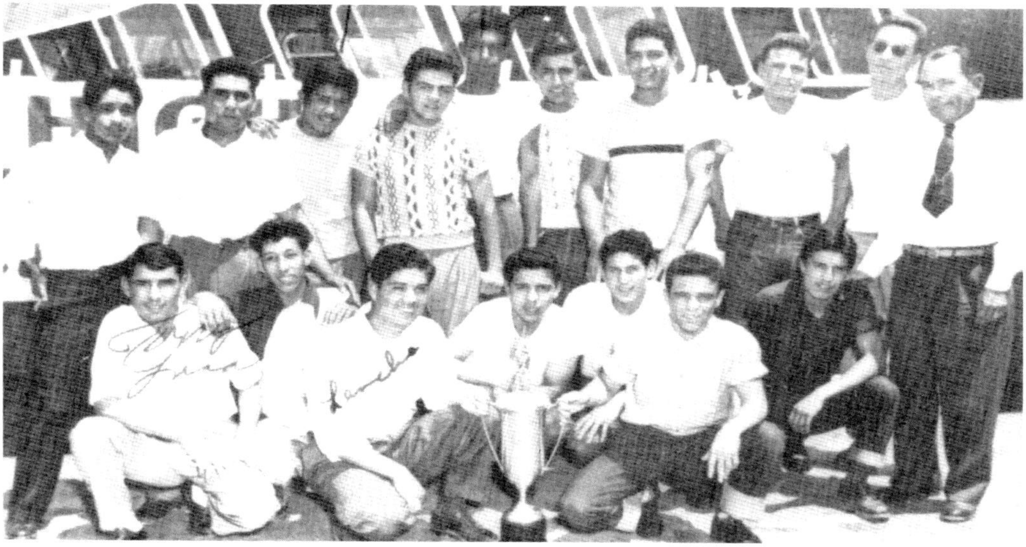

These are the 1949 state champions from Bowie High School. In no particular order are Ramón Camarillo, José Corona, José Galarza, Rodolfo García, Fernando Gómez, Guillermo Gómez, Trini Guillen, Ernesto Guzmán, Xavier Holguín, Tony Lara, Alfonso López, Carlos Macías, Lorenzo Martínez, Andy Morales, Rubén Porras, Rubén Rodríguez, Gustavo Sambrano, manager Eddie Ramos, and coach Nemo Herrera. This photograph was taken on their arrival in El Paso after winning the championship game in Austin. Another important person was Dulcenombres Mendoza, who was the school custodian. His job was to maintain the dusty sandlot baseball field behind the main building. (Courtesy Pete G. Flores.)

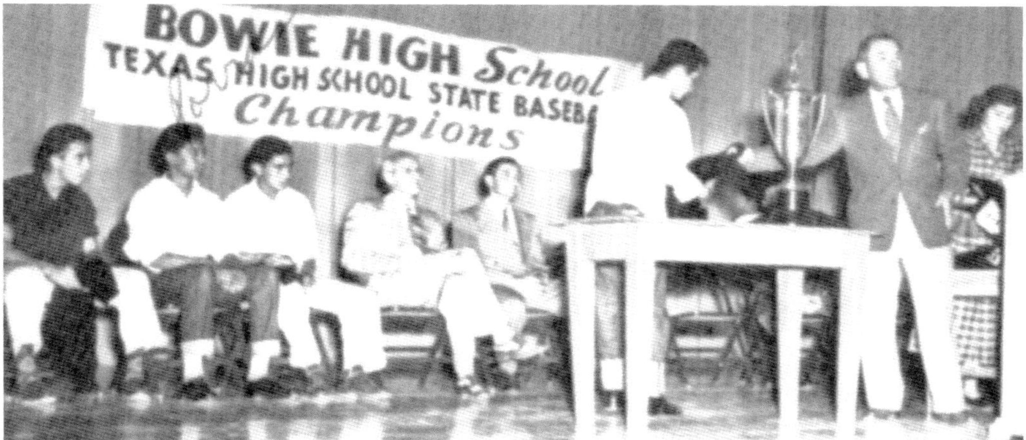

Nemo Herrera (right) presents the championship trophy to the high school at an assembly. Coach Herrera practiced for hours on the field with his players. He would pick up all the equipment after practice and clean the field. He would get a wire net, tie a rope at each end, strap it over his shoulders, and rake the field. He walked slowly back and forth across the infield until it was completely smooth, then he would get a small can of white powder to mark the base lines. He did this routine every day during the season. (Courtesy Pete G. Flores.)

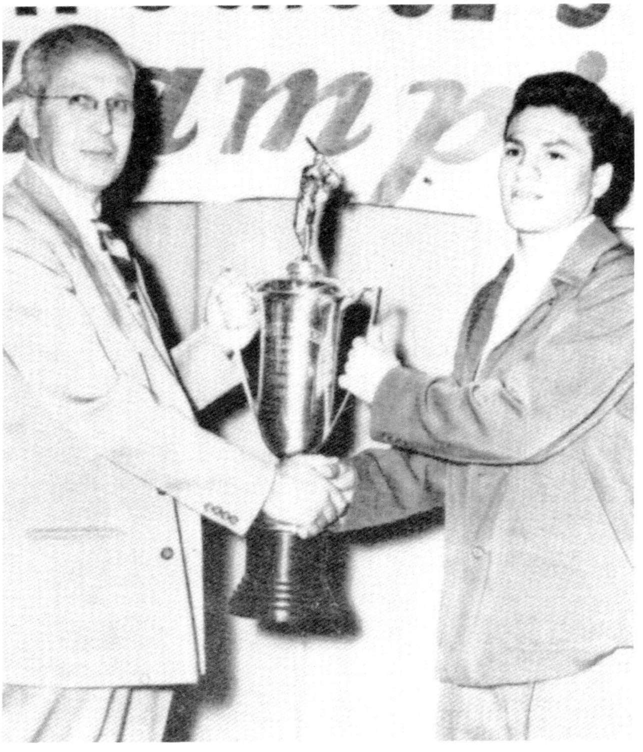

Third baseman José "Rocky" Galarza (right) presents the trophy to school principal Frank Pollit. Rocky Galarza was born in El Segundo Barrio. He became a star at Bowie High School playing football, and was all-district in basketball and baseball. He attended Durham College and later taught and coached boxing. He trained over 200 boxers, several of whom won titles, including Ernie Lazcano. He started Rocky's Youth Program to keep kids away from drugs. He touched the lives of many young people before he died in 1997. A basketball camp, Basketball in the Barrio, is sponsored each year in his memory. (Courtesy Pete G. Flores.)

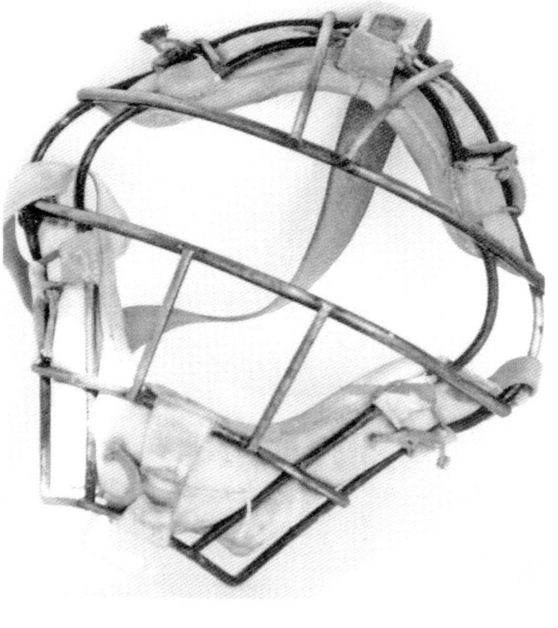

This is the catcher's mask worn by teammates Ramón Camarillo and Carlos Macías. Ramón was a studious young man. He loved to read, and his knowledge of basketball and baseball were immeasurable. He played on local teams, including the Juárez Indios and El Dorado de Chihuahua. He and his wife, Aurora, were married for 61 years. He passed away in 2011. Carlos Macías was born near the Mexican border. He learned to work at an early age. He served in the military and retired from the Phelps-Dodge metal processing plant. He still shares stories with the last remaining teammates, who meet at a local restaurant. Never far from their memories is the harsh poverty they experienced growing up. (Courtesy Pete G. Flores.)

This is one of the uniforms worn by the 1949 Bowie Bears. Pitcher Javier J. Holguín was from the poorest section of El Paso, called Chihuahuita, and attended Aoy School and Bowie. He served in Korea and later worked as a truck driver for Falstaff Beer. He played for several teams, including the El Paso 40-60 Club and the softball team Drifters. He loved playing Santa Claus for the neighborhood children. Javier passed away in 1989. Another pitcher on the team was Rubén Porras, who also served in Korea. He attended Texas Western College. Porras won the Babe Ruth Sportsmanship Award, given to a graduating senior who has been outstanding in sportsmanship throughout high school. He also played minor-league ball. He was the senior class president. Porras passed away in 1996. (Courtesy Pete G. Flores.)

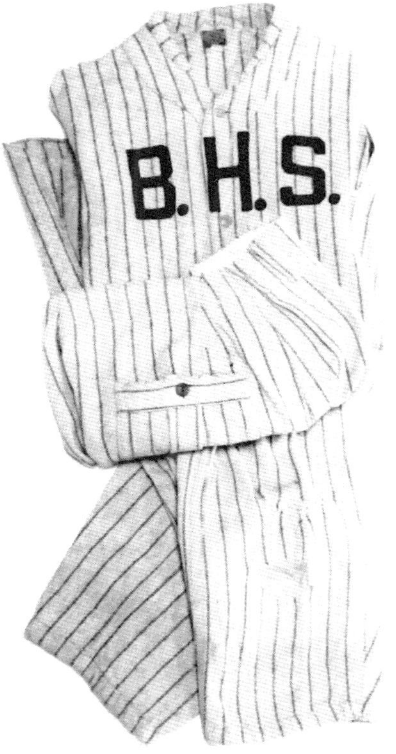

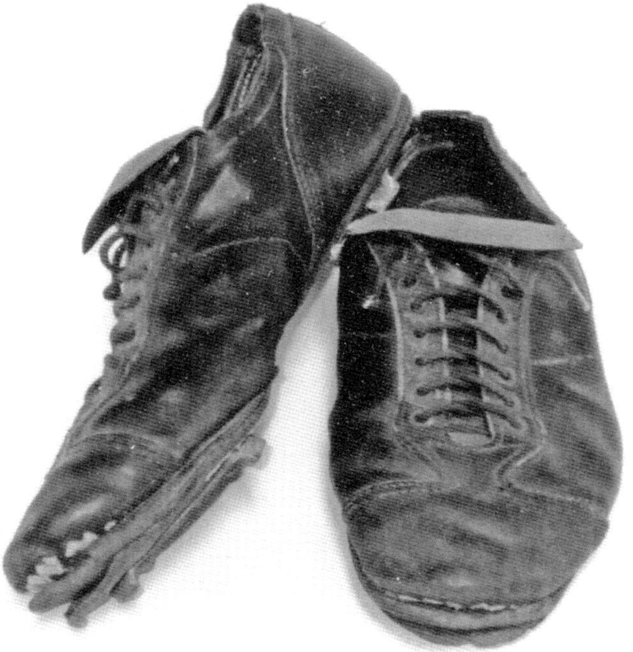

These are the cleats worn by the Bears in 1949. Lorenzo Martínez was born a stone's throw from the border on Cordova Island, now Chamizal National Memorial. He, too, served in Korea. He worked for Goodyear Tire Company and the US Post Office. He and his wife, Bertha, raised three sons and one daughter Lorenzo passed away in 1996. Pitcher Trini Guillen won the championship game against Austin High School. After graduating, he joined the US Air Force. He later earned a degree in economics and became an executive with the Southern Pacific Railroad. He died in 1999. (Courtesy Pete G. Flores.)

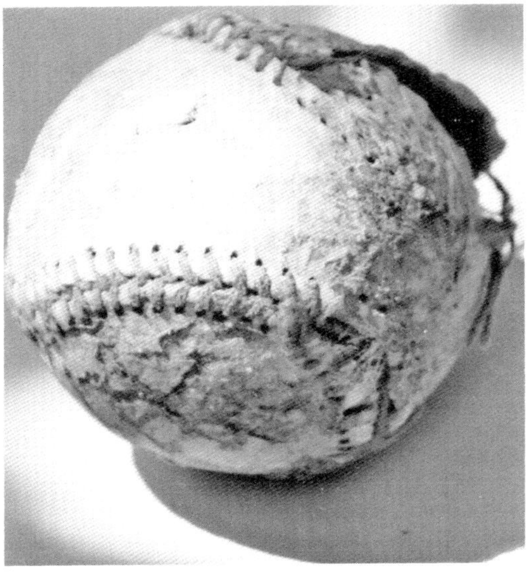

This is a practice ball from the 1949 season. Rodolfo García played second base and later joined the US Air Force, serving during the Korean War. He retired from the Southern Pacific Railroad after 30 years. He played for local teams including La Tuna. His son, Victor, continues his legacy by playing semipro baseball in El Paso. Rodolfo passed away in 2008. Fernando Gomez played centerfield and saved games with his speed and amazing catches. He served for over 22 years in the US Air Force in Korea and Vietnam. Fernando did not have a glove for the 1949 playoffs, but a friend lent his and told him that the glove would win a championship for the team. (Courtesy Pete G. Flores.)

This is a glove and ball from that amazing season when Bowie High School, against all odds, won the initial Texas high school baseball championship. José Corona played left field. He was small compared to his teammates, but his speed and agility helped win games. He served in the US Air Force and retired from Kroger Properties Company after 25 years. He loved meeting his former teammates to share stories over a cup of coffee. He lived in the area called Lincoln, in the southeast area of the city, and walked for miles to attend Bowie. José passed away in 2011. (Courtesy Pete G. Flores.)

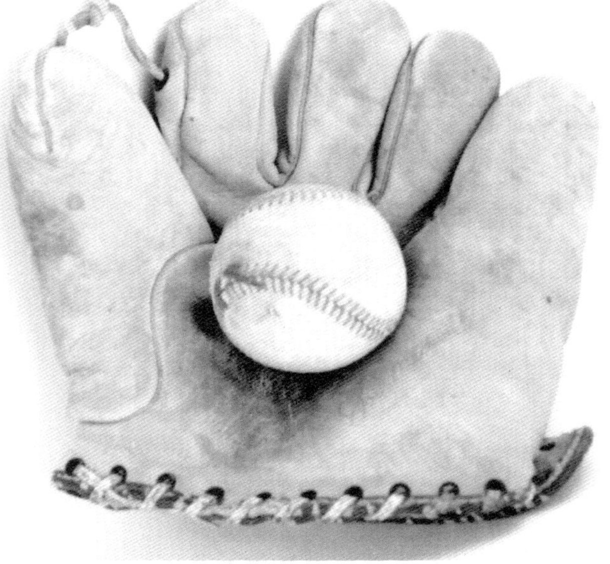

Andy Morales played second base and on the football team. His neighborhood was referred to as El Barrio del Diablo (The Devil's Neighborhood). He was inducted into the El Paso Football Hall of Fame in 1996. After high school, he joined the Navy. He was offered a contract with the Washington Redskins, but decided to earn a college degree. (Courtesy Pete G. Flores.)

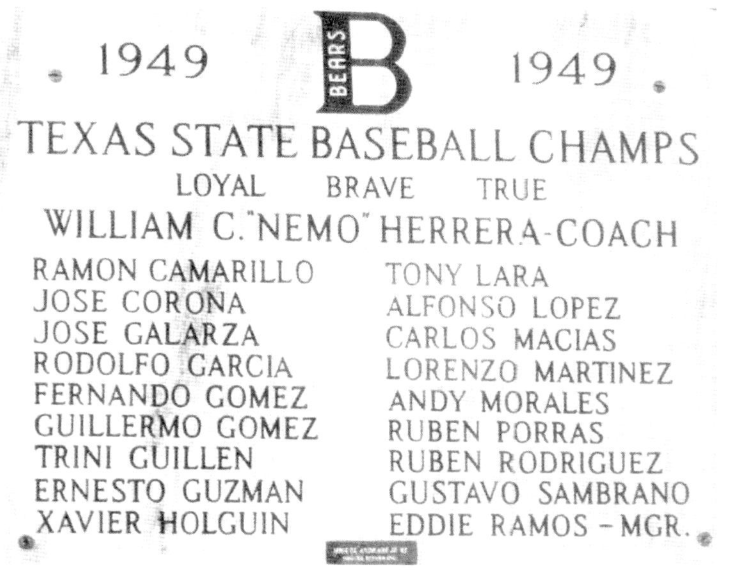

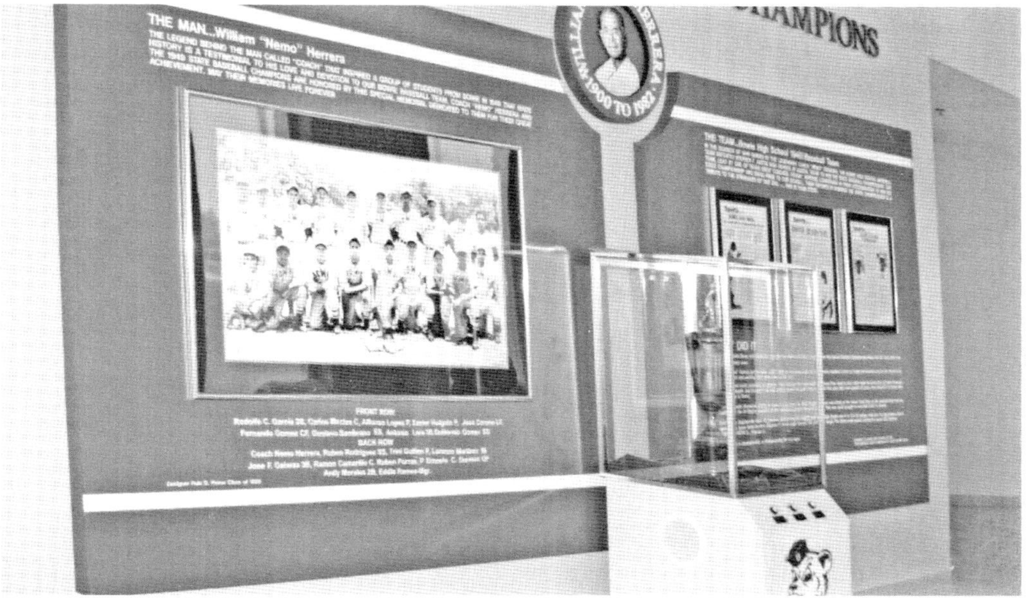

The 1949 state championship memorial at Bowie High School was unveiled on January 29, 2009. The championship trophy, which was described by Coach Herrera as three feet tall, lay hidden from view for 63 years but now rests in a specially designed trophy case. Within the beautiful glass-enclosed case is a series of recordings by Coach Herrera and radio announcer John Phelan on the championship game against Austin. There is a team photograph and sports pages documenting the championship run. This memorial is a symbol of the legacy and the events that changed the lives of these players. (Courtesy Pete G. Flores.)

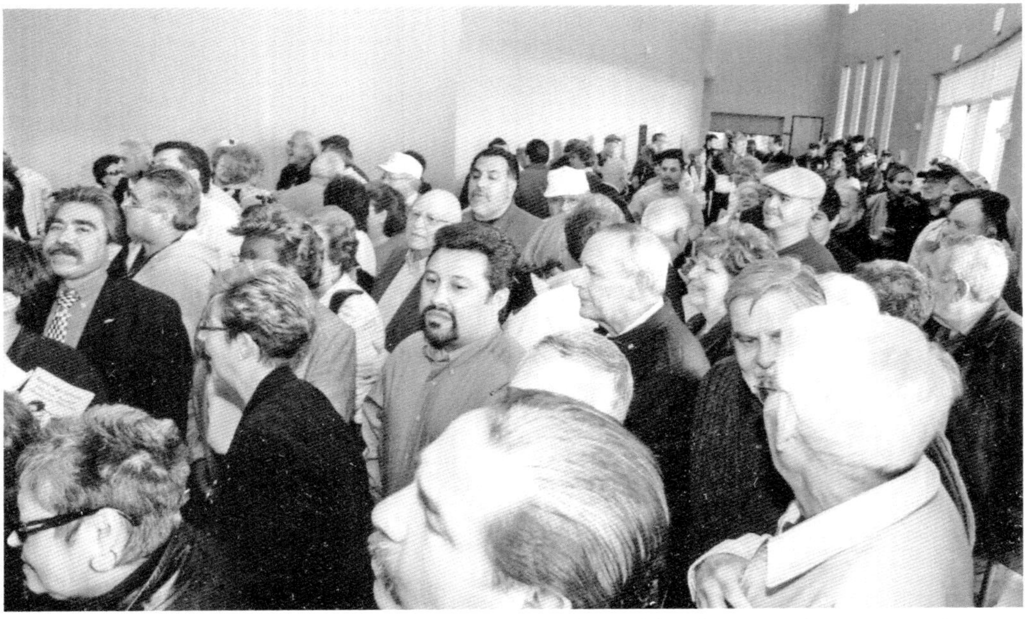

This is part of the large crowd that attended the unveiling of the championship memorial paying tribute to the 1949 Bowie Bears. These hard-nosed players and remarkable coaches have given great honor and immense pride to their families, friends, diehard fans, and neighborhoods. Those in attendance represent several generations. (Courtesy Pete G. Flores.)

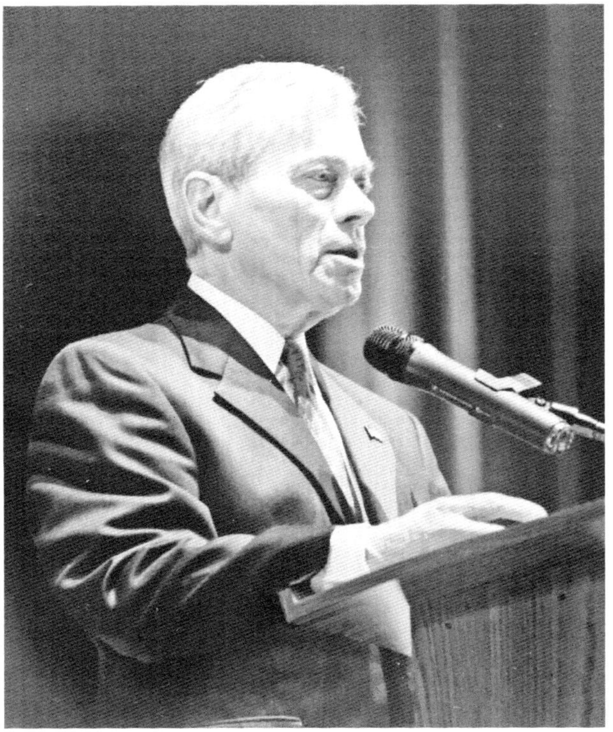

At the memorial dedication, the son of Coach Herrera, Col. Charles Herrera, addressed the crowd and thanked them for honoring his father and the players. Charles bears a remarkable resemblance to his father. He said that his father knew more about the players than their parents and that he would have put the championship at the very top of his accomplishments. Former councilman Beto O'Rouke, who now serves in the US Congress, read a proclamation from the City of El Paso. Old memories were recalled, and those glorious moments seemed to come alive once again. They had remained waiting for that spark that would ignite them once more. (Courtesy Pete G. Flores.)

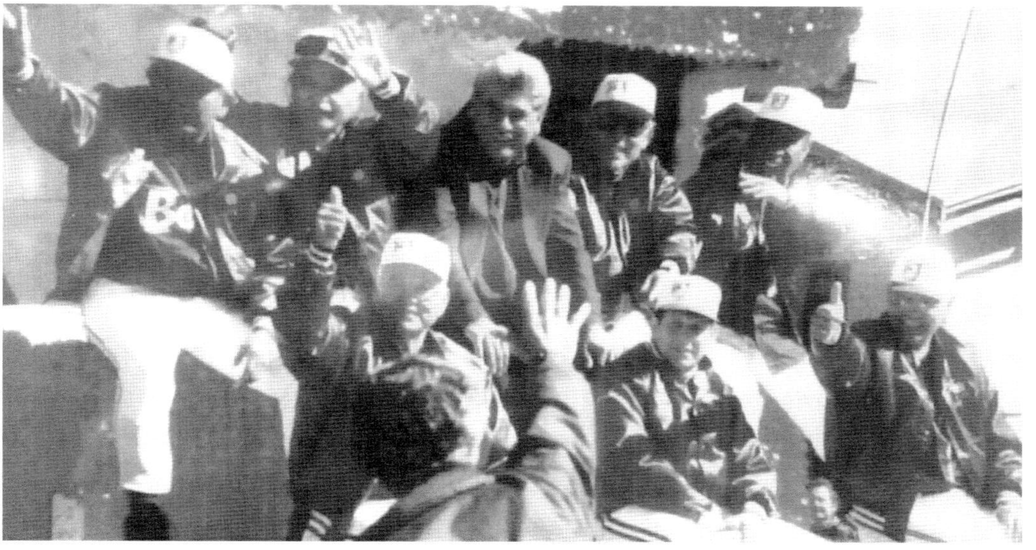

Besides the memorial, the surviving players were honored guests in the Sun Bowl Parade. The Fort Bliss army post honored them during Hispanic Heritage Week, and in 2011, *Sports Illustrated* published an extensive article on the 1949 Bowie Bears. State Farm insurance agents raised money for a sign dedicating the Bowie baseball diamond in the name of coach Nemo Herrera. From a group of 17, only three remain. The team members still share their thoughts amongst themselves and relive their memories of the great championship game. (Courtesy Pete G. Flores.)

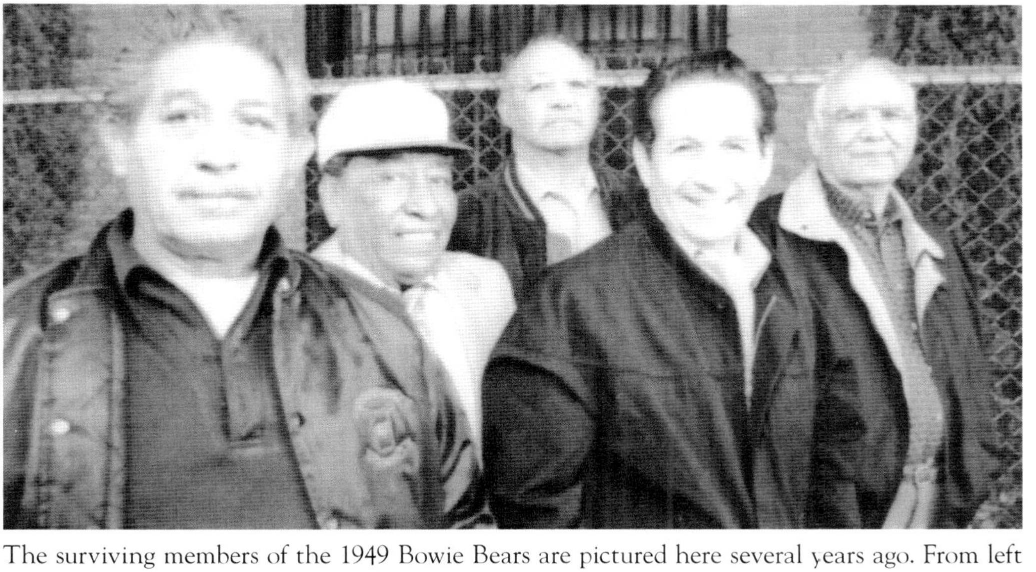

The surviving members of the 1949 Bowie Bears are pictured here several years ago. From left to right are Carlos Macías, José Corona, Andy Morales, Alfonso López, and Tony Lara. Pete G. Flores, who wrote a book about the 1949 Bears and was their schoolmate, noted that aside from the sandlot baseball and football games, these young men played in the narrow inner-city streets. Their entertainment consisted of an occasional swim in the murky waters of the Franklin Canal. What they had was all they knew. (Courtesy Pete G. Flores.)

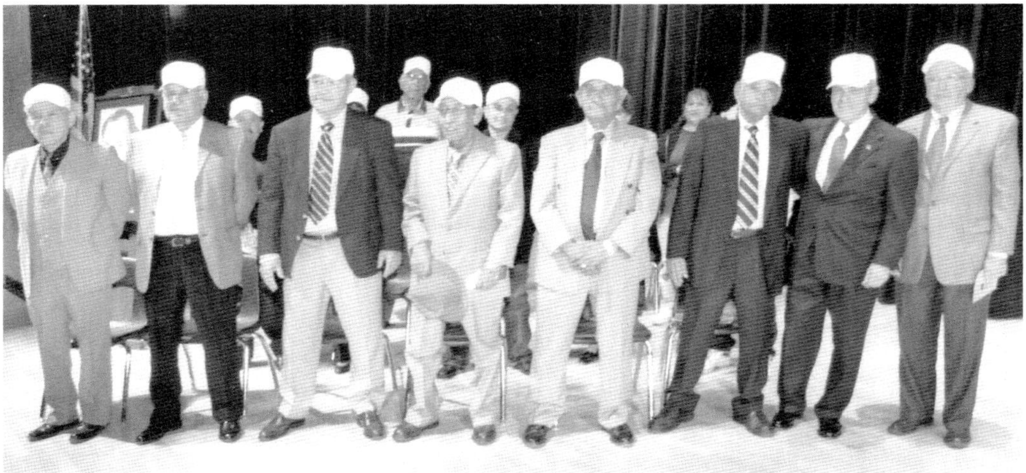

Several players were honored at this special event. From left to right are Gustavo Sambrano, Tony Lara, Andy Morales, José Corona, Carlos Macías, Guillermo Gomes, Charles D. Herrera, and William Herrera. Pete G. Flores wrote that the boys were forced to depend on each other for distraction, and they never lacked playmates and friends. They remembered the good times and the bad times of their childhood. (Courtesy Pete G. Flores.)

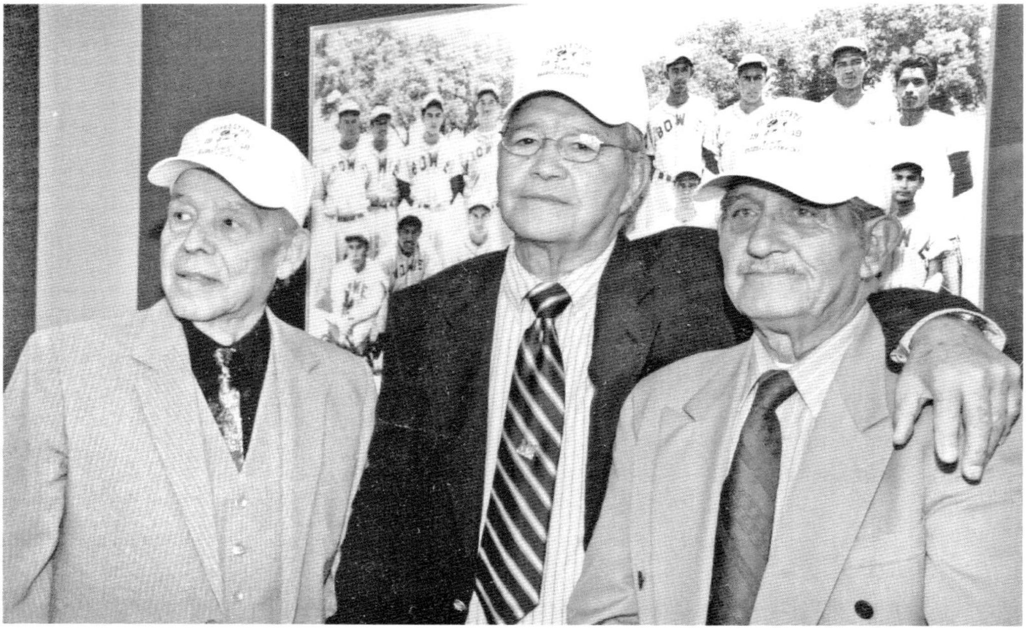

Three of the Bowie High School champions, from left to right, are Gus Sambrano, Andy Morales, and Carlos Macías. Pete G. Flores noted that the players' parents gave them few material things, since they could barely afford to provide them with even the basic necessities. But more important, their parents gave them love in abundance and the wisdom and strength of character to help them survive and thrive. In time, vivid and glorious memories fade away, but these memories left indelible marks in their hearts. (Courtesy Pete G. Flores.)

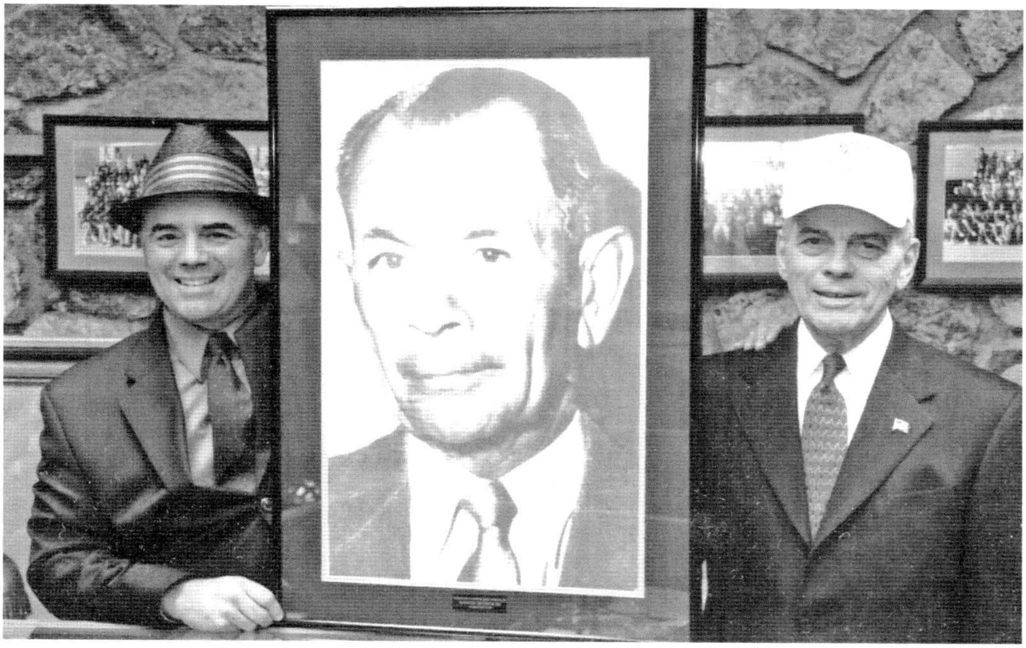

Here are three generations of the Herrera family. The portrait is of the legendary Bowie coach William C. "Nemo" Herrera. His son Charles Herrera is on the right, and Charles's son Ken Herrera is standing on the left. Ken lives in Wildomer, California. (Courtesy Pete G. Flores.)

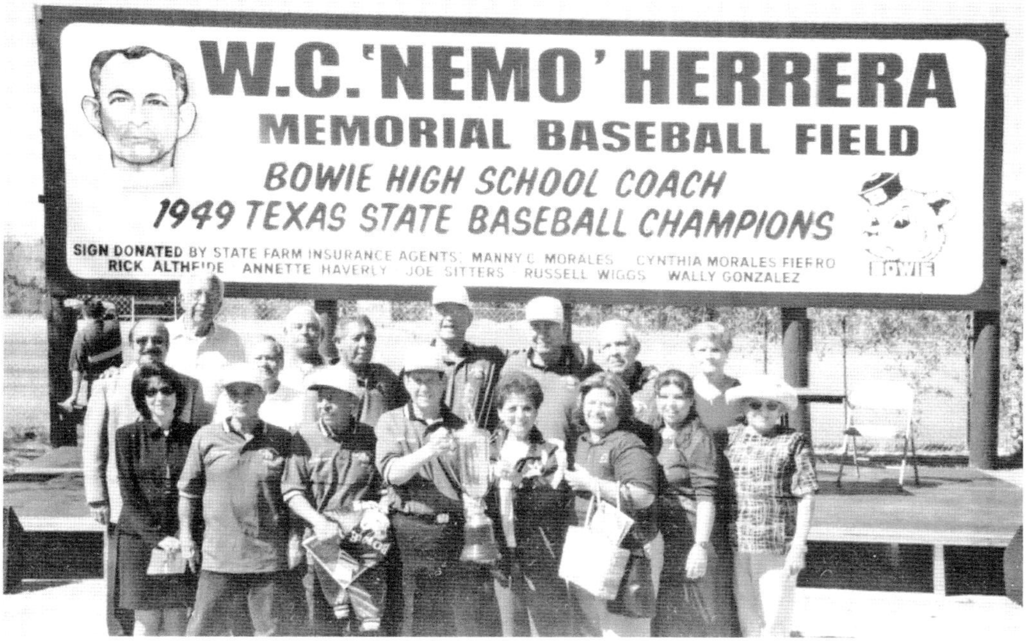

This memorial sign was dedicated around 2011 to honor Coach Nemo Herrera. The funds for the sign were raised by local State Farm insurance agents. (Courtesy Pete G. Flores.)

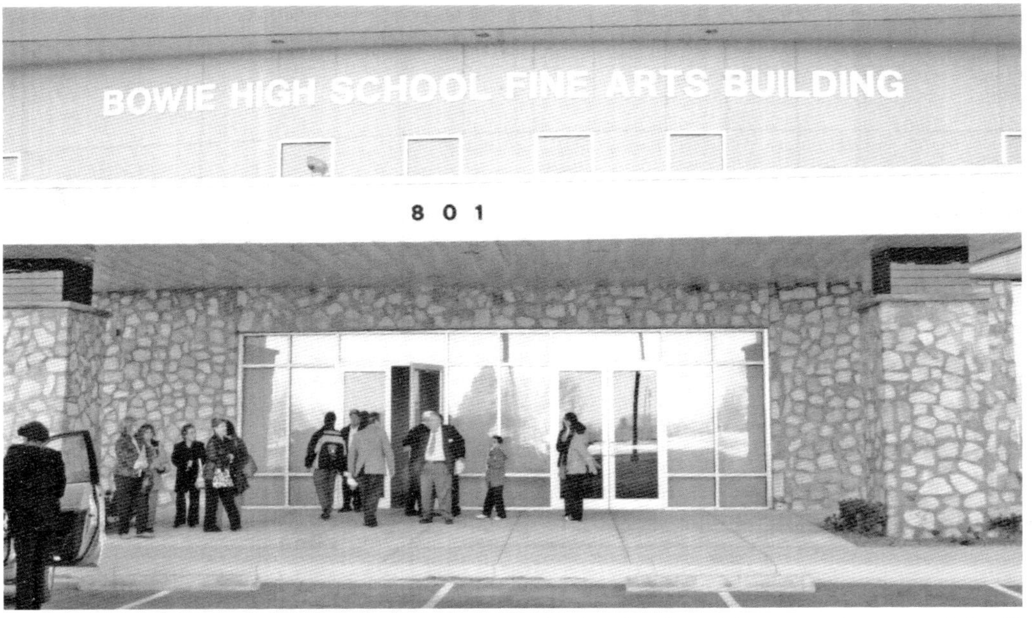

Bowie High School is one of the oldest operating high schools in El Paso and is part of the El Paso Independent School District. It is located in the Chamizal neighborhood in the south central part of the city, next to the border with Mexico and not far from the Bridge of the Americas linking El Paso with Ciudad Juárez. The school is across San Marcial Street from Chamizal National Memorial. School colors are royal blue and white, and its motto is "Once A Bear, Always a Bear." Its main rival is Jefferson High School. The new high school was built in 1973. (Courtesy Pete G. Flores.)

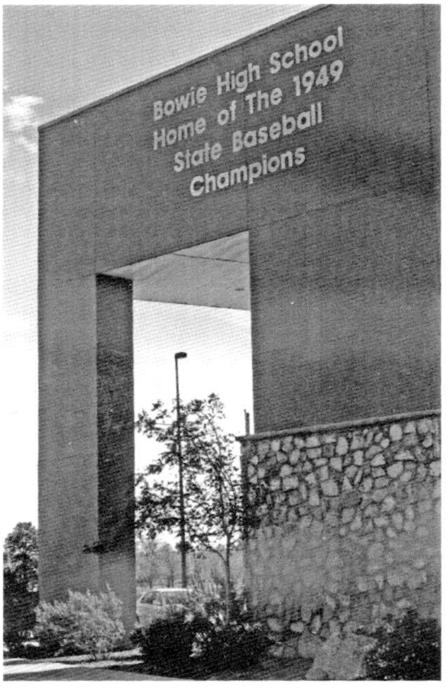

Over the last several years, Bowie High School has sponsored events and dedicated reminders on the school grounds honoring the 1949 Bowie Bears, including a baseball field and scoreboard. Besides paying tribute to the 1949 team, in 1948, Bowie dedicated a memorial to the 40 students who lost their lives during World War II. An ROTC color guard concluded each school day that year with a retreat ceremony, lowering the flag that flew above the cenotaph. In September 2016, Bowie High School also officially dedicated the gym in honor of one of its legendary players and coaches, basketball hall-of-famer Nolan Richardson. Richardson is a Bears legend who played basketball for Don Haskins at UTEP and gained national fame as the head coach of the NCAA championship team at the University at Arkansas. (Courtesy Pete G. Flores.)

5

The King Ranch

With its headquarters located near Kingsville, approximately 200 miles south of San Antonio in a region celebrated as the birthplace of the American cowboy, the King Ranch is the largest ranch in Texas. It comprises 825,000 acres and was founded in 1853 by Capt. Richard King and Gideon K. Lewis; it includes portions of six counties. The ranch was designated a national historic landmark in 1961. Kingsville is located in a hot, humid area between the Nueces and Río Grande at the tip of Texas. The cowboys had a complex relationship with the ranch ownership and the Mexican American employees referred to as *Kineños*, or King's men. The Kineños came from families that had served the ranch for most of a century. Their families were prominent in supplying players for the ranch teams. For over a decade beginning in 1947, the Mexican Americans on the ranch fielded a semipro baseball team that is still remembered by longtime residents of the region. The semitropical conditions allow baseball to be played almost the entire year. Kingsville had a history of baseball participation from its founding and a culture that encouraged baseball among Mexican Americans. At the time, heckling during games was loud, continuous, and bilingual. Baseball was the only form of entertainment besides religious holidays. Ranch workers would get together on Sundays at Assault Park to cheer on the King Ranch baseball team. The Cowboys competed against minor-league and semipro teams from Mexico and Texas. Their most memorable games were against the San Antonio Brooke Army Medical Center teams. When men such as Bob Turley and Don Newcomb, two of the greatest pitchers in baseball history, came to Kingsville, thousands of fans turned out. The culture outside the diamond included travel, drinking, gambling, and parties. Eventually, the quest for baseball dominance led to a tri-ethnic team including Anglos and African Americans.

The African Americans mixed with team members and fans at a time when many Americans would not sit next to them. Ellen Goodman, writing for the *San Antonio Express News*, hit it right on the nose when she wrote that "Sports is the male icebreaker and a leveler of class, race and age. It's what many men who have little in common have in common." The Cowboys expose a unique example of what semipro baseball was like on the King Ranch before the homogenization of television. In general, the King Ranch, Kingsville, and the workers were more like the rest of the country than some would think. The arrangement refutes the assertion of exploitive feudalism alleged by many critics. It is this paternalism that has caused many people to suggest the ranch workers were ignorant of worldly ways. This cannot be true, considering they were thinking, active people, handling money, making up schedules, working up rosters, and organizing the finest semipro teams ever.

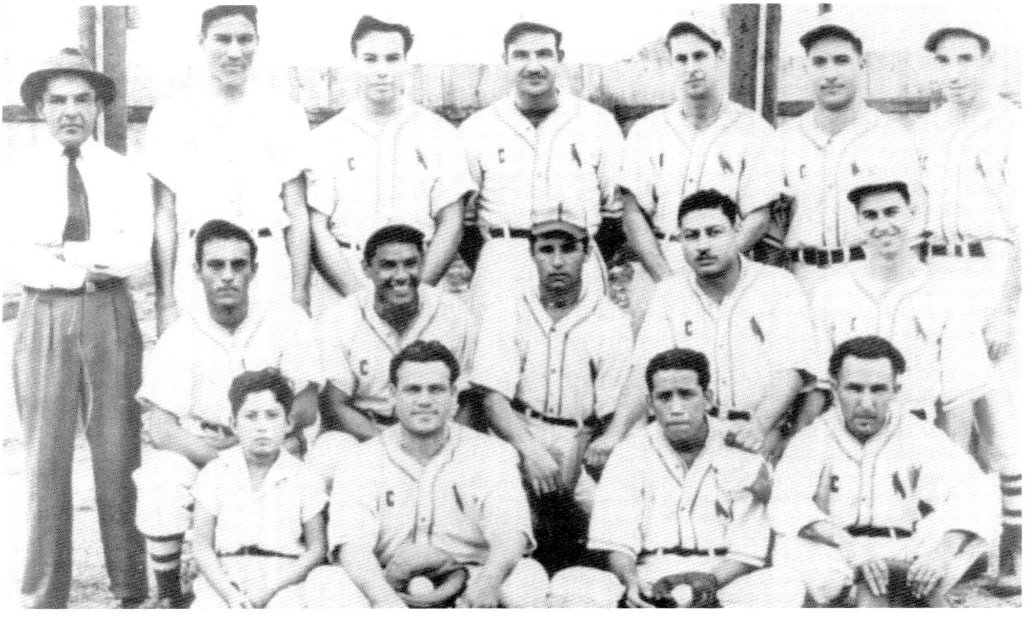

The semipro 1936 Kingsville Cardinals cornered the market on the town's top-notch players. They built a field on East Corral Street. Luís Canales went on to umpire many years for the King Ranch Cowboys. From left to right are (first row) Felipe Herrera, Luís Canales, Juan Flores, and Federico Peña; (second row) unidentified, ? Acosta, ? Lozano, Moisés Leyva, and Pipo Ruíz; (third row) manager Augustine Peña, Ramiro Gutiérrez, Flavio Ochoa, Daniel García, unidentified, Lupe Valdez, and Andy Alañiz. (Courtesy Donavan "Captain D" López.)

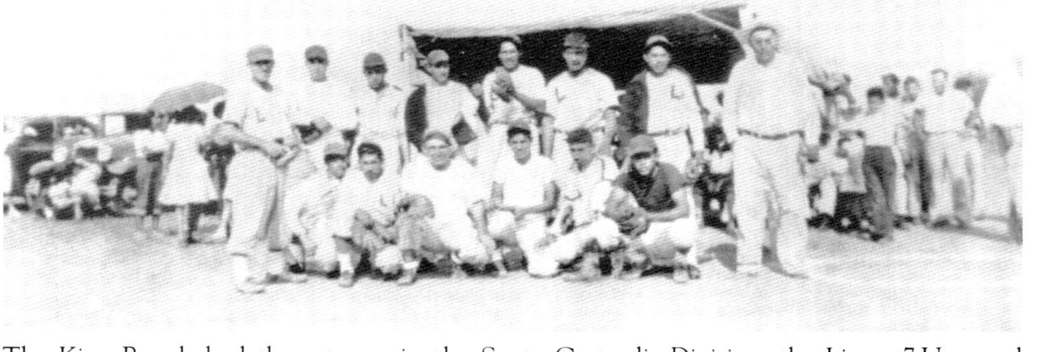

The King Ranch had three teams in the Santa Gertrudis Division: the Lions, 7-Ups, and Cowboys. It was not until the ranch built the colony near the headquarters in Kingsville that there were sufficient people to support a semipro baseball team. In this 1948 Lions photograph, cars line up along the edge of the early field near the covered dugout. From left to right are (first row) Tellyle Treviño, Cipriano Escobedo, Cipriano García, Jesús Muñiz, Billy Buentello, and Abundio Rodríguez; (second row) Coach Jesús García, Julián Sáenz, Beto Mendietta, Alberto Treviño, David Borrego Sr., Francisco Gutiérrez, Alberto Buentello, and manager Refugio Rodríguez. (Courtesy Cipriano García.)

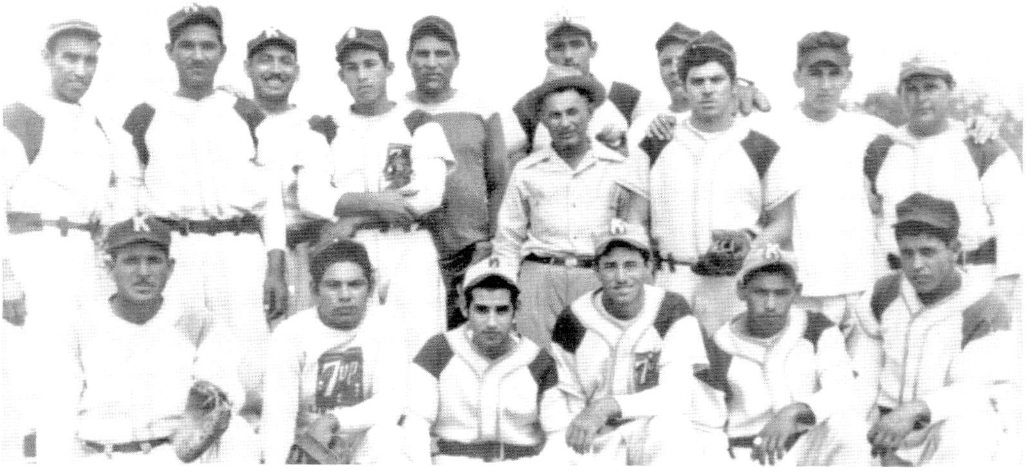

In 1949, the King Ranch 7-Ups pose in their new uniforms. Many of these photographs were taken by *Kingsville Record-News* staff photographer Jimmie Dodd, whose collection is located at the University of Texas in Austin. From left to right are (first row) Jesús García, Alberto Buentello, Romeo Pérez, Alberto Treviño, Billy Buentello, and Alberto Cortéz; (second row) Césario Cavazos, Jesús Muñiz, Cipriano García, Gilberto Rodríguez, Ramiro Gutiérrez, manager Jesús Garza, Lorenzo Mendietta, Neri Gutiérrez, Guadalupe Juárez, Gilberto González, and Clareció Muñoz. (Courtesy Jesús García.)

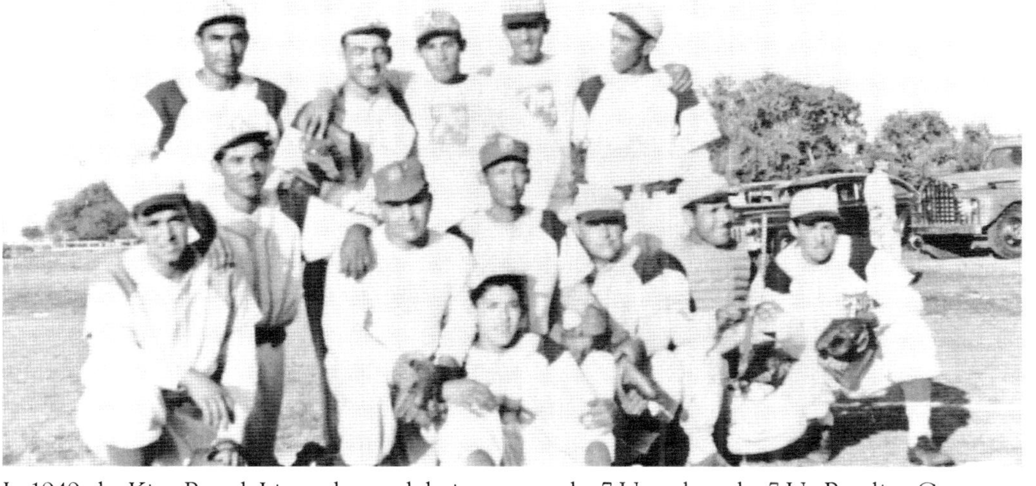

In 1949, the King Ranch Lions changed their name to the 7-Ups when the 7-Up Bottling Company sponsored the team, but they are remembered by the name adopted in 1952, the Cowboys. The King Ranch 7-Ups are pictured at Assault Park in 1950 with one of the company trucks that players, fans, and family members would squeeze into. Many players had their own vehicles and caravanned to out-of-town games. From left to right are (first row) Gilberto Mendietta; (second row) Julián Sáenz, Jesús Muñiz, Clareció Muñoz, Militon Aguirre, Neri Gutiérrez, Jesús García, and Alberto Treviño; (third row) Miguel Ochoa, Cipriano García, Abundio Rodríguez, Lorenzo Mendietta, and Césario Cavazos. (Courtesy Jesús García.)

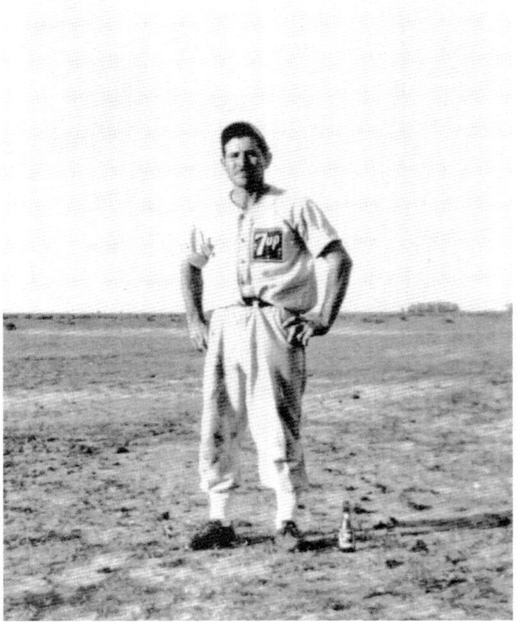

The culture outside the diamond included travel, drinking, gambling, and parties, but many ranch players, such as Alberto Treviño and Jesús García, did not drink. Jesús García poses in his King Ranch 7-Ups uniform next to a 7-Up soft drink in 1949. Sunday afternoon at Assault Park was as much a *pachanga* as a ball game. For a 3:00 p.m. game, many people arrived at noon to claim a favorite shade tree and to barbecue, talk, and drink beer. The concession stands had washtubs full of iced-down Falstaff, Southern Select, and Jax. (Courtesy Jesús García.)

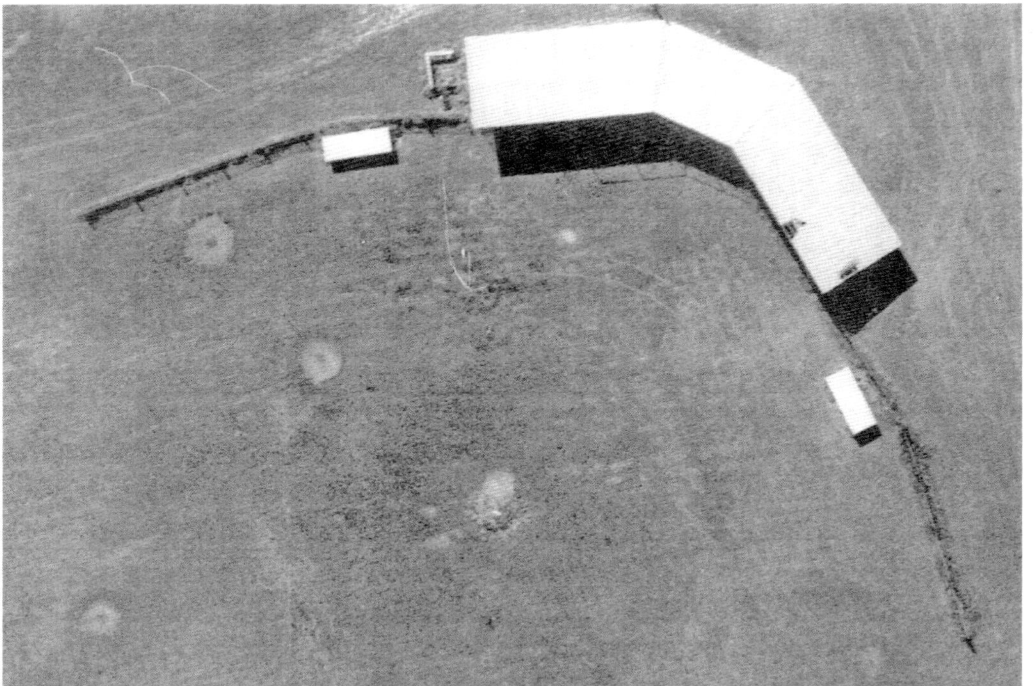

Ranch workers would get together on Sundays at Assault Park to cheer on the King Ranch Cowboy baseball team. This aerial photograph of Assault Park was taken in 1970. The grandstand, dugouts, and fence were removed in the 1980s. (Courtesy King Ranch Archives.)

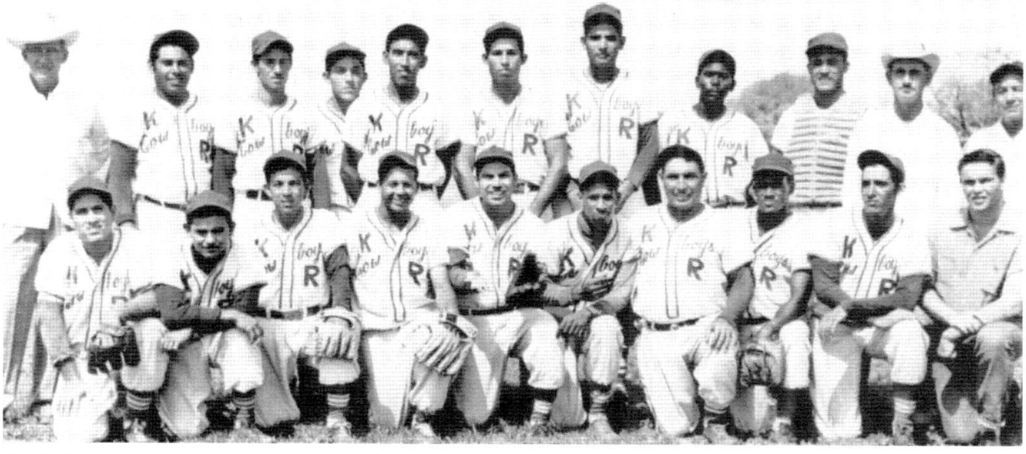

By 1954, the King Ranch Cowboys had gathered the best talent in the area. From left to right are (first row) Enrique Bazan, José "Lefty" Arredondo, Alberto Cavazos, Gustavo Garza, Guadalupe Juárez, Johnny Pinchback, Cipriano García, Willie Moore, Gonzalo González, and unidentified; (second row) coach Refugio Rodríguez, Alberto Buentello, Alberto Treviño, Gilberto Mendietta, Césario Cavazos, Gilberto Rodríguez, Lorenzo Mendietta, J.J. Jackson, Noe Marmelejo, president Adán Muñoz, and Frank Quintanilla. (Courtesy Jesús García.)

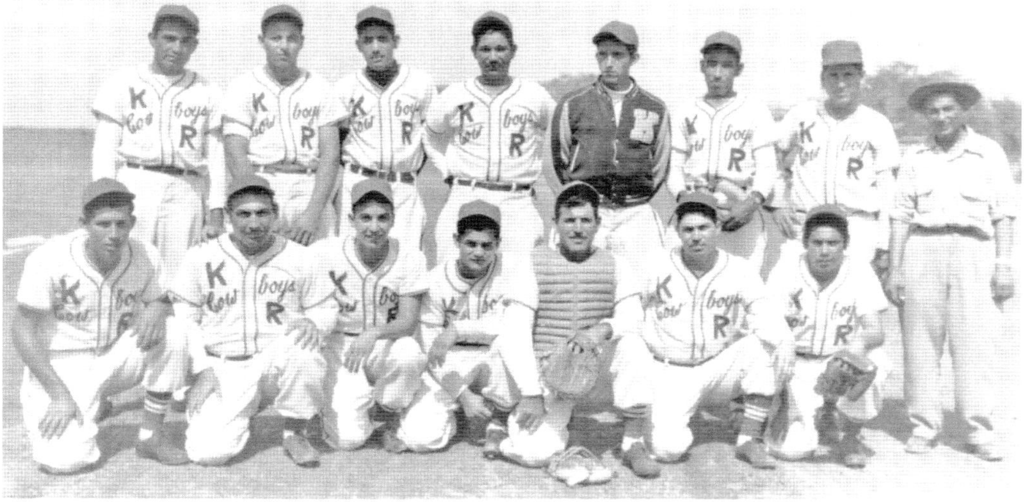

In 1953, these Cowboys—with the addition of a few ringers—played the San Antonio Brooke Army Medical Center Comets and lost 3-8. The Comets were always stocked with top minor-league professionals and sometimes a Major-Leaguer or two playing baseball while serving their country. The Cowboys managed three runs off George Susce, a Boston Red Sox pitcher. Comets Bob Turley and Don Newcombe, two of the best pitchers in Major-League history, drew over 2,000 fans to the game. From left to right are (first row) Gilberto Rodríguez, Cipriano García, Amando Sáenz, Antonio Rodríguez, Jesús García, Guadalupe Juárez, and Alberto Buentello; (second row) Miguel Ochoa, Andrés Soto, Lorenzo Mendietta, Jesús Muñiz, Gonzalo González, Césario Cavazos, Enrique Bazan, and manager Jesús Garza. (Courtesy Cipriano García.)

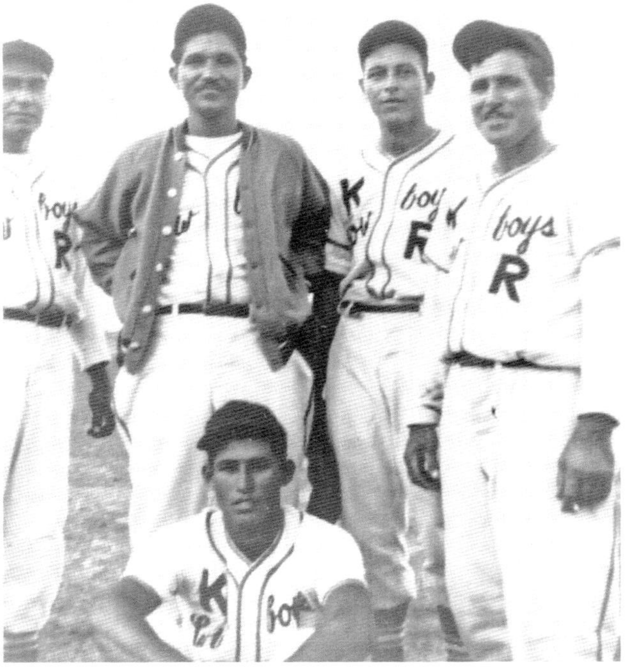

Pictured from left to right in 1953 are (first row) Abundio Rodríguez; (second row) Miguel Ochoa, Jesús Muñiz, Andrés Soto, and Jesús García. The team often used the profits collected to purchase uniforms and team jackets. Muñiz is wearing one of the jackets. García had once coached the team, but his love of the game led him to stay active on the field. The players, boosters, and parents often pitched in and worked around the diamond. The people who pitched in for the Cowboys included Choche Mayorga, Guadalupe García Sr., Emiterio Silguero, Refugio Rodríguez, Julián Buentello, Valentín Quintanilla, Champo Cortéz, and Jesús Muñiz. (Courtesy Jesús García.)

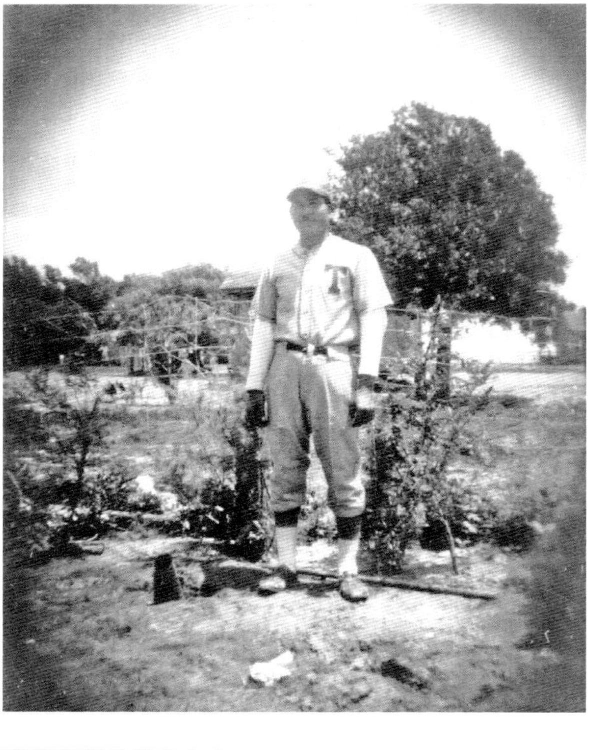

In 1945, Kingsville Toro Jesús García poses in his front yard, which is enclosed in King Ranch square range fence. He played for the Toros before coaching and playing on a very young King Ranch Lions team. The Lions were the first formal team to play on the King Ranch. For one of their away games, the players squeezed into ranch work trucks to play in Banquete, about 25 miles away. Once they arrived, the opposing fans started heckling them because of how young the Lions were. After the ranch team defeated them, the Banquete players and fans had a newfound respect for them. They quickly requested a rematch. This occurred many times during those early years. (Courtesy Jesús García.)

Luís Canales had plenty of semipro experience by the time of this photograph in the early 1950s at home plate in Assault Park, on historic King Ranch. He had previously played for several of the better semipro teams in Kingsville. The field was named for the King Ranch horse that won the Triple Crown in 1941. This photograph gives a great view of the grandstands that the players, boosters, and ranch employees built with donated material. The grandstand could hold approximately 400. (Courtesy Cipriano García.)

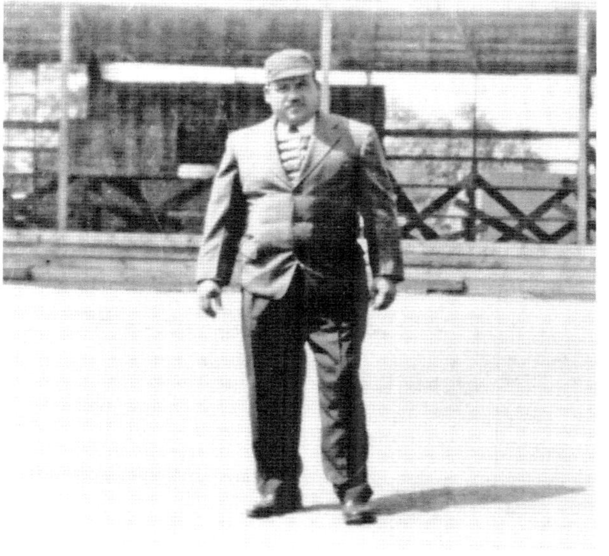

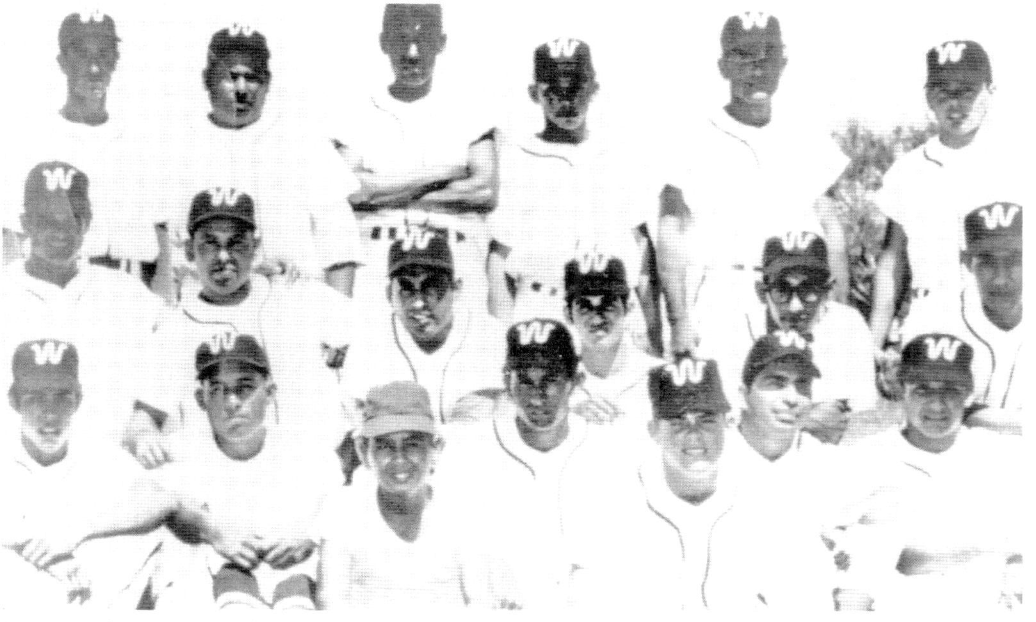

By 1961, the King Ranch Cowboys were in decline. The veteran players were all in their 30s, and semipro baseball across America faced new challenges with competition for fans. In Kingsville, there was a new bowling alley, golf course, and softball and youth baseball leagues, as well as the devastating combination of television and air-conditioning. Attendance was an issue. From left to right are (first row) Nano Borrego, Abundio Rodríguez, batboy Rene Villarreal, Chino Rodríguez, Stephen "Tio" Kleberg, Valentín Quintanilla, and Fernando Rodríguez; (second row) Antonio Rodríguez, Julián Buentello Jr., Cipriano Escobedo, Jesús García Jr., Raúl Buentello, and Rene Borrego; (third row) Alberto Treviño, Alberto Buentello, Lorenzo Mendietta, Raúl Rodríguez, Chito Mendietta, and Coche Buentello. (Courtesy Jesús García.)

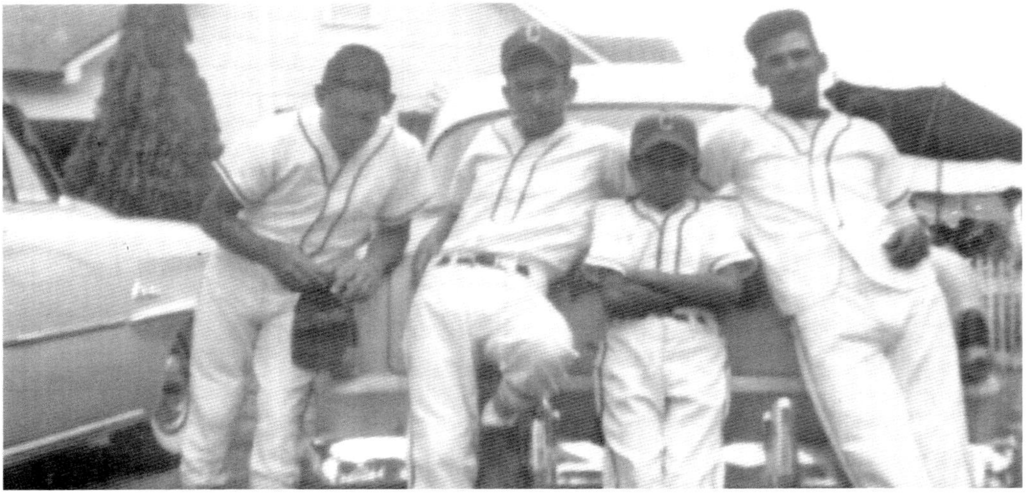

Just before a 1956 home game, these Laureles-Chapman Cowboy players are proudly leaning on 16-year-old Héctor M. Treviño's 1955 Chevrolet in front of Manuel Treviño Sr.'s house on Laureles Ranch. Héctor's 12-year-old brother, Gabriel Treviño, with his arms crossed, seems to be just as proud. Gabriel was batboy at the time and later played second base and shortstop for the Laureles-Chapman Cowboys. From left to right are Ernesto Quintanilla, Héctor M. Treviño, Gabriel Treviño, and Manuel Treviño Jr. (Courtesy Lupe Quintanilla.)

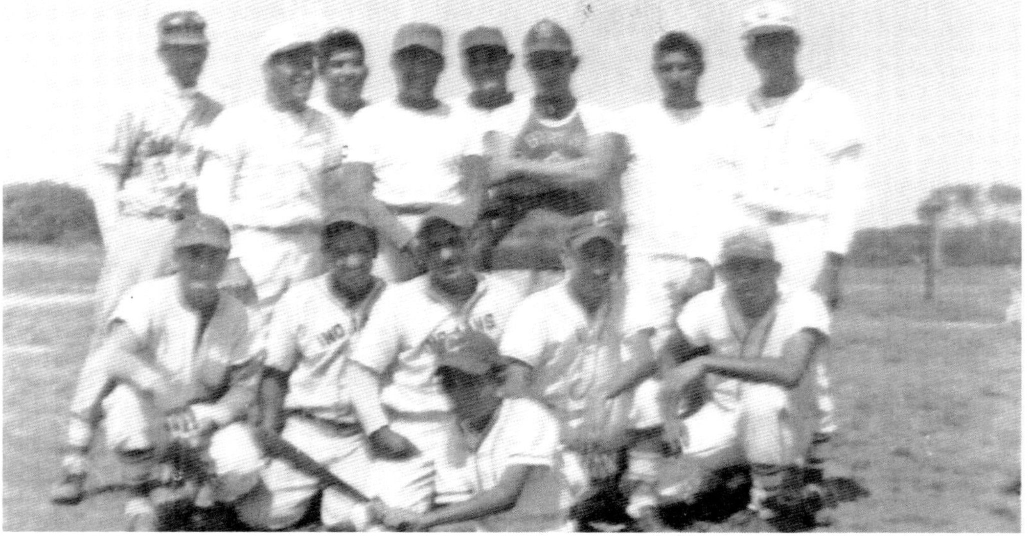

The 1956 Laureles-Chapman Cowboys played on a diamond between the Laureles and Chapman Ranches. These ranches were different divisions of the King Ranch and are approximately 15 miles south of Corpus Christi. From left to right are (first row) batboy Gabriel Treviño; (second row) Rudy Chapa, two unidentified, Héctor Treviño, and Ernesto Quintanilla; (third row) Juan Zaragosa, Domingo García, Mike Ríos, unidentified, ? Chavana, Evaristo García, Amadeo Lozano, and Manuel Treviño Jr. The unidentified players are from Corpus Christi. (Courtesy Lupe Quintanilla.)

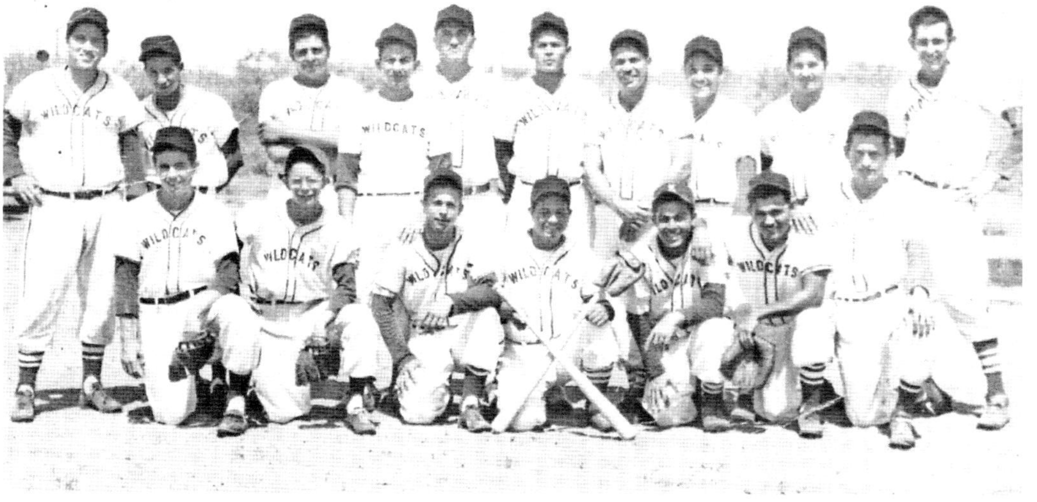

The Cowboys had a strong rivalry with the Kingsville Wildcats. The Wildcats started playing on an empty field behind what is now Kleberg Elementary School. St. Martin's Catholic School now sits where the diamond was. The Wildcats relocated to Wildcat Park, just north of Corral Street between Sixth and Fourteenth Streets. This 1959 picture was taken in front of the chicken wire backstop. From left to right are (first row) Armando Salazar, Oscar Cabra, Raúl Reyes Sr., Gustavo Garza, Baldemar Ramos, José "Lefty" Arredondo, and Moisés Aguilar; (second row) player-coach Enrique Bazan, Arturo Flores, Ramón Solís, "Sugar" Rodríguez, Humberto García, Alex Solíz, Guadalupe Juárez, Álvaro Flores, Adán Flores, and Lalo Soto. (Courtesy Enrique Bazan.)

Tules Sánchez, photographed in 1945 at 27, played for the Missouri-Pacific All-Stars. The All-Stars were a railroad-sponsored team, and most of the players worked for the Missouri-Pacific Railroad. There were several departments and a roundhouse in Kingsville. The All-Stars played other semipro teams and regularly participated in railroad leagues consisting of company teams from the surrounding area. Tules Sánchez later played for the King Ranch Cowboys and took over as manager in 1958. (Courtesy Tules Sánchez.)

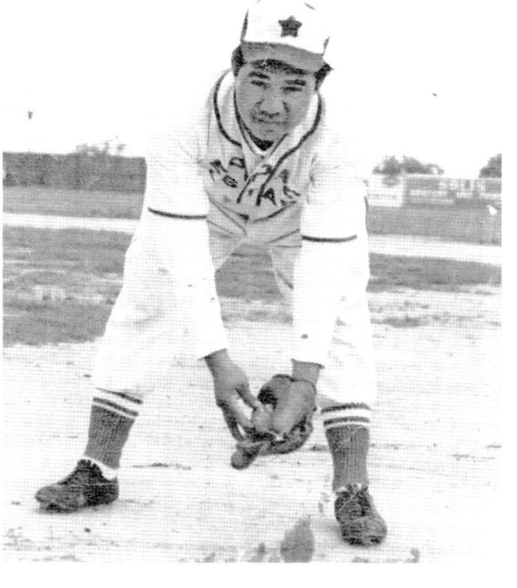

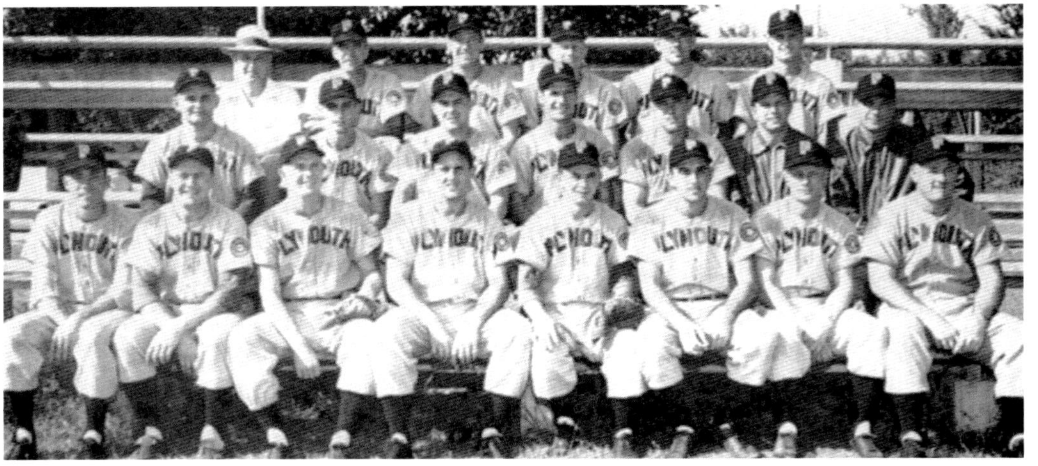

One of the best teams the Cowboys competed against was the Sinton Plymouth Oilers. Although the Cowboys never bested them, they had some very competitive games. The close scores proved the Cowboys could compete with one of the best semipro teams around. These 1951 Oilers became the first Texas team to win the National Baseball Congress (NBC) Championship, held in Wichita, Kansas. The Oilers were a heavy semipro team comprised of former professional and college players. In 1950, a young Pat Hubert (first row, second from left) pitched the first no-hitter in NBC championship history. (Courtesy NBC World Series.)

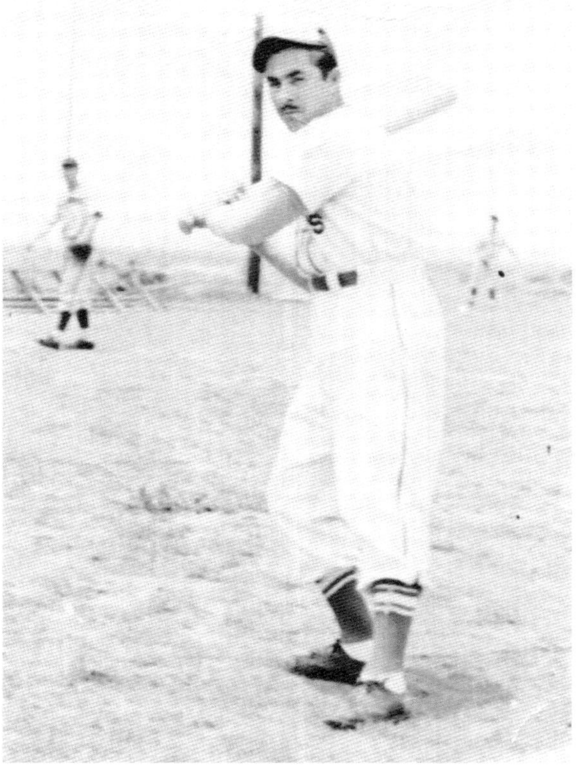

Alberto "Beto" Garza poses in his Kingsville Toros uniform just before a game against the Naval Air Station Kingsville team. The naval club had a diamond on the base, designated as the Texas A&I University (now Texas A&M University–Kingsville) East Campus. The school converted some old barracks into classrooms, and a baseball diamond evolved near the facility. The King Ranch Cowboys played many military teams, including the Corpus Christi Cabniss Field; Kingsville Naval Auxiliary Air Station Flyers; San Antonio Brook Army Medical Center Comets; Corpus Christi Blue Angels; Nuevo Laredo, Mexico, 31st Battalion; Refugio VFW; Victoria Air Force Base Jets; Corpus Christi Naval Air Station Comets; Laredo Air Force Base; and Harlingen Air Force Base Hustlers. (Courtesy Cristella Garza Mendietta.)

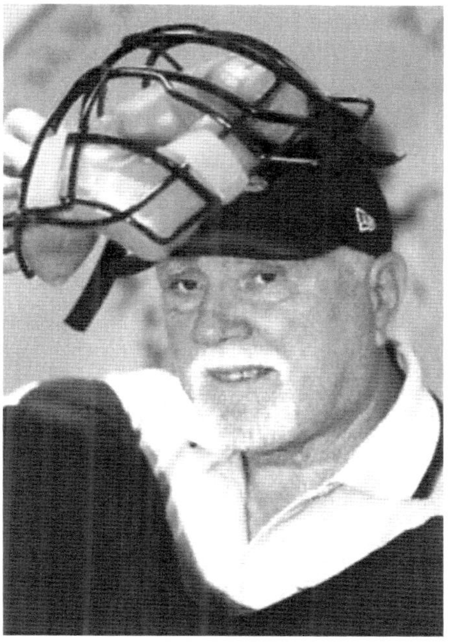

Joseph L. Cusack loved watching the Cowboys and officiated with many of them, including Balde Delgado, Joe Mendietta, Mario Delgado, and Cipriano García. Cusack called his first Little League game in Hawaii in 1958. He has officiated baseball, softball, volleyball, basketball, and soccer. He is the president of the local softball chapter of the Texas Association of Sports Officials. He has been an umpire for kids and their grandparents and officiated state high school volleyball and softball tournaments and the Softball World Series. He is currently an assistant to the dean of students and was named a "bringer of light" to the Texas A&M University–Kingsville campus. He volunteers as usher and greeter at St. Gertrude's Catholic Church. (Courtesy Pete García/*Alice Echo News Journal*.)

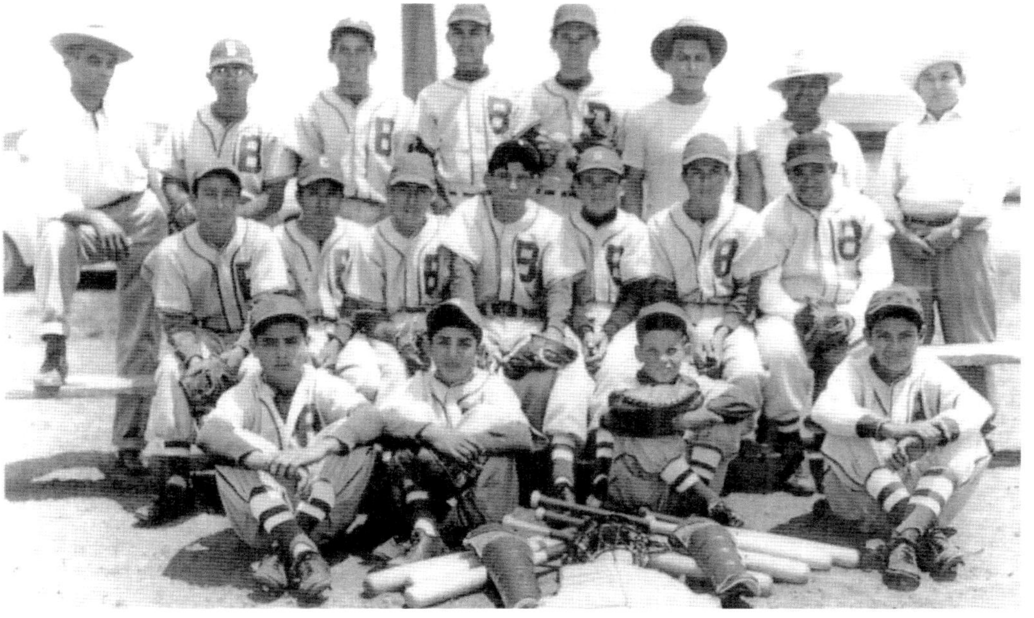

Although the Bishop Wildcats never defeated the Cowboys, they developed a heavy semipro team. This 1961 team played against Robstown, Taft, Three Rivers, Sinton, Corpus Christi–West Oso, and the Rio Grande Valley. From left to right are (first row) Willie Segovia, Héctor Ramírez, Homero Vela, and Romeo Álvarez; (second row) Lee Solíz, Mique Rangel, Manual Solíz, Librado Rodríguez, Andrés Vela, Keno Rangel, and Baldemaro Ortiz; (third row) Carlos Gutiérrez Sr., coach Joe Alvarado, Abel Zepeda, Juan Hernández, John Garrett, coaches Manuel Támez and Pedro Alvarado, and treasurer Lionel Ramírez. (Courtesy Mario Álvarez.)

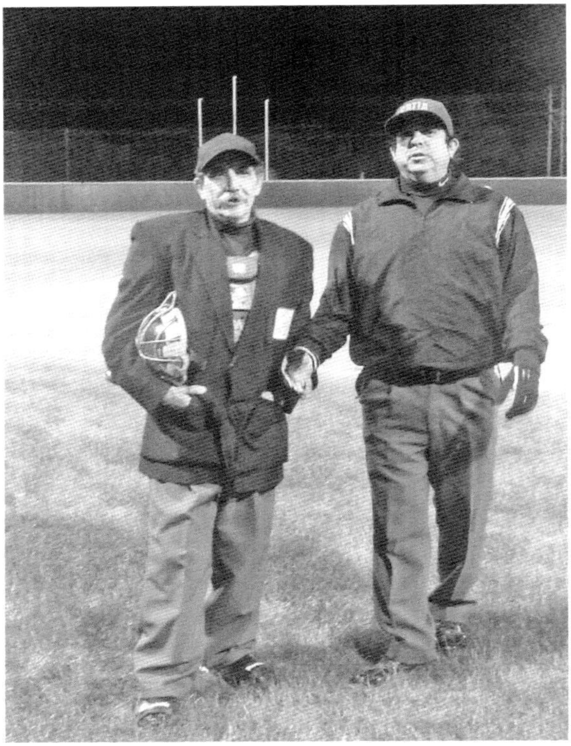

Donavan "Captain D" López has a long history with baseball. Besides writing three books on the subject and playing for over 40 years, he is a University Interscholastic League college and professional umpire. He is pictured here (at right) in 2017, umpiring with his older brother, Daniel López, in a high school match at Alice High School. López's father Pablo López, brother Donnie Amador López, and nephew Donnie Paul López all umpired. Daniel López is the president of an umpire association that covers the amateur baseball schedules in Kingsville, Alice, Premont, Kingsville, Corpus Christi, Riviera, Bishop, Robstown, and Benavidez. It is often said that where there is a baseball game in South Texas, one will find a López umpiring it. (Courtesy Donavan "Captain D" López.)

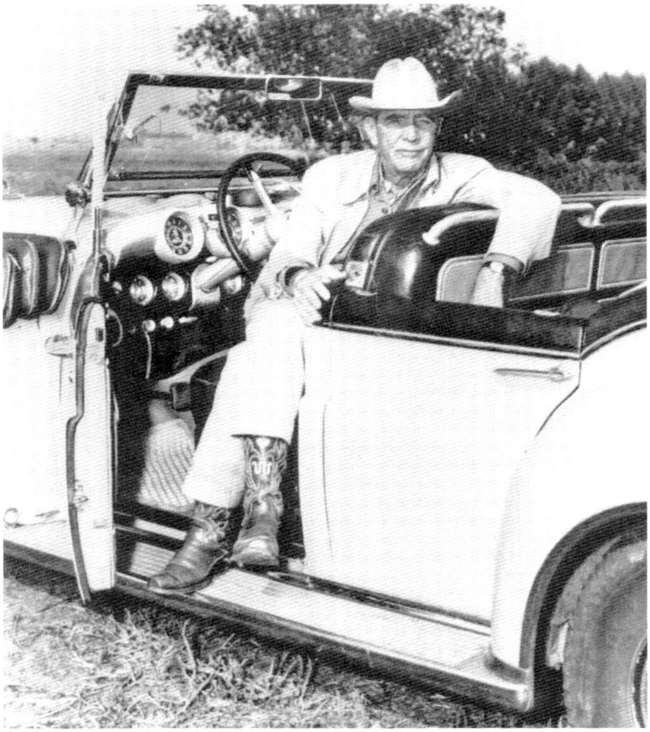

Baseball on the ranch, as distinguished from the city of Kingsville, had a long history. One of the owners of the ranch, Richard Kleberg Sr., was a baseball enthusiast. He pitched for the 1907 Kingsville 5000. By the 1930s, formal games were played between departments on the ranch. The dairy barn, racehorse department, and slaughterhouse department played on a cleared pasture near the home of ranch veterinarian Dr. J.K. Northway. At times, tryouts were held to select the best players to compete against other ranches. In 1942, King Ranch defeated a team from Hebbronville. (Courtesy King Ranch Archives.)

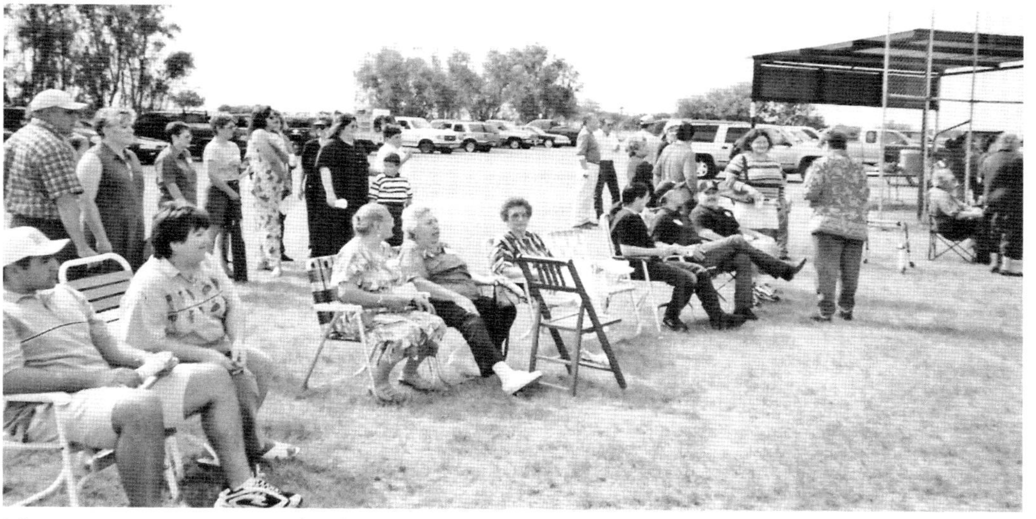

Many came out to support the dedication of Assault Park on the King Ranch on April 19, 2001. The Santa Gertrudis Independent School District was established in 1917 and currently operates two schools: a combined elementary and junior high and Academy High School, originally a collaborative program of Santa Gertrudis ISD, Driscoll ISD, and Texas A&M University–Kingsville. The school began with a freshman class in 1994–1995 and expanded to serve grades 9 through 12 by 1997–1998. Both schools practice at Assault Park. (Courtesy Lupita Borrego.)

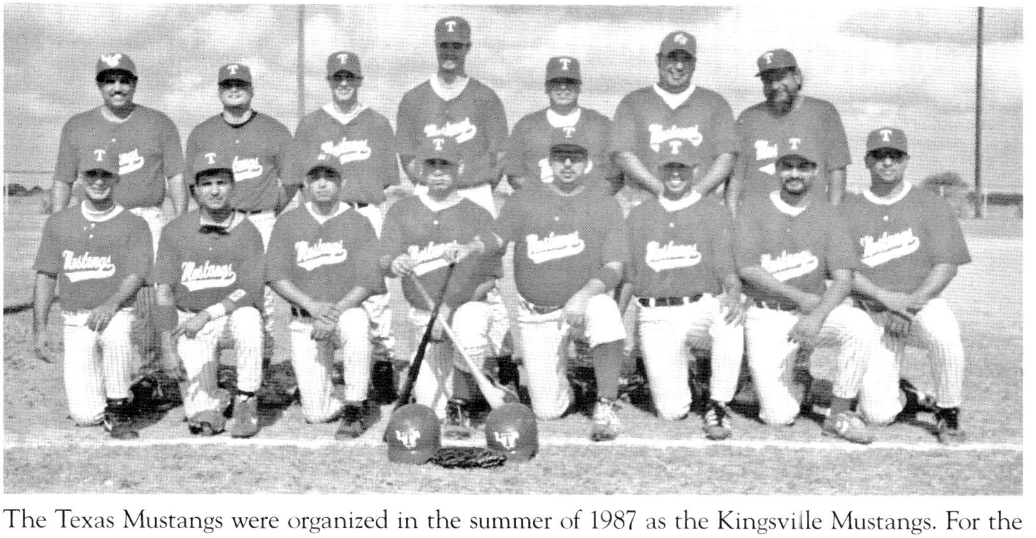

The Texas Mustangs were organized in the summer of 1987 as the Kingsville Mustangs. For the 1997 season, they were named the Kingsville Eagles. The Mustangs were organized by Donavan "Captain D" López to give players the opportunity to continue playing after high school. These 1998 Mustangs are, from left to right, (first row) Gabe Sáenz, Benny Sánchez, Joey Jara, J.V. Riviera, player-coach Donavan "Captain D" López, John Joslin, Beto Mejía, and Romey Utley; (second row) sponsor Roland Bazan, Matt Benavides, Danny Díaz-DeLeón. Frank McDaniels, Gian Guerra, Gabby Morales, and coach Moe Henry Alvarado. (Courtesy Donavan "Captain D" López.)

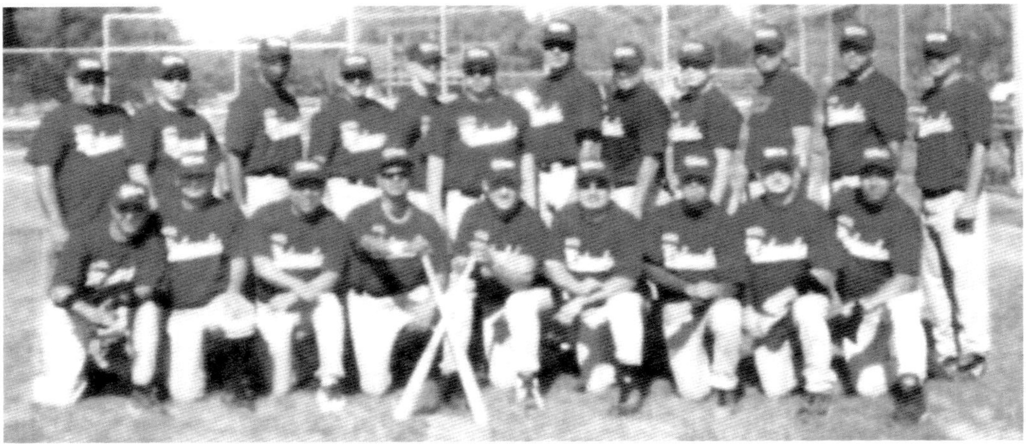

In 2003, the semipro Alice Merchants played the professional Coastal Bend Aviators at Zeke Mora Field in Alice. The Aviators were a minor-league team that played in Robstown from 2003 to 2007. They were members of the Central Baseball and the American Association Leagues. Rene Zarate played against the King Ranch Cowboys. From left to right are (first row) Mike Silguero, Gabby Sáenz, Joe Hernández, Benito Sánchez, Ramón Flores, Eloy Cantú, Pete Treviño, Trino Carbajal, and Leo Zarate; (second row) manager Rene Zarate, Cris Casares, Victor Williams, coach John Farias, Brian Boerjan, Donavan "Captain D" López, Mike McDonald, Tydie Castillo, Raúl Guerra, unidentified, Anthony Cortéz, and Gabe Pulido. (Courtesy Donavan "Captain D" López.)

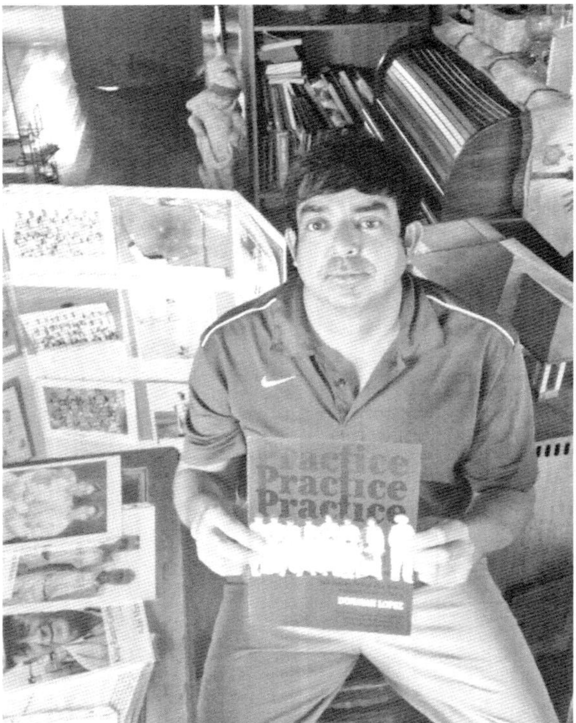

Donavan "Captain D" López poses with his book *Practice! Practice! Practice!* for the *Corpus Christi Caller-Times.* The newspaper ran the front-page story "Cowboys on the Diamond" on July 18, 2016, in a periodical called *South Texas Snapshot.* López learned about the King Ranch Cowboy team and players while growing up. He played Little League, American Legion, high school, college, and semipro baseball in Kingsville. After graduating from H.M. King High School in 1987, he played for Texas A&I University from 1987 to 1989 and continued playing semipro baseball well into his 40s. (Courtesy *Corpus Christi Caller-Times.*)

Kingsville native Donavan "Captain D" López (left), with the guidance of Dr. Harry Russ Huebel, researched the King Ranch Cowboys for his history master's thesis while attending Texas A&I University, now Texas A&M University–Kingsville. Huebel was chair of the thesis committee. His research took five years, during which he interviewed players, fans, and family members and researched articles from the *Corpus Christi Caller-Times*, the *Kingsville and Bishop Record News*, and the *Alice Echo–News Journal*. (Courtesy Donavan "Captain D" López.)

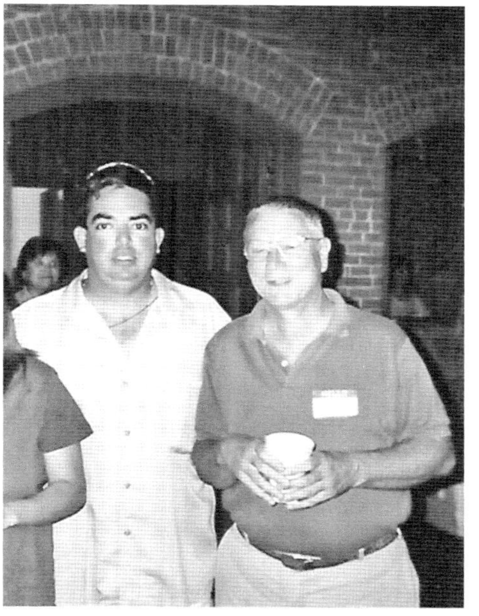

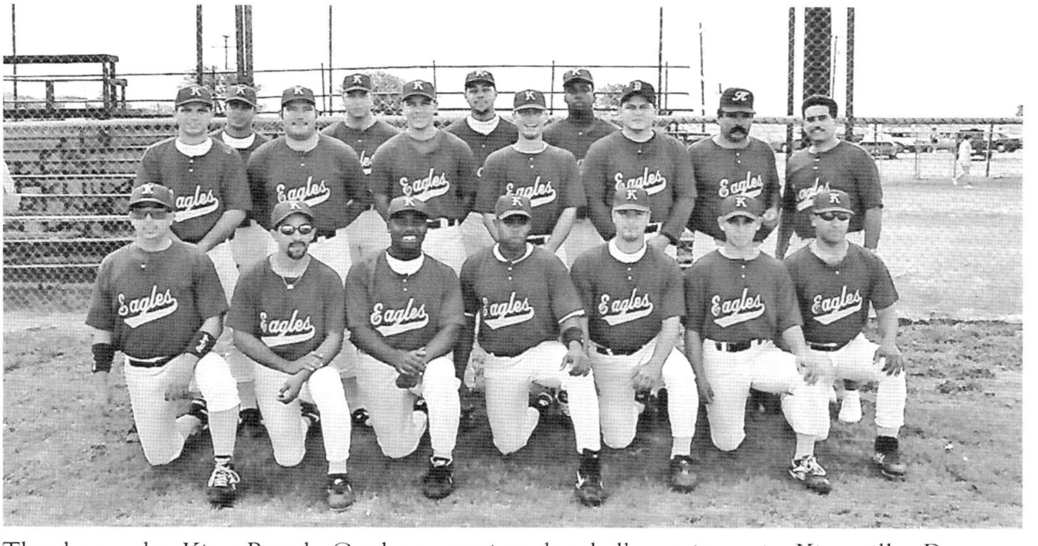

Thanks to the King Ranch Cowboys, semipro baseball continues in Kingsville. Donavan "Captain D" López played and coached semipro teams for more than 25 years. A team sponsor and owner of Henry's Glass Shop, Rolando Bazan, is the son of Enrique Bazan, who coached and played for the Cowboys. The 1997 Kingsville Eagles are, from left to right, (first row) team captain Donavan "Captain D" López, Jo Jo Espinoza, Dedrick Porter, unidentified, Mark Mungia, John Joslin, and Romey Utley; (second row) Jake Hoffsteter, Gabby Morales, Gabe Pérez, Asmel Acum, Rico Treviño, manager Roel García, and sponsor Rolando Bazan; (third row) Héctor Lebrón, Omar Allende, Able Montilla, and David Chisolm. Porter, Mungia, Utley, Pérez, Acum, García, Lebrón, Allende, and Montilla also played on the inaugural Texas A&I University baseball team. (Courtesy Donavan "Captain D" López.)

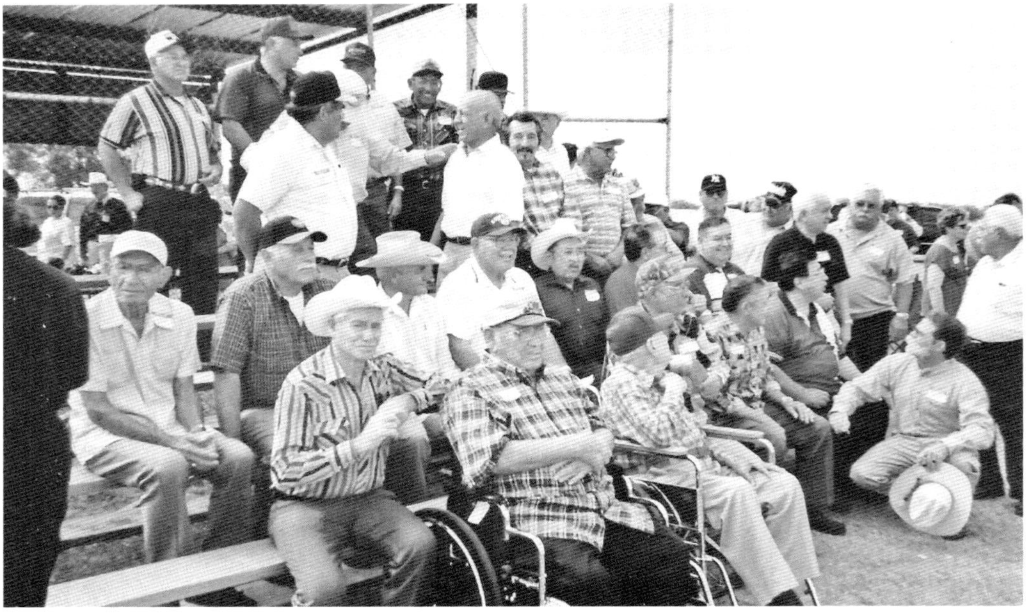

Many King Ranch Cowboys earned greater accolades. Stephen "Tio" Kleberg was a member of the board of directors for King Ranch Inc., Humberto "Chino" García was Kingsville chief of police, Mario Delgado was a Kleberg County justice of the peace, Adán Muñoz Jr. was Kleberg County sheriff, José Mendietta was administrative director for Kingsville ISD, and Rene Villarreal was a Kingsville city commissioner. Several became public school educators. Eliseo Ramos Jr. had the Hebbronville high school field named in his honor, the greatest honor any player can receive. Many volunteered in Little Leagues as coaches, umpires, and board members. (Courtesy Lupita Borrego.)

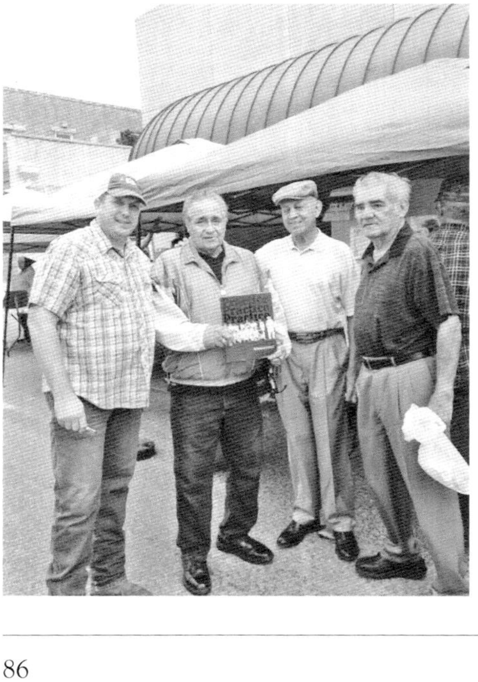

On November 21, 2015, Donavan "Captain D" López and the Robert J. Kleberg Public Library conducted a book signing and exhibit at the King Ranch Hand Festival in historic downtown Kingsville. López, along with several players, family members, and opponents of the Cowboys, signed copies of his book *Practice! Practice! Practice!: The History of the King Ranch Cowboys Baseball Team*. Members presented stories, memories, and baseball memorabilia. Lupita Borrego, King Ranch Cowboys reunion coordinator, also presented pictures and memorabilia from the 2001 reunion. From left to right are Sean Mitchell, Rene Zarate, Mario Delgado, and José Mendietta. (Courtesy Donavan "Captain D" López.)

6

The Lone Star State

Noted scholar of Latino/a sports Jose Alamillo argued recently in his article "Beyond the Latino Sports Hero: The Role of Sports in Creating Communities, Networks and Identities," that the value of athletes and coaches of such backgrounds comes from their "relation to both family and community . . . we must go beyond seeing individual Latina/Latino as Hero, Star, and Superhero." There are many examples we can point to: for example, the first female to broadcast a Major League baseball game, Jessica Mendoza (an Olympic gold medalist in her own right), each week comes into millions of homes throughout the nation and demonstrates a level of intellectual and sporting talent few could have imagined in the past. She is a hero who is making it possible for Spanish-surnamed athletes to break new ground in sport. As the photographs and stories herein demonstrate, baseball has been important to the maintenance and development of an ethnic consciousness among Mexican Americans for the past 100 years. Most of the athletes mentioned here did not play for money, but rather competed for camaraderie, recreation, and as a way to challenge assumptions about the athletic and organizational capabilities of their communities. Two current examples, from opposite ends of the state of Texas, highlight how this trend continues to the current day.

The first is the story of Eric Gutíerrez from Sharyland, who helped Texas Tech to its first ever College World Series appearances. Coming out of the town of Mission, he was overlooked, even though he batted .600 in his senior year. There were three strikes against Gutíerrez: his height, his family's inability to afford traveling squads, and, as his head coach at Texas Tech noted, "he wasn't recruited because he's practically from Mexico." Like many Mexican Americans, Gutíerrez managed to overcome by outworking his competition. He was named all-American as a senior and is now in the Miami Marlins system. Texas Tech has also benefitted, as its nationally ranked squad now features talented (and overlooked) Mexican American athletes from both the Valley and El Paso.

Larry Hernandez began coaching in 1971 and started the El Paso Bandits in 1989 at Ponder Park. The squad won its first title in 1990 and has racked up 20 more national and regional championships since. Dozens of Hernandez's boys have gone on to play collegiate ball and even professionally. Almost 200 have earned National Honor Society awards at their high schools. Five have become coaches in their own right, assuring that El Paso baseball will continue to thrive.

These stories are just samples of how baseball continues to benefit both family and community of Mexican Americans throughout Texas. And the action on the field is pretty darn exciting as well!

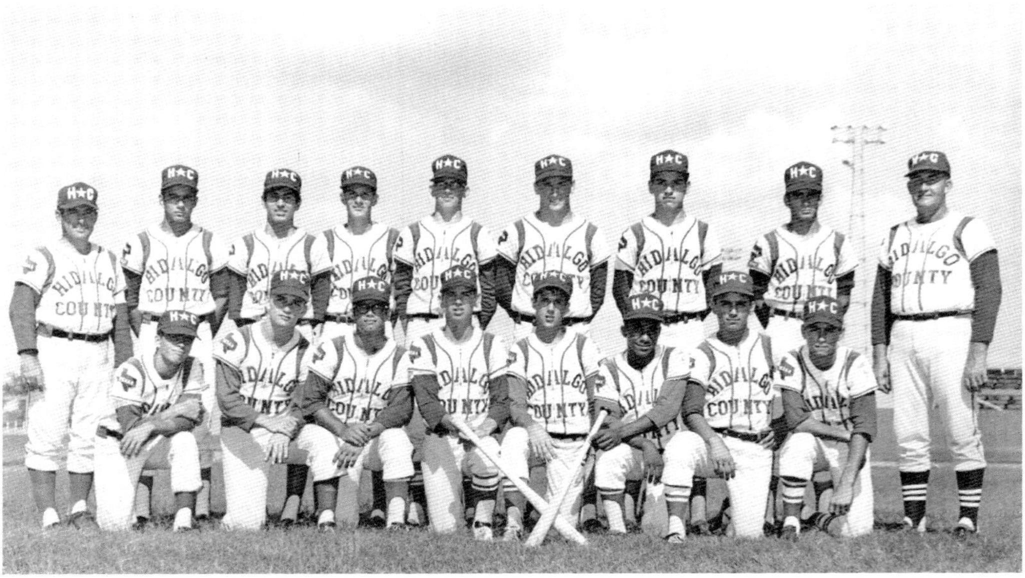

The 1968 Hidalgo County Colt League All-Stars were managed by Rubén Ayala Sr. and coached by Bill Ward. The team attempted to duplicate the World Series run by the 1962 Hidalgo County Colts, who won the tournament in Shawnee, Oklahoma. In a close and competitive elimination game, the Hidalgo County team from South Texas lost to a San Antonio squad 1-0. Besides Ayala's volunteer work with baseball, he also served as municipal judge in his hometown of Edinburg, Texas. (Courtesy Gloria Guerra Ayala.)

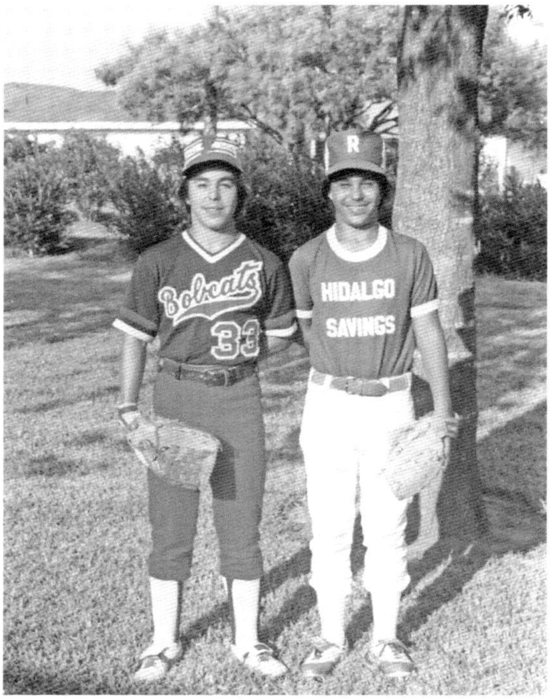

Brothers Rubén Jr. (left) and Jaime Ayala (right) played baseball at numerous levels in their hometown of Edinburg. Rubén played varsity baseball for the Edinburg Bobcats, while Jaime played Little League for Edinburg's Hidalgo County Savings in 1979. Rubén went on to play for the Pan American University Broncs. Both brothers went on to serve devotedly in law enforcement. Jaime is currently the assistant police chief with the Fort Worth Police Department. Rubén served with various police departments in South Texas. Sadly, he suddenly passed away in March 2016. (Courtesy Gloria Guerra Ayala.)

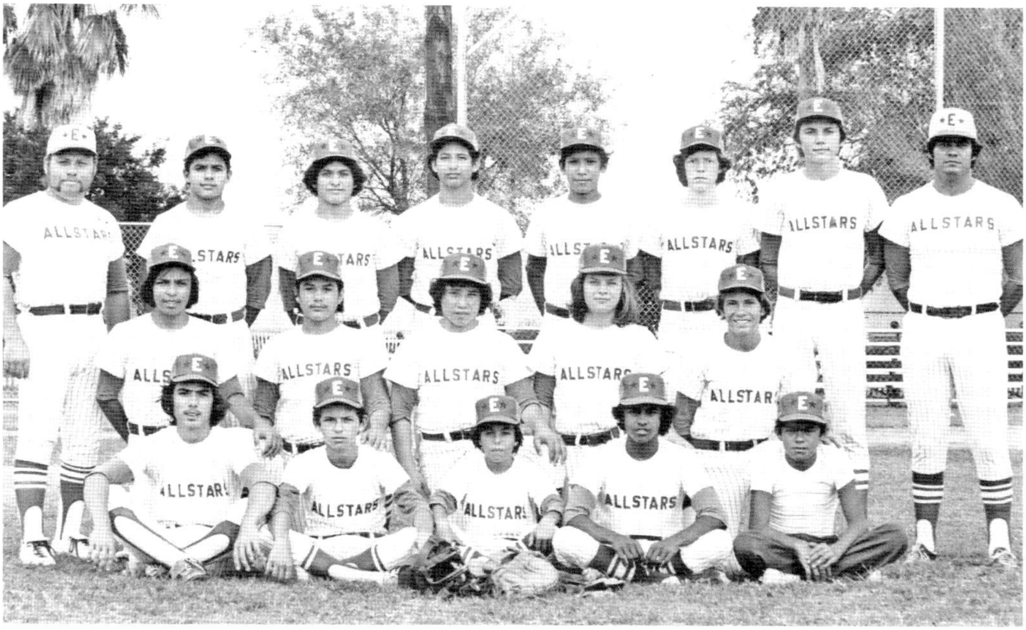

The 1975 Edinburg All-Stars include José González, Arnoldo García, Zacarías Olivarez, David Ochoa, Rafael Garza, David Olivarez, Rene Flores, Severiano Rubio, Fernando De La Garza, Rubén Ayala Jr., Emedel Molina, Philip Money, Travis Benke, Ramón Esquivel, and David Gormillón. Frank Balli and Adán Rendón coached the team, while Don Naiser served as bus manager. This photograph was taken at a playoff game against Pasadena, Texas, on August 6, 1975. (Courtesy Gloria Guerra Ayala.)

Abel Casas Sr. (left) played centerfield for the Mission 30-30 Rifles, a semipro team in South Texas in 1946. The legendary Leo Najo, Bernardo Peña, and José Carreon Garza founded the 30-30s along with other players. The Chicago White Sox drafted Najo in 1925. Semipro teams like the 30-30s set a precedent for integration and a limited interaction among Mexican Americans and Anglo Americans in the Río Grande valley. (Courtesy Abel Casas Jr.)

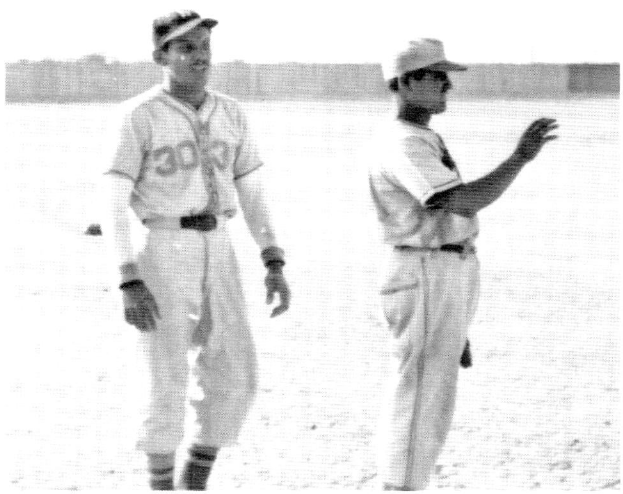

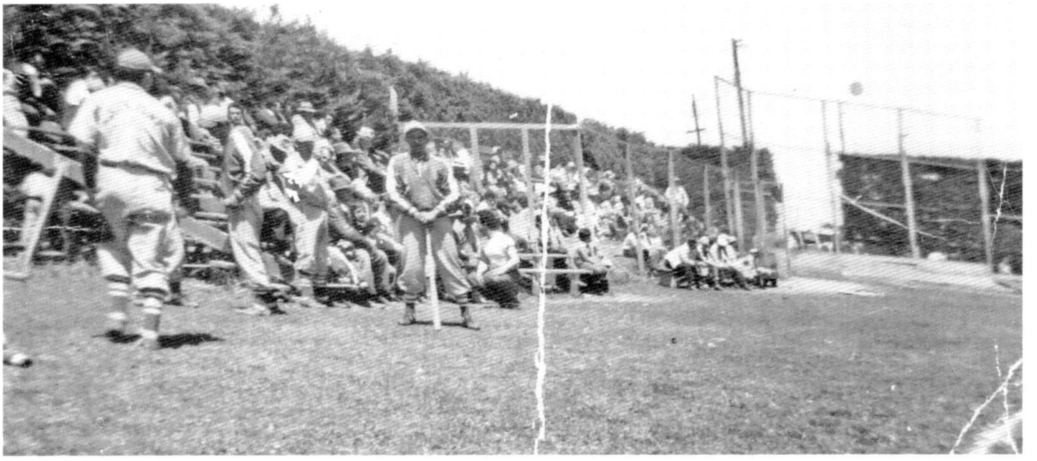

This 1947 photograph was taken at the inaugural season of the Mission 30-30 Rifle Baseball Park in Mission, Texas. During the 1946 season, the 30-30s played primarily on the road, as they lacked a home field. The team eventually nestled at the 30-30 Ballpark in Southwest Mission, the traditional Mexican American part of town. Legendary Dallas Cowboys coach Tom Landry, a Mission native, suited up for the 30-30s and hit the first home run at the 30-30 ballpark that year. (Courtesy Abel Casas Jr.)

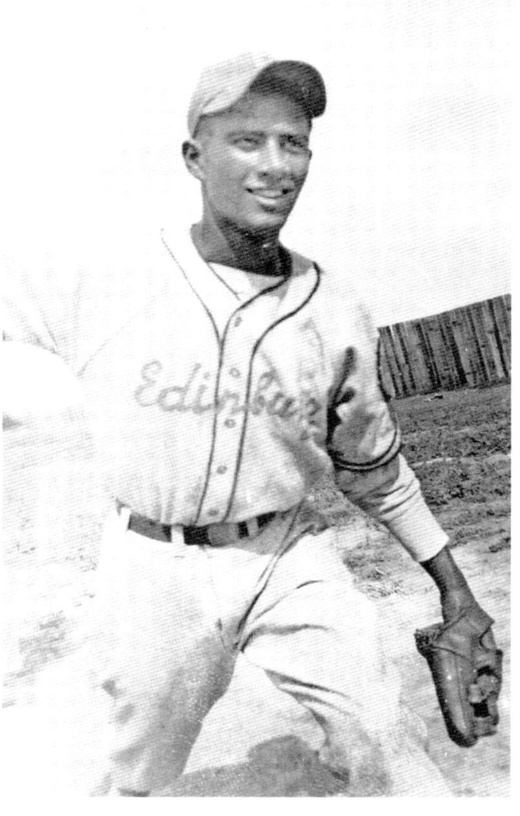

Francisco "Cisco" Estévis pitched for the varsity Edinburg High School Bobcats in 1951. The team won the District AA championship that year. In 1952, the Bobcats won District 16 AA and faced the Mission Eagles, who dominated Single A ball. Estévis dueled it out against Reynaldo "Rey" Valadez, and Estévis won. He went on to pitch for the Pan American Broncs. One of his teammates was Valadez. Estévis was later drafted and served toward the end of the Korean War. He attended New Mexico Highlands, serving as an assistant baseball coach. One of his longest stints was with the varsity Weslaco High School Panthers. Baseball served as an avenue for social and racial unification in Edinburg. There was a sizable African American community that played ball with Mexican Americans. African Americans attended George Washington Carver School in Edinburg between 1938 and 1961. (Courtesy Vicente and Francisco Estévis.)

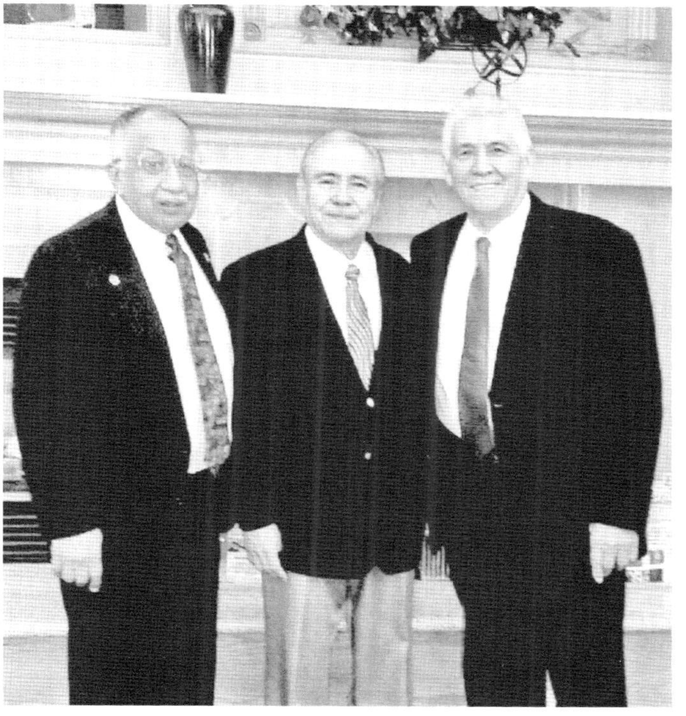

From left to right, Juan Roque, Licenciado Arturo Estrada, and Bert Lozano all umpired for decades. In 2014, they attended an annual celebration entitled Los Mejores Ampayers de Mexico y del Sur de Tejas (The Best Umpires of Mexico and South Texas) in Monterrey, Nuevo León. They were awarded El Trofeo Ampayer Arturo Estrada Sánchez. Roque is originally from California and now lives in the Río Grande valley. Licenciado Estrada is from Monterrey, and Bert Lozano is from Mission, Texas. (Courtesy Bert Lozano.)

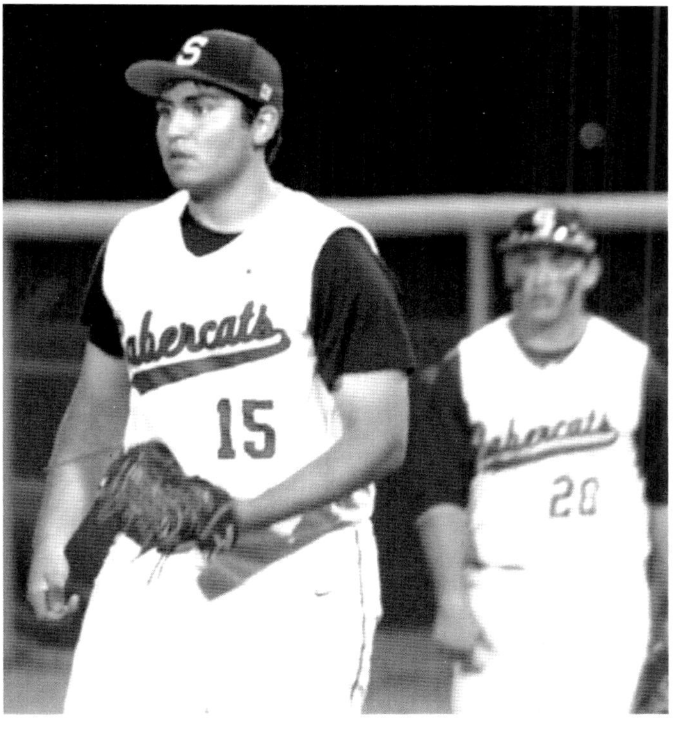

Arnulfo "Arnie" Salinas Jr. is a native of Edinburg, Texas, where he pitched for the varsity Robert Vela High School Sabercats. After graduating in 2015, Salinas pitched for the Coastal Bend College Cougars. He played for the Cougars for two years. However, like many Mexican Americans from the Río Grande valley, Salinas had to leave his community for more opportunities. He transferred to Texas A&M International College in Laredo, where he will seek to continue his aspirations of pitching at a higher and more competitive level. (Courtesy Arnulfo Salinas Sr. and family.)

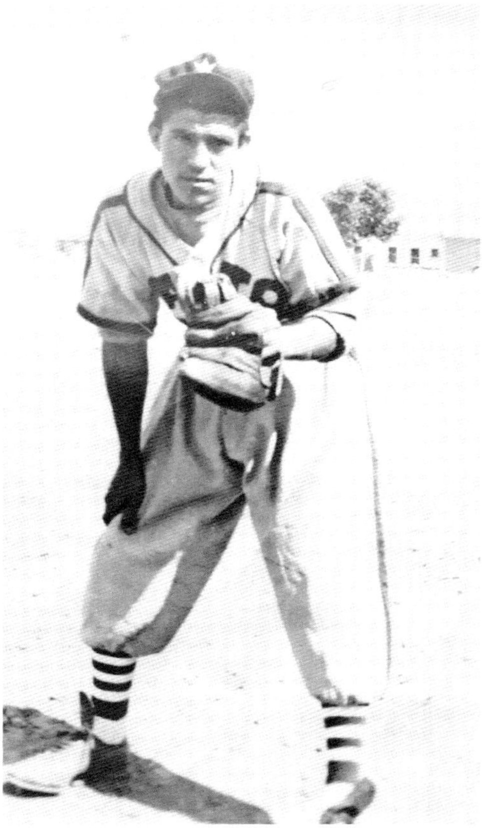

Jesús Badillo was born in Torreón, Mexico, and moved at a very early age to Juárez. He participated in the Bracero program but found time to play baseball. He was an ace pitcher for the Gato Negro and Juárez Indios teams during the 1940s. During his time with Gato Negro, he was scouted to play with the professional Arizona-Texas League, where he enjoyed great success. In the early 1950s, he, his wife, Elvira, and children Maria Cruz, Erasto, and Jess moved to Compton, California, where Maria Teresa was born. Erasto attended the Claremont Colleges, while Jess graduated from California State University at Long Beach. Maria Cruz enjoys a successful career, and Maria Teresa is employed with the Anaheim Angels. (Courtesy Jess Badillo.)

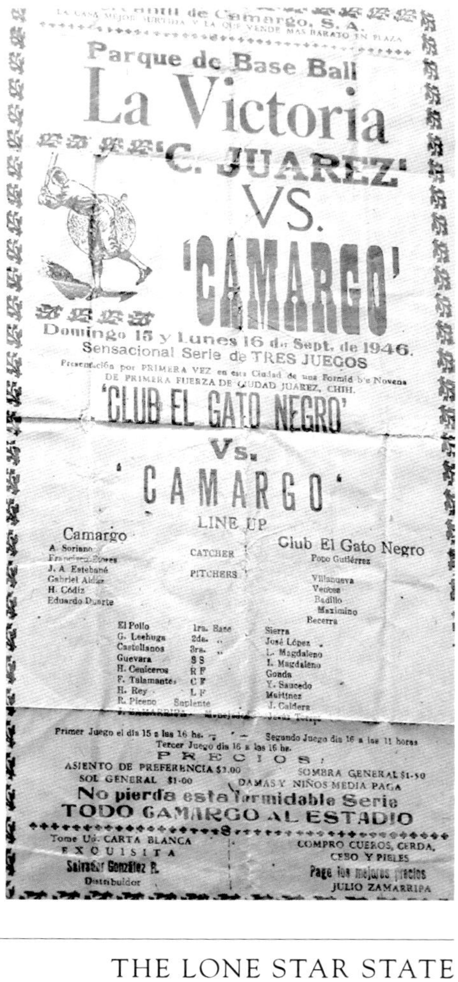

This 1940s baseball poster announcing a game between La Victoria and Camargo is part of a collection of the Badillo family. Jesús Badillo played in this game. He loved to tell baseball stories to his children when they were young. One tale was about a baseball owner who promised the players a steak dinner at his home if the team won a critical game. They did, and the owner, true to his word, invited them to his home. But he first fed them large bowls of soup, endless selections of *botanas* (appetizers), and several drinks. By the time they were asked how they wanted their steaks, they were so full that they left without eating them. Badillo did not live long enough to meet any of his grandchildren or great-grandchildren. His granddaughter Jenna played La Habra softball, and his great-grandson Joaquín played little league in Whittier, California. (Courtesy Jess Badillo.)

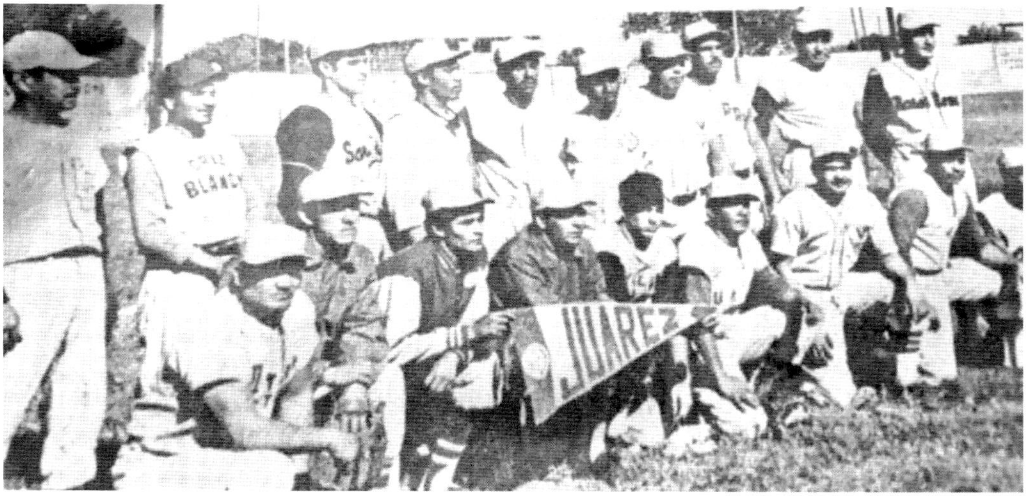

Although life was good to Jesús Badillo (first row, second form left) and his wife, Elvira, in Juárez, they wanted more opportunities for their children and decided to move in 1956 to California, where Jesús was a steelworker and a proud member of the AFL-CIO. He passed away at 47 in 1975. Jesús taught his family many valuable lessons about life by example. He watched the Dodgers on television and listened to them on the radio. (Courtesy Jesús Badillo family.)

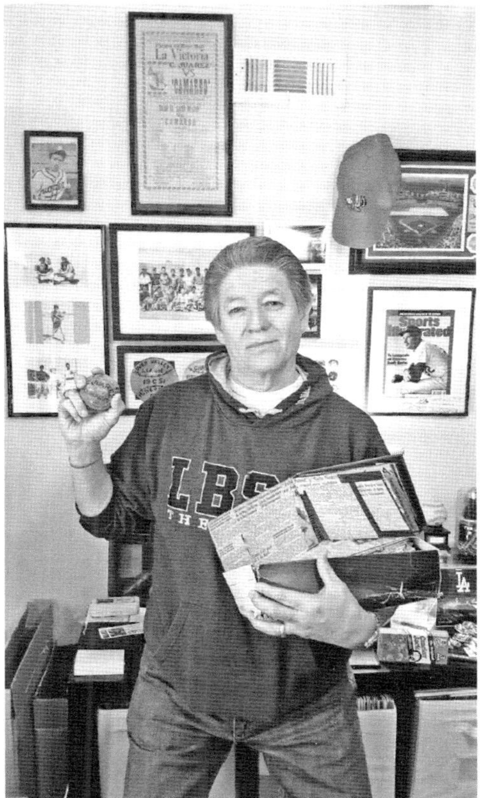

Jess Badillo holds his father's scrapbook and one of his baseballs. On the wall are photographs from when Jesús Badillo played in Juárez and El Paso. While attending California State University at Long Beach, Jess often spoke with his father about life, politics, and baseball. As a result, he became very involved in the Chicano civil rights movement and developed a profound love of books, music, and art. He served as a community service commissioner for La Habra, California. He has met several renowned authors, including Victor Villaseñor, Luís Rodríguez, and Sandra Cisneros, and iconic figures such as Dolores Huerta, Helen Chávez, and Lalo Guerrero. He credits his parents' sacrifices for his life's experiences and successes. (Courtesy Jess Badillo.)

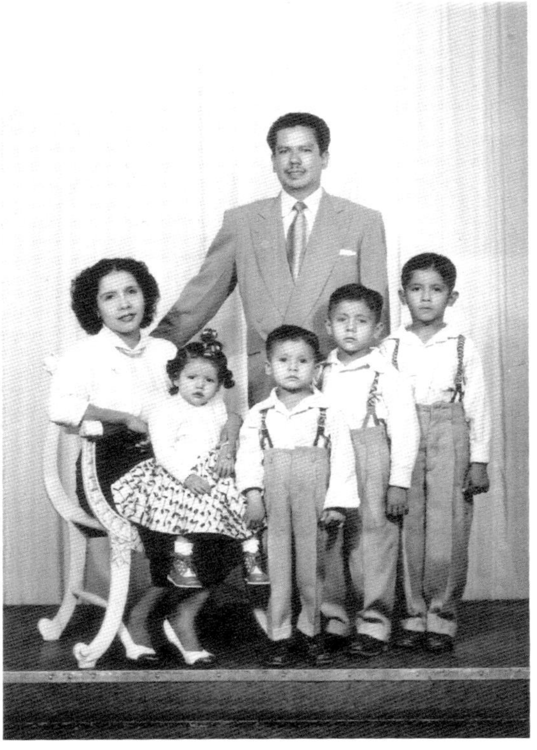

The Caballero family posed for this photo at a studio in Ciudad Juárez, Mexico, about a year before they immigrated to El Paso in 1958. Sitting is Rafaela Alonso Caballero and standing is her husband Arnulfo Caballero. From left to right are their children Graciela (on mother's lap), Carlos, Gonzalo, and César. César attended a Catholic school in El Paso in the morning and a school in Ciudad Juárez in the afternoon. The family eventually moved into a two-room apartment on the Southside of El Paso on the corner of Seventh and Florence Streets. After a year, they moved into a larger apartment and opened a laundry and cleaning business, Caballero Cleaners. While living in El Segundo Barrio, César and his brothers would play sandlot ball on weekends and summers at Armijo Park across from their home. (Courtesy César Caballero.)

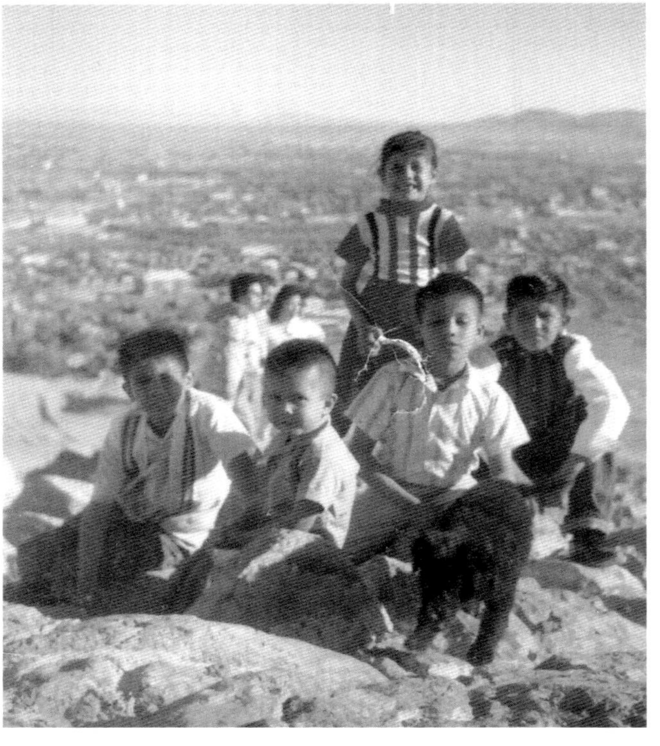

The Caballero children are seen here with their dog Lobo at Lookout Point on a hill next to Franklin Mountain, with a panoramic view of downtown El Paso. From left to right are Carlos, Mario, Graciela (standing), Gonzalo, and César. César attended both Jefferson Junior and High Schools. In high school, he joined the band and orchestra and served as drum major during his senior year. He attended Texas Western College, the University of Texas at Austin, and Texas Tech University. For the past 10 years, he has served as the director of the Latino Baseball History Project. (Courtesy César Caballero.)

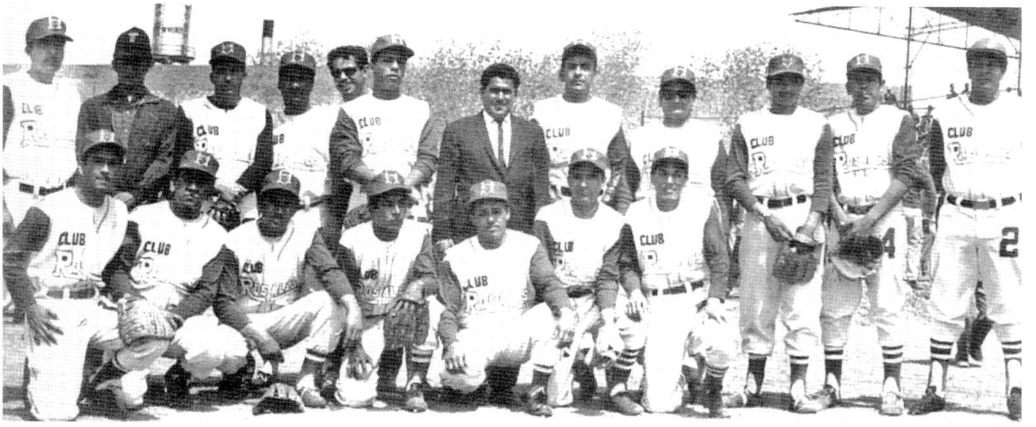

The 1968 Diablos Rojos (Red Devils) were sponsored by Club Rosales in Ciudad Juárez. Their games were played at Ceveceria Cruz Blanca Stadium. From left to right are (first row) Tomás Minjarez, Francisco Hernández, Manuel Puea, Manuel Aceves, Ángel Muñoz, Mundo Télles, and Ángel Rojas; (second row) manager Francisco Cadena, Ramón Gallardo, Jesús Araiza, Óscar Alvarado, Jaime Villa, Ramón Flores, Rodolfo Adame, brothers Pedro Seánez and Jesús Seánez, and three unidentified. Pedro Seánez's two boys, Richard and Greg, were the batboys. (Courtesy Seánez family.)

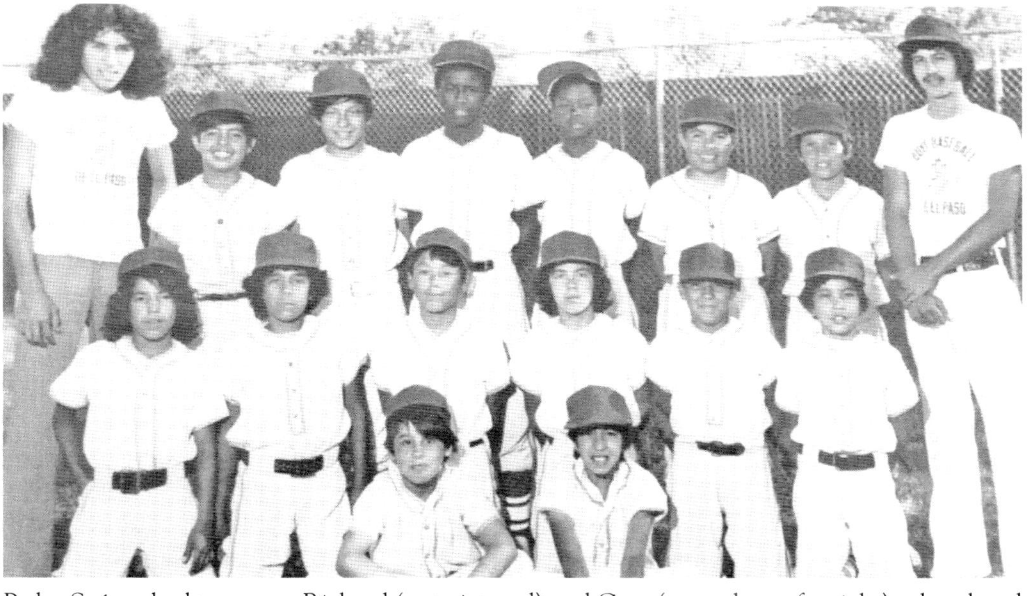

Pedro Seánez had two sons, Richard (not pictured) and Greg (second row, far right), who played for the 1970s El Paso Hawkins team. Other players on this Rams team included Alex Escalante, Richard Porras, and Albert Mendoza. Greg was a gifted athlete who played with the Rubén Salazar Park Reds in East Los Angeles and later played baseball and football at Roosevelt High School as an infielder and quarterback. Rubén Salazar was a news reporter killed by the Los Angeles Sheriff's Department during an anti–Vietnam War protest on August 29, 1970, in East Los Angeles. (Courtesy Greg Seánez.)

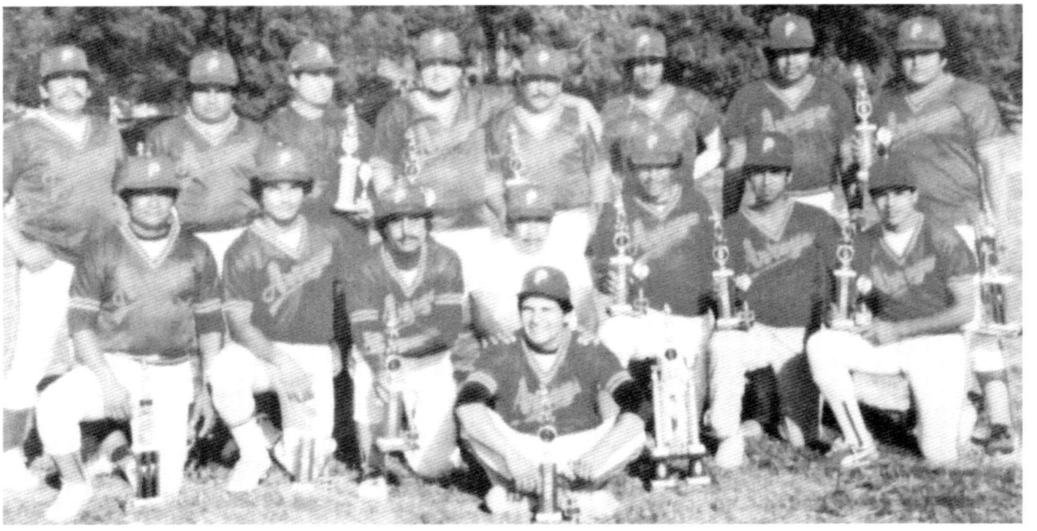

Mike Brito, a longtime Dodgers scout, has sponsored a baseball league for 50 years. Thousands have participated in the Mike Brito League. This 1983 East Los Angeles team, Arroyo Colorado, includes players whose parents migrated from Ciudad Juárez. The team bears the name of their neighborhood in Juárez. Among those pictured are Richard Seánez (first row, far right) and his father, Pedro Seánez (second row, far left). Other team members include the González brothers—Alfredo, Rubén, and Charlie—as well as Alfred Rodríguez, Ángel Fonseca, and manager Víctor Rodríguez. (Courtesy Seánez family.)

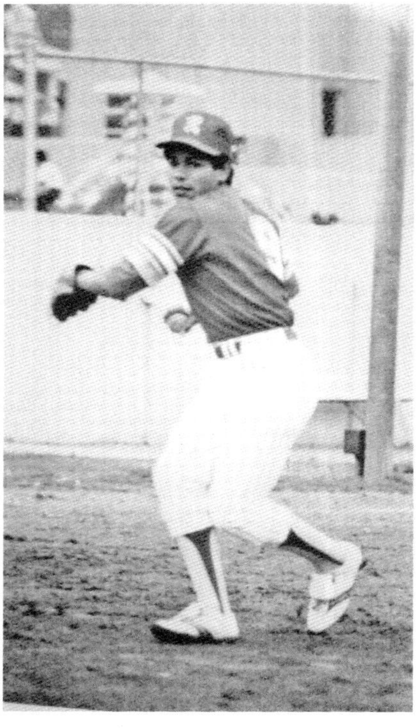

Richard Seánez is seen here playing for the Roosevelt baseball team in East Los Angeles in 1979. As a young boy growing up in El Paso, Seánez could not wait for Sunday mornings when the family would cross over the border bridge into Ciudad Juarez to watch his dad, Pedro, and his dad's two younger brothers Jesús "Tio Pilo" and Roberto play baseball games at Cerveceria Cruz Blanca and Jaime Canales Lira stadiums. Richard recalls that the crowds were always loud and fully engaged cheering on players such as "El Bon Bon" Gallardo, Negris Aceves, Skinny Cadena, Andy Alvarado, and Cliserio Torres to victory. After attending Cal State Los Angeles, Richard Seánez has worked at several law firms and participates in venture capital projects both domestic and international. He is married to Marty Seánez and has three children, Luke, Sarah, and Lauren. The family resides in Chino Hills, California. (Courtesy Richard Seánez.)

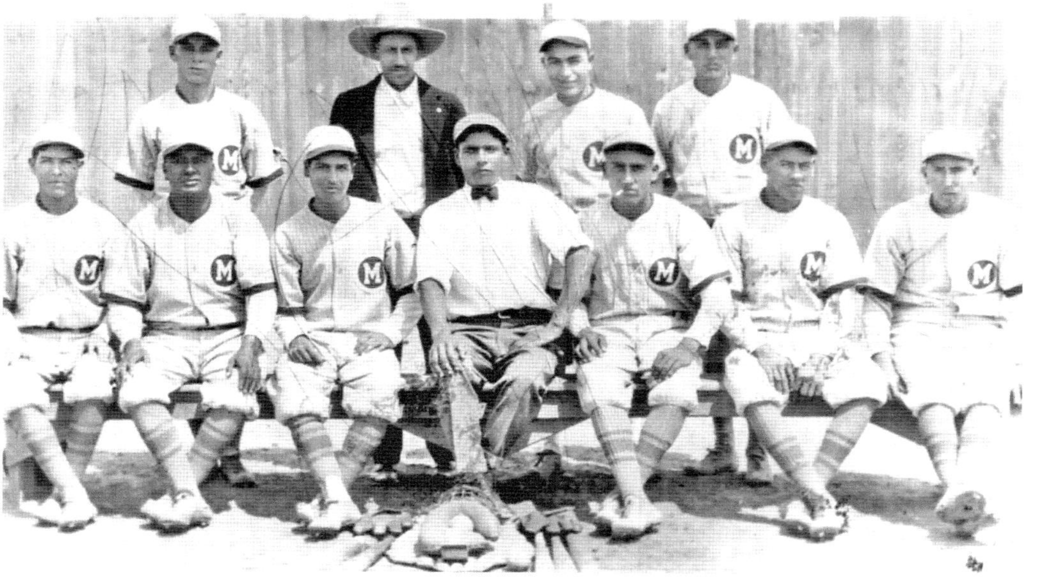

Little is known about this 1930s semipro team from Marfa, Texas. Note the cigarette dangling from one player's mouth and the pile of cash sitting on top of the catcher's mitt, which likely represented the players' share of ticket sales from a big game. Semipro teams drew huge crowds on holidays. In 1948, the Big Spring Tigers, an independent team managed by Tacho Martínez, hosted a 16 de Septiembre celebration at their local ballpark. Exhibition games with Major-League teams were also huge draws. In 1951, the St. Louis Browns played a memorable exhibition game at Kokernot Field in Alpine, even bringing along a chaise lounge for Satchel Paige to rest on. (Courtesy Marfa Public Library.)

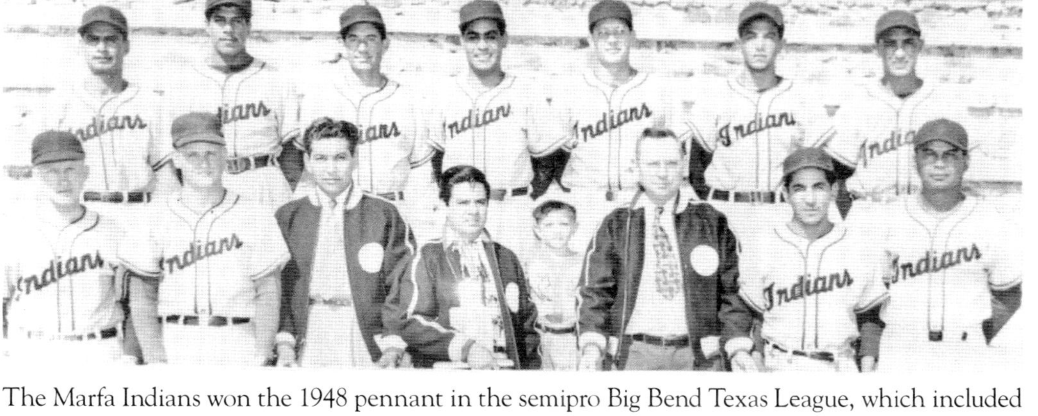

The Marfa Indians won the 1948 pennant in the semipro Big Bend Texas League, which included teams from Balmorhea, Fort Davis, and Alpine. Marfa's star pitcher was Joe Sanches, and its best hitter was Fred Luján. After winning a game over the rival Alpine Cowboys in 1948, a barbecue dinner in the team's honor was hosted by local judge C.F. Lee. Pictured are Russell Guevara (second row, fifth from left), coach L.B. Martin (first row, sixth from left), business manager Charlie Franco (first row, fourth from left), scorekeeper Robert Luján (first row, third from left), and team mascot Larry Lee Vásquez (first row, fifth from left). (Courtesy Marfa Public Library.)

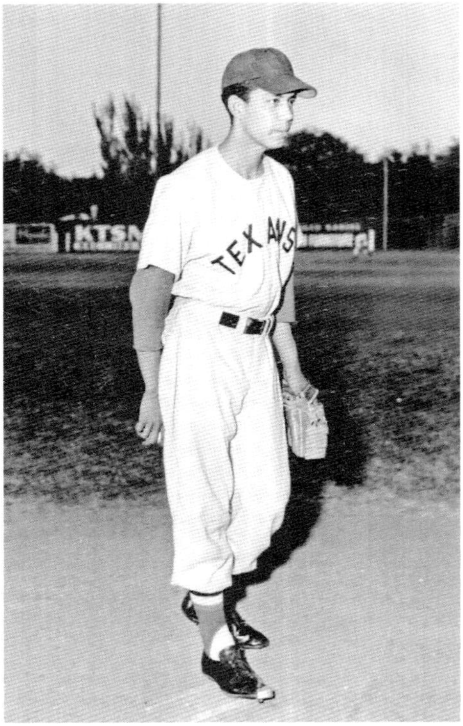

Rubén Porras, one of El Paso's best homegrown pitchers, is shown in the uniform of the minor-league El Paso Texans, who played in the Class C Southwest International League. A key member of Bowie High School's 1949 state championship team, Porras led the Bears to the playoffs again in 1950 before graduating in 1951. He turned down a scholarship to the University of Idaho to sign a professional contract with the Texans. He was inducted into the El Paso Baseball Hall of Fame in 1991. In 1949, neither of El Paso's daily papers sent a reporter to the tournament, so people back home followed Bowie's progress through the collect calls Coach Nemo Herrera placed to KTSM Radio. These calls were taped at the radio station and are now housed at the high school along with the championship trophy. After defeating Waco, Coach Herrera is heard on one of the tapes saying proudly about his players, they "just don't know when to quit." (Courtesy El Paso Chihuahuas.)

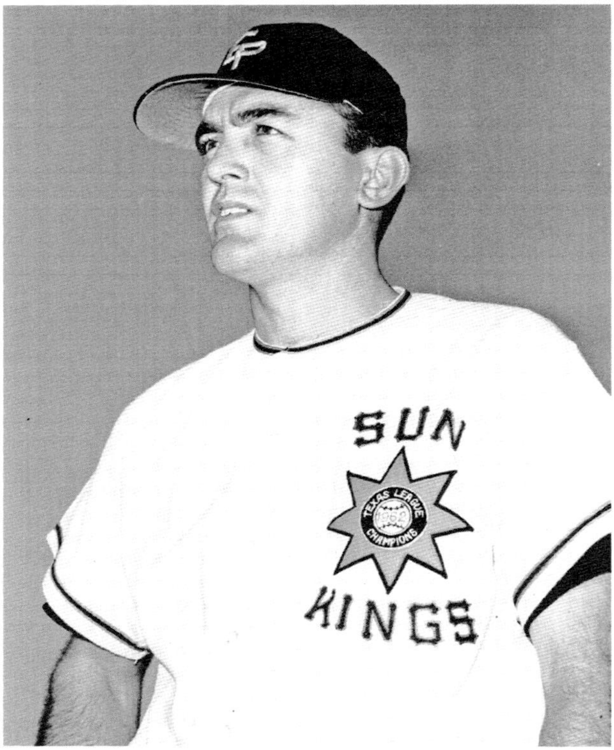

Baldemar "Pete" Carmona was a native of Nuevo Laredo, Tamaulipas, just across the Río Grande from Texas. He spent the late 1950s and early 1960s playing shortstop for various minor-league teams throughout the Texas border region, performing in Sweetwater, Paris, Del Rio, Corpus Christi, Victoria, and Harlingen, before joining the El Paso Sun Kings at age 29 in 1962. He batted .295 with a .382 on-base percentage for El Paso that year, and the *El Paso Herald-Post* labeled him a "valuable veteran." However, his performance dipped the following year, and he never played affiliated baseball again. (Courtesy El Paso Chihuahuas.)

Omar Quintanilla, shortstop for the Texas Longhorns, rounds the bases after hitting a three-run homer against Miami in the 2002 College World Series. After a storied career at El Paso's Socorro High School, Quintanilla batted .329 as a college sophomore in 2002, helping the Longhorns reach the College World Series for the first time since 1989. Quintanilla went four for five in the national championship game to help clinch the title for Texas and was named to the NCAA All-Tournament Team. As a sophomore, Quintanilla was a second-team All-American. (Courtesy *El Paso Times*.)

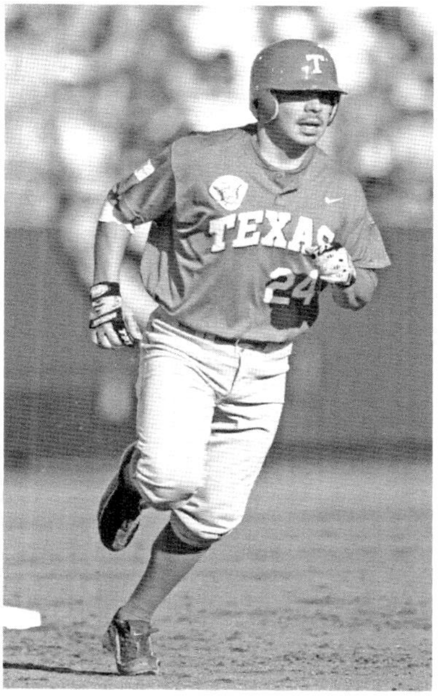

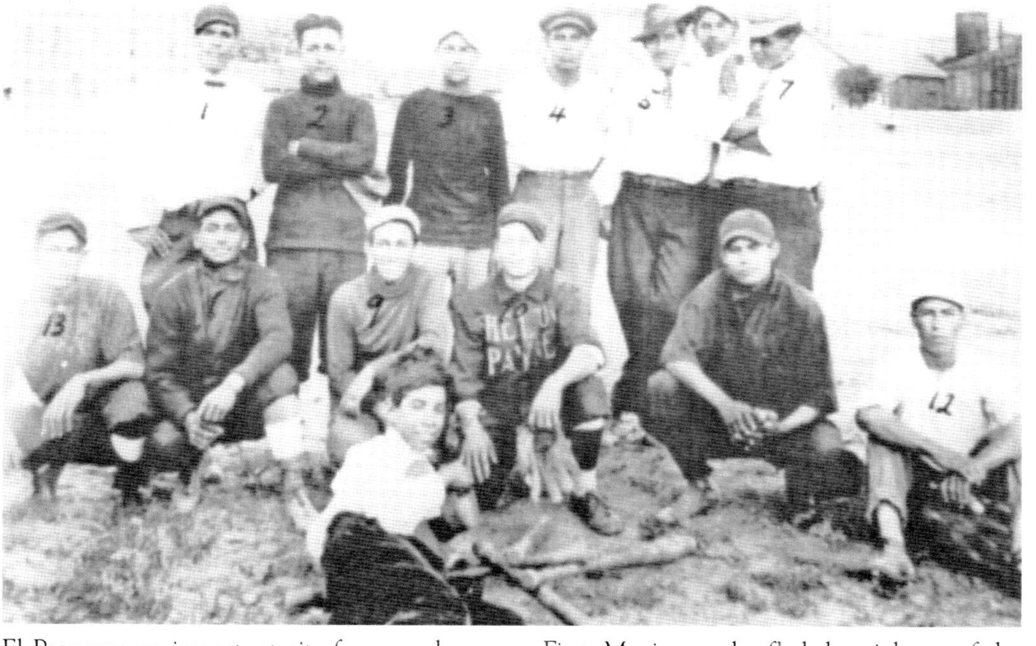

El Paso was an important city for several reasons. First, Mexicans who fled the violence of the Mexican Revolution between 1910 and 1917 passed through there. Second, once they entered El Paso, there were met by countless labor contractors promising work with the railroads, steel mills, packinghouses, agriculture, auto industry, icehouses, cement factories, salt mines, and other occupations throughout the United States. Many Mexican Americans from California to New York can trace their family history to El Paso. Third, baseball became a popular sport there before 1900. This is a Mexican pick-up team in El Paso in 1913. (Courtesy Latino Baseball History Project.)

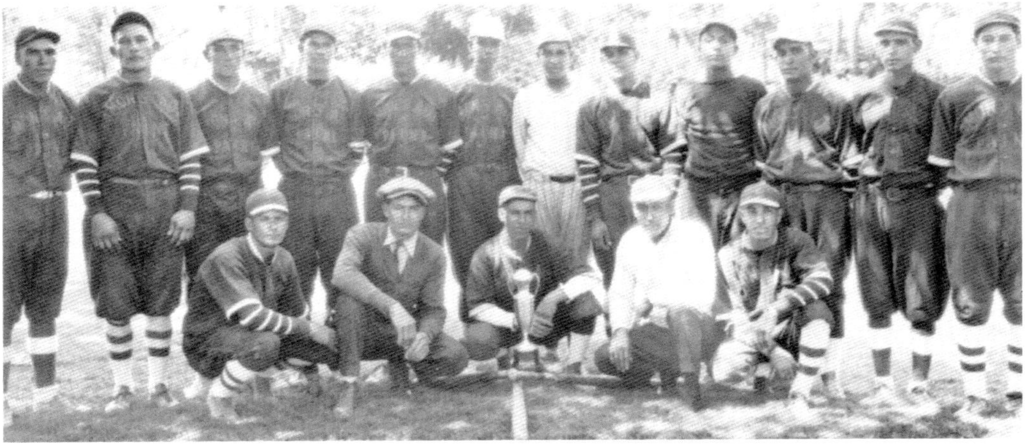

Baseball promoter Manuel Regalado organized Ramon's Auto and Paint in El Paso in 1924. After arriving in Los Angeles in 1926, he began to enjoy even greater success. He was so notable that the Los Angeles Spanish-language newspaper *La Opinión* frequently called Regalado the mastermind and the "McGraw" of local Mexican American baseball—a reference to the famous New York Giants hall-of-fame manager John McGraw. Regalado was also in the forefront in arranging and scheduling games between teams from El Paso and Juárez and teams from East Los Angeles. This interstate rivalry endured for years. (Courtesy Regalado family.)

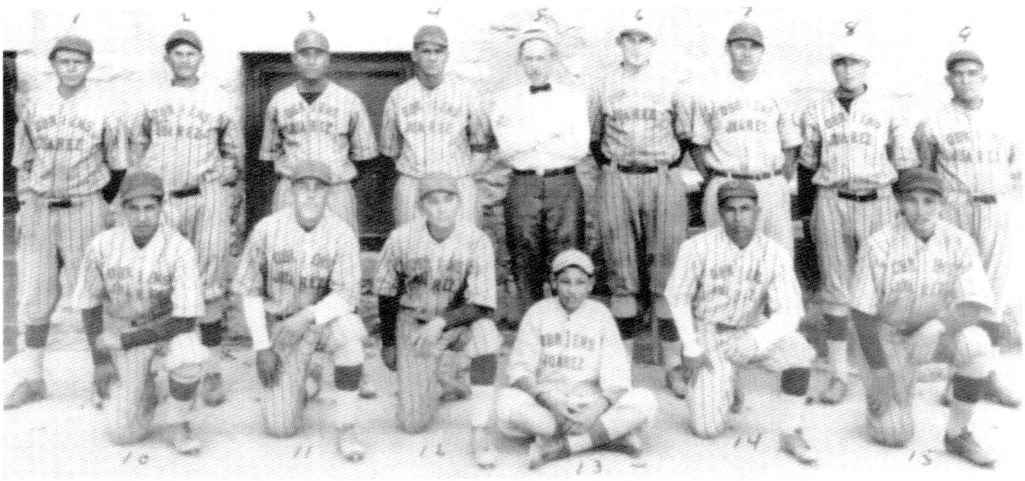

After retiring as a player, Manuel Regalado organized and managed several successful teams in Ciudad Juárez and El Paso, such as the Ciudad Juárez O'Brian Greenlegs in 1921. Jimmy O'Brian (second row, center) and Manuel Regalado (second row, third from right) continued as a sponsor and manager, respectively, of the team in 1923, pictured here at the Beal School in El Paso. Regalado's son Rudy later played three years for the Cleveland Indians, including in the 1954 World Series. Manuel is also the grandfather of Sam Regalado, a renowned baseball scholar. (Courtesy Regalado family.)

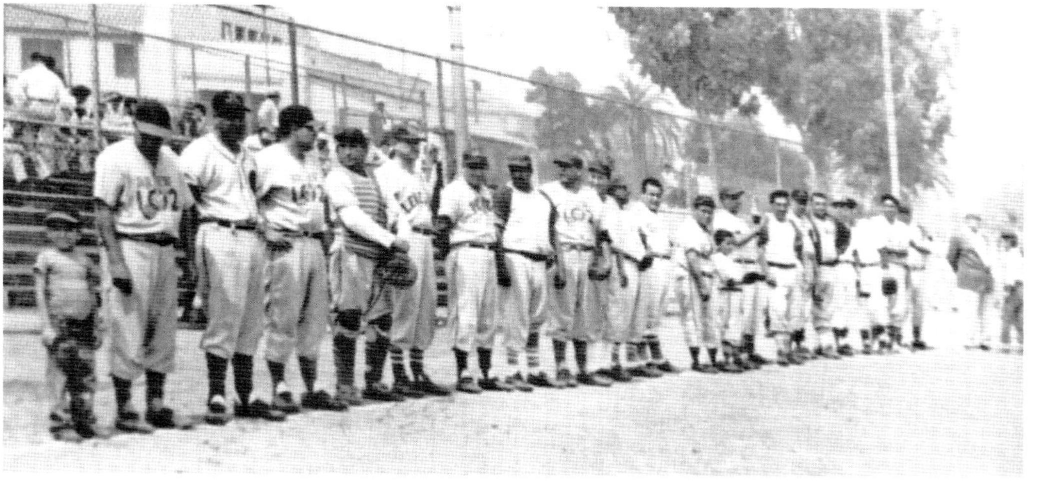

Many former barrio and ex-professional players refused to quit the game as they grew older and instead joined the Los Angeles 40-60 Club. The Los Angeles and El Paso 40-60 club scheduled goodwill games twice a year at each other's venues, often on Memorial Day or Labor Day. The games in El Paso attracted family and friends from Ciudad Juárez who would cross the border to attend the games and dances that followed. Manuel Regalado (sixth from left) is wearing his son Rudy's Cleveland Indians jersey at Evergreen Park in East Los Angeles around 1956. (Courtesy Regalado family.)

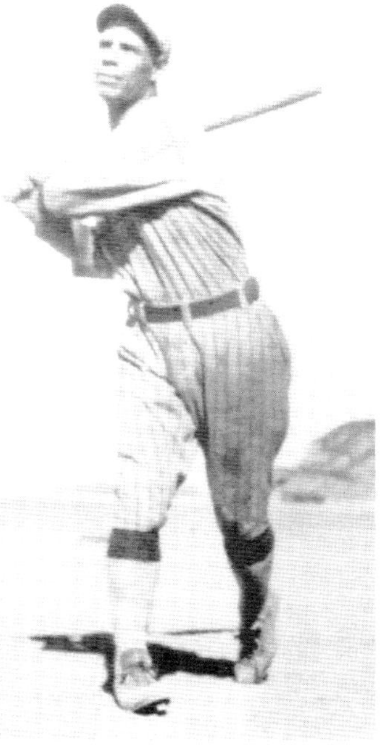

Robert "Lakes" Lagunas was a significant player from the 1920s through the 1940s (*lagunas* is Spanish for "lakes"). He played shortstop for El Paso teams in the Texas-New Mexico League, where he endured considerable prejudice and discrimination as a result of being the only Mexican on some teams. He described Texas as "still fighting the Battle of the Alamo" and remembered racial discrimination even from fans. After an exhibition game against the St. Louis Cardinals, Baseball Hall of Famer Rogers Hornsby refused to shake his hand because of his Mexican background. Lagunas's brother, Raymond, was also an outstanding player. They both played in Mexico for many years, especially for Juarez, Hermosillo, and Chihuahua teams. Robert Lagunas had two sons, Bob and Art, who were remarkable players in youth ball, at El Rancho High School in Pico Rivera, California, at Orange Coast College, Los Angeles State College, and the military. (Courtesy Bob Lagunas.)

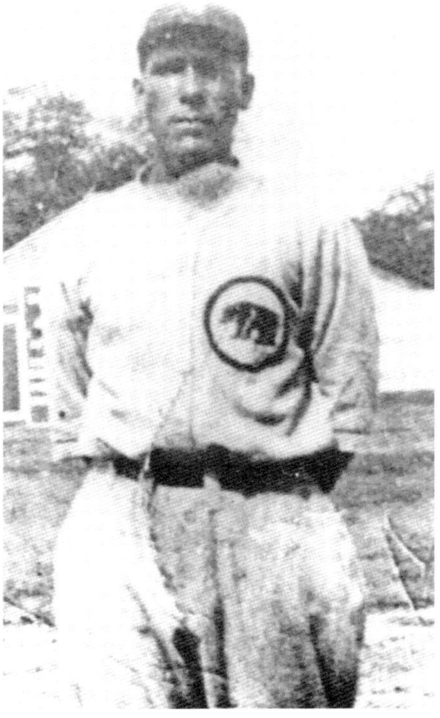

Lino Aguilar (1901–1967) started playing in the 1920s as a successful pitcher for the Juárez Indios and played for several teams along the border. He was invited to try out with the Washington Senators but was rejected because he was considered too old for the Major Leagues. After a brilliant career, he was elected to the Ciudad Juárez Baseball Hall of Fame. Some of his children stayed in Juárez, while others moved to El Paso and Los Angeles. Aguilar became a cook after his playing days. Grandson Alfonso Aguilar Jr. said Lino's love for the game was passed onto him, because he starting playing at a young age. Alfonso played 11 years of youth and high school ball, including for the Wilson High School varsity team in El Sereno and two years with the Mike Brito League at Evergreen Playground in East Los Angeles. (Courtesy José Cruz Aguilar.)

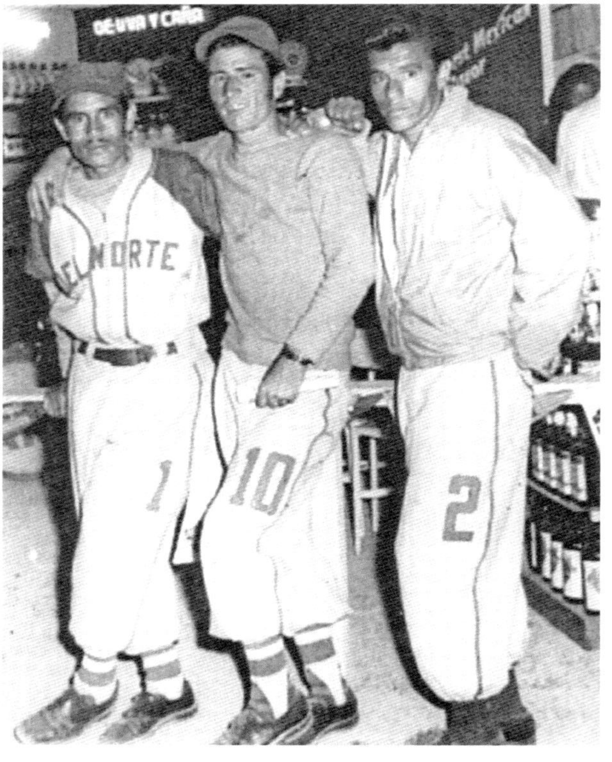

This c. 1958 photograph was taken in a Ciudad Juárez liquor store after a game. The three Del Norte players are, from left to right, Gabriel Enriguez, his brother Cecilio Enriguez, and unidentified. The Enriguez brothers were born on a ranch outside of Durango, Mexico. They grew up playing ball in Juárez and ultimately played for the Del Norte team sponsored by Auditorio Nacional. Gabriel pitched and played second base while Cecilio was the catcher. Gabriel continued playing ball after moving to Los Angeles with his wife, Soledad, and their two children, Gabriel Jr. and Blanca. (Courtesy Enriguez family.)

7

Coast to Coast

From its modest early stages in 2006, the Latino Baseball History Project planning committee adopted short- and long-term goals promoting the long and rich history of Mexican American baseball and softball. The short-term initiatives consisted of a book series, quarterly newsletter, baseball reunions, luncheons honoring players and their families, first-pitch ceremonies, library exhibits, symposiums and forums, collecting vintage photographs and other memorabilia, press conferences, college courses, and oral histories. By any reasonable measure, the project has been successful due in large part to its dedicated volunteers, institutional affiliation with the John F. Pfau Library at California State University at San Bernardino, and the tireless energy and enthusiasm of the players themselves and their adoring families. While the initial intention of the project was to narrow its organizational energy at the local, regional, and state levels in California, there was a conscious effort to integrate a national perspective from the start.

The long-term goals were more ambitious: to expand the book series to include other states, to work on regional and national projects with other groups interested in Mexican American and Latino baseball and softball, to include articles in newsletters that reflected a national perspective, and to reach out to both the Baseball Hall of Fame and the Smithsonian Institution. From its start in 2006, the project has incorporated a national perspective in all its activities. Today, a decade after its launch, the project has its books in the library of the Baseball Hall of Fame, and in 2015, the Latino Baseball History Project, along with several other national groups, teamed up with the Smithsonian Institution for a memorabilia-collecting initiative, a future national tour focusing on the history of Mexican American and Latino baseball and softball, and eventually, an exhibit in Washington, DC. These national arrangements are establishing an amazing network of players, families, community groups, scholars, universities, historical societies, government agencies, museums, the media, and professional baseball. Within 10 short years, the Latino Baseball History Project has become a major player in collecting, preserving, and promoting the numerous remarkable contributions of Mexican Americans to baseball and softball both nationally and internationally.

From the very beginning, nearly every book has included a chapter entitled Coast to Coast to showcase Mexican American baseball and softball throughout the country to confirm that wherever Mexicans settled, baseball has served as a political tool to combat racial, class, language, and gender discrimination. The project has now published four Texas books along with its California series and is currently working on a book on Kansas City. The books also present photographs of teams and players in Mexico, addressing critical issues regarding the border. Each book is deliberately structured to link local, regional, state, national, and international levels of baseball between its covers. Here is yet another glimpse of this national story.

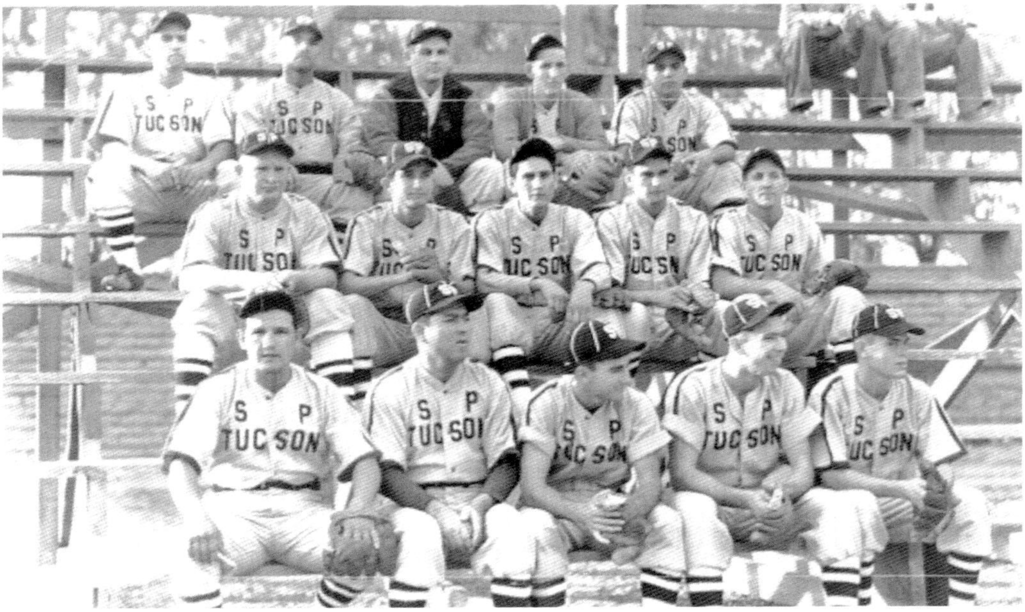

Arnold Riesgo (second row, far right) caught for the 1939 Southern Pacific Railroad team. He was born and raised in Tucson, Arizona. He played for many teams in the region and also in Nogales, Mexico, where he met his wife, Maria Dolores Campodonico. They were married in 1950 and had four children. Riesgo went on to play for the San Jose (California) Red Sox and the Winston-Salem Cardinals. He was a player and team manager in Hazlehurst, Georgia. He went by many nicknames during his remarkable career, including Mickey and Yogi in reference to two great Major-League catchers, Mickey Owens and Yogi Berra. (Courtesy Mary Alyce Riesgo Carrasco.)

RED SOX REPORTER

Riesgo, Lenn, Earn Places On All Stars

Two Red Sox players, Mickey Riesgo, catcher, and Ed Lenn, first baseman, were chosen on the Sports Writers' 1947 California League all-star team. Here is the team as selected.

PLAYER	POS.	TEAM
Lau Vezilich	IF	Fresno
Ralph Samhammer	OF	Ventura
James Trew	OF	Visalia
Willie Enos	UOF	Modesto
Edwin Lenn	1B	San Jose
Edward Samcoff	2B	Stockton
Don Alfano	SS	Visalia
Bert Bonami	3B	Fresno
Harry Clements	UIF	Stockton
Lilio Marcucci	C	Stockton
Arnold Riesgo	C	San Jose
PITCHER		TEAM
Ray Hathaway	P	Santa Barbara
Lloyd Hittle	P	Stockton
Don Belton	P	Stockton

Arnold Riesgo was known for an unusual amount of diamond savvy, a rifle for an arm, and deadly accuracy in gauging foul balls. He also had a keen eye as a batter, with an outstanding average, and once hit three home runs in a game in Bakersfield, California. Everywhere he played, he was very good. He was voted the most popular player when he played for the San Jose Red Sox. He played on several all-star teams, including one against the Nogales (Mexico) Internationals. In 1947, he made the all-star team while playing in the California League. (Courtesy Mary Alyce Riesgo Carrasco.)

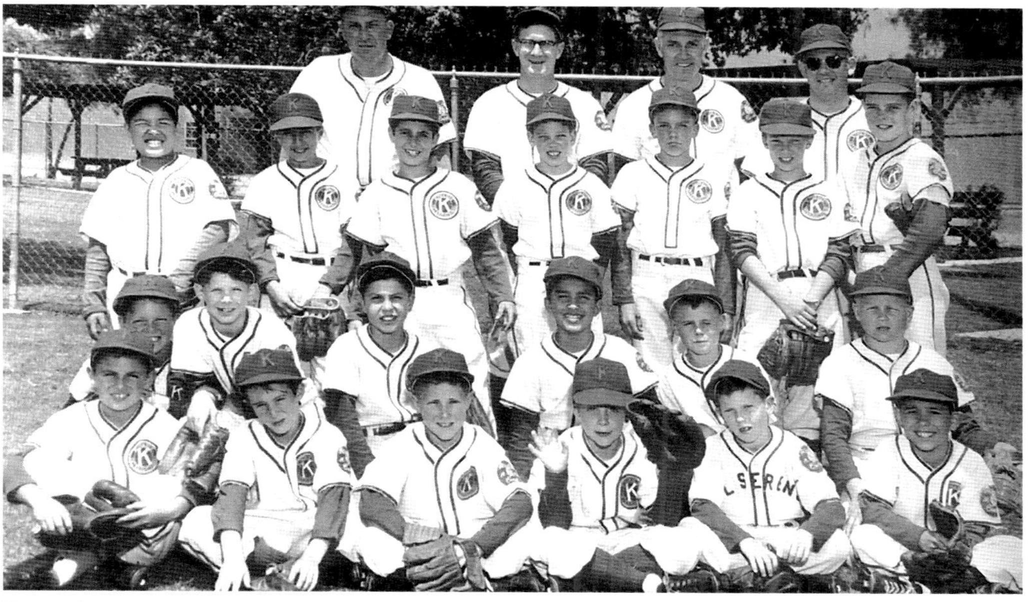

Tony Ortega's parents were both born in Mexico. His father, Michael, immigrated to Los Angeles and grew up in the area known as Dogtown because the city dog pound was nearby. His mother, Amelia, grew up near the famous San Antonio Winery. Amelia and her four sisters crushed grapes the old-fashioned way—with their feet. Michael played in the 1920s with several industrial teams and was invited by the Chicago Cubs for a tryout as a catcher. In the Hollywood classic *Alibi Ike*, starring Joe E. Brown, Michael is catching the ball from Brown. The scene was shot at Downey Playground in East Los Angeles. Tony Ortega is third from left in the second row on this 1957 El Sereno team. (Courtesy Tony Ortega.)

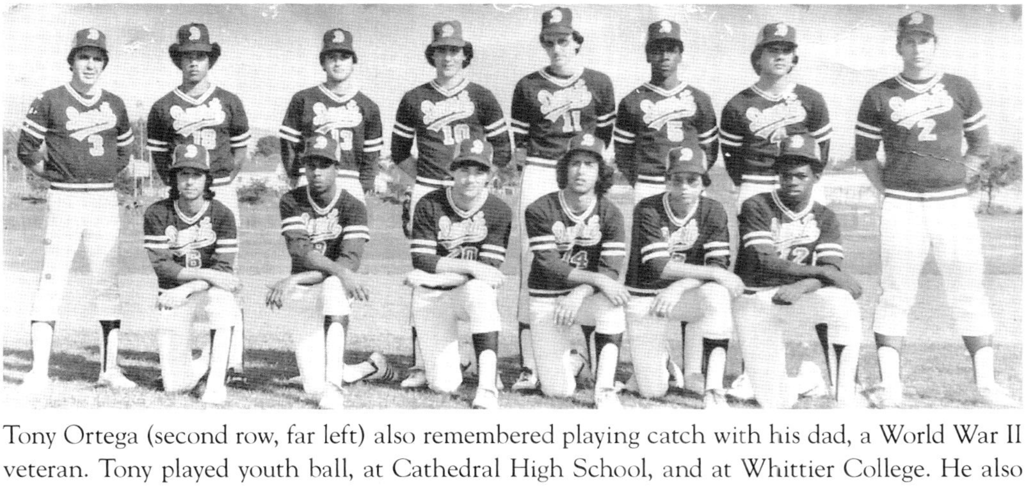

Tony Ortega (second row, far left) also remembered playing catch with his dad, a World War II veteran. Tony played youth ball, at Cathedral High School, and at Whittier College. He also played football at Whittier. As a youth, he played against black teams that included future Major-Leaguers Bob Watson, Willie Crawford, and Bobby Tolan. Hall-of-famer Chet Brewer coached Tony for four years. Tony coached for many years. He is seen here as manager of the Duarte High School squad. (Courtesy Tony Ortega.)

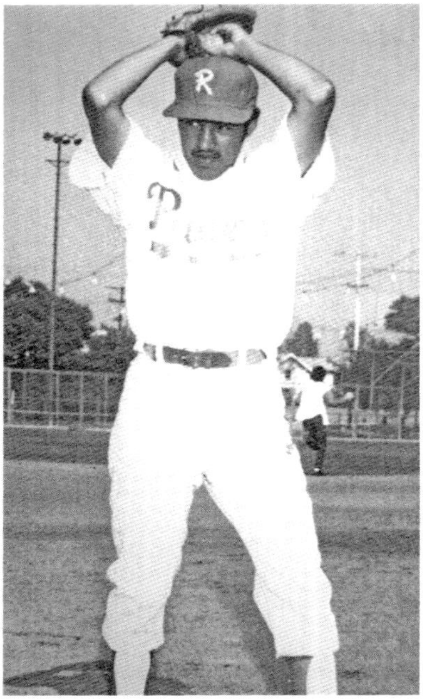

Frankie Sandoval had a distinguished career at Roosevelt High School, Los Angeles City College, California State College at Los Angeles, and in the Mexican leagues. In 1974, he was Player of the Year pitching for Los Angeles City College. Sandoval acknowledges outstanding coaches including Ernie Rodríguez, Milo Lizalde, and Mexicans Javier Espinoza and Jaime Favela. He met Sandy Koufax in 1985, when both pitched batting practice to Dodgers hitters. Koufax was very impressed with Sandoval's pitching and nicknamed him "Little Sandy," a play on his last name. Frankie Sandoval was the batting practice pitcher with the Dodgers for their World Series victories in 1981 and 1988. (Courtesy Frankie Sandoval.)

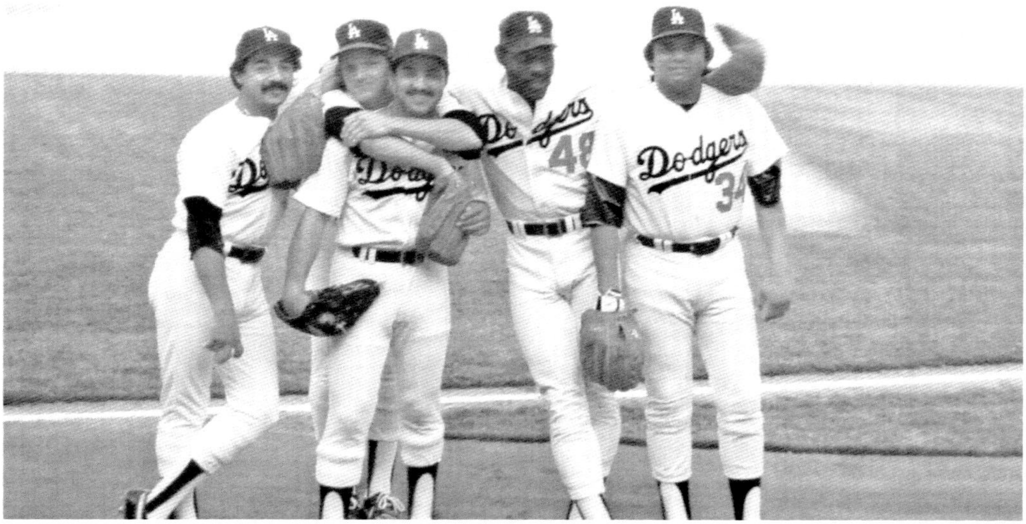

Frankie Sandoval is seen with four Dodgers pitchers. From left to right are Bobby Castillo, Steve Howe, Sandoval, Dave Stewart, and Fernando Valenzuela. Both Howe and Valenzuela won the National League Rookie of the Year awards, Dave Stewart has five World Series rings, and Bobby Castillo had an outstanding baseball career with the Dodgers and Minnesota Twins. He won a World Series title with Los Angeles. Sandoval was the batting practice pitcher and went on the road with the team to Montreal, Cincinnati, Philadelphia, New York, Pittsburgh, San Francisco, and San Diego. (Courtesy Frankie Sandoval.)

Alex Guzmán (left) and Louie Gómez played for the Rampart Reds under Eddie Fierro. The Reds were part of the Los Angeles Police Department youth outreach program. Police teams were formed in several Los Angeles neighborhoods. Guzmán played against the Hollenbeck Police Department team that included his friend Al De La Rosa. Both Guzmán and Gómez played at Nightingale Junior High School and baseball and football at Belmont High School in the late 1960s. Guzmán played football at East Los Angeles Community College (ELAC) and at Sacramento State University. At ELAC, he was the quarterback; his brother Rubén was the center. Gómez played at the University of California at Los Angeles and signed with the Minnesota Twins. He also played with the Toronto Blue Jays and Atlanta Braves. (Courtesy Alex Guzmán.)

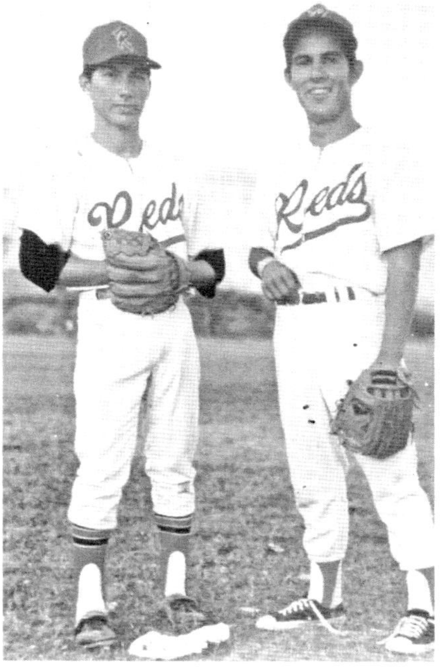

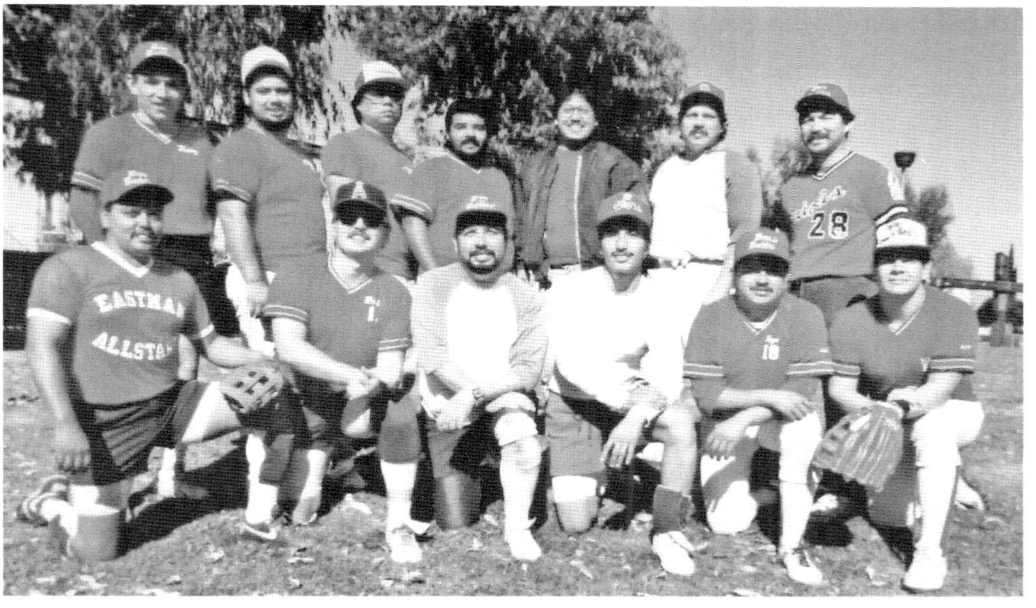

Like many players, Alex Guzmán started on slow- and fast-pitch softball teams. His uncles played football at Lincoln High School in the 1930s, including star Tony "Turk" García. This 1988 softball team was called La Familia because they were almost all related. The team played at Reggie Rodríguez Park in Montebello. From left to right are (first row) Manny Alvidrez, Ralph Guzmán, Félix Reyes, Anthony Reyes, José Rodríguez, and Louie Barragán; (second row) Manny Medina, Fidel Trujillo, James Caling, Stevie Orozco, John Reyes, and brothers Rubén and Alex Guzmán. (Courtesy of Alex Guzmán.)

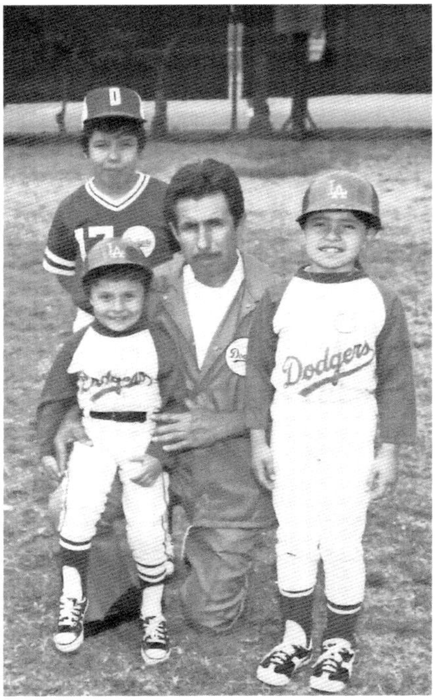

Andrés Nieto is pictured in 1977 with his children Andy (standing, left), Angie, and Tony (standing, right) at the Monterey Park Sports Club picture day. His youngest son, Adrian, is not shown. Andy played at California State University at Fullerton and with the Chicago White Sox and Detroit Tigers organizations. He later coached at the University of Southern California and currently is a teacher and coach at Damien High School in La Verne. Angie is a registered nurse and played softball at Schurr High School in Montebello. Tony played at USC and for the Cincinnati Reds. He is now a teacher and coach at California High School in Whittier. Andrés Nieto was an excellent basketball player and coach in Mexico during the 1940s and 1950s and has coached Mexico's top basketball players, including some who played in the Olympics. He also played baseball in Mexico. (Courtesy Nieto family.)

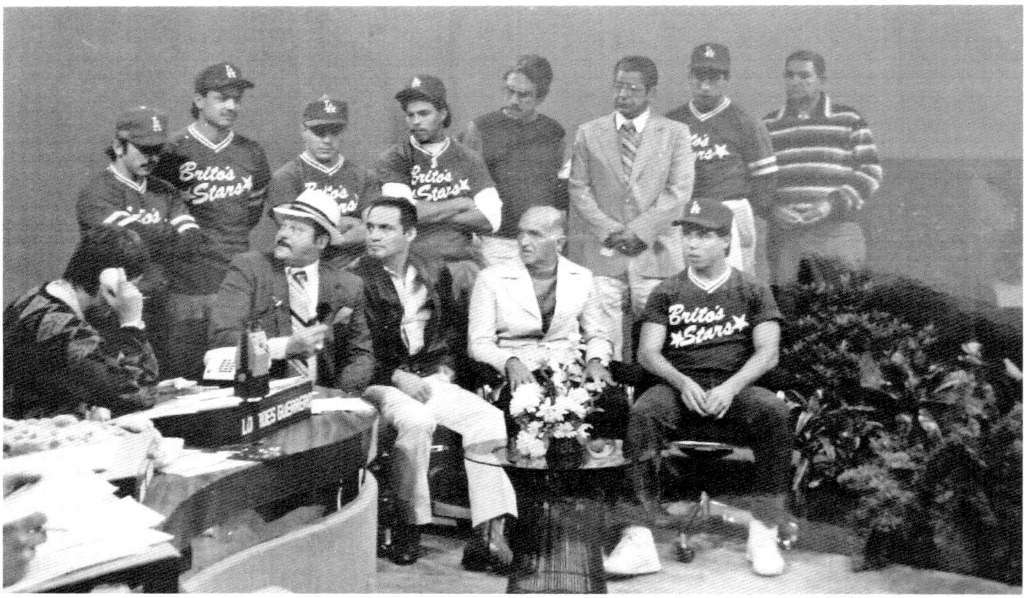

Andy Nieto (seated far right) was a member of the Mike Brito All-Star Team. Brito, a long-time Dodger scout who signed Fernando Valenzuela and Bobby Castillo, took this team of college and minor-league players to Mexico City in the winter of 1989. *Hoy Mismo*, a morning show in Mexico City similar to *Good Morning America*, interviewed the team. Andy, who was then playing for the White Sox, spoke on behalf of the team since he was by far the most fluent in Spanish. (Courtesy Nieto family.)

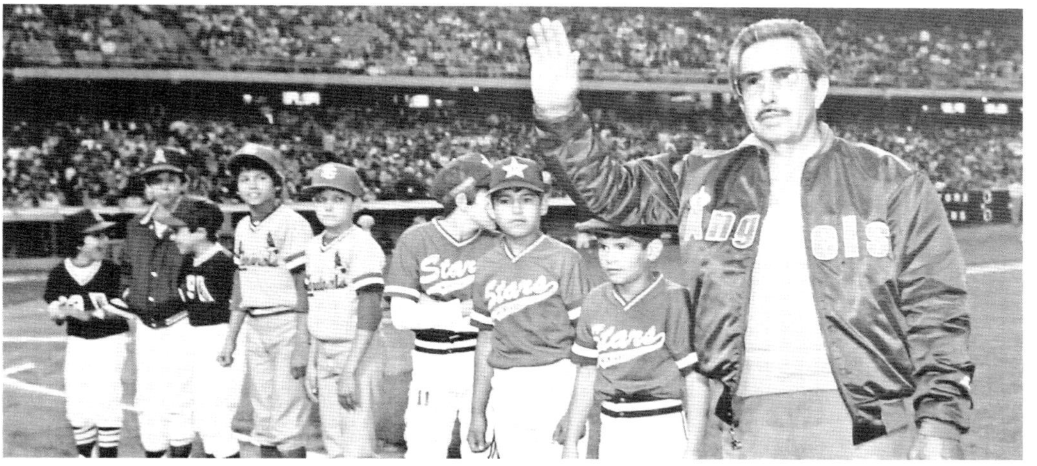

In 1982, Andrés Nieto founded the Monterey Park Angels, the first travel baseball team in Monterey Park, California. His team is pictured participating in pregame ceremonies at Dodger Stadium in 1983. Third from left is his son Tony, who returned to Dodger Stadium eight years later as a member of the USC team. Andrés Nieto (far right) has received countless certificates, honors, and tributes both in Mexico and the United States for his tireless dedication to basketball and baseball. His children and grandchildren all played ball while his wife, Ana, served as team mom along with many other duties. (Courtesy Nieto family.)

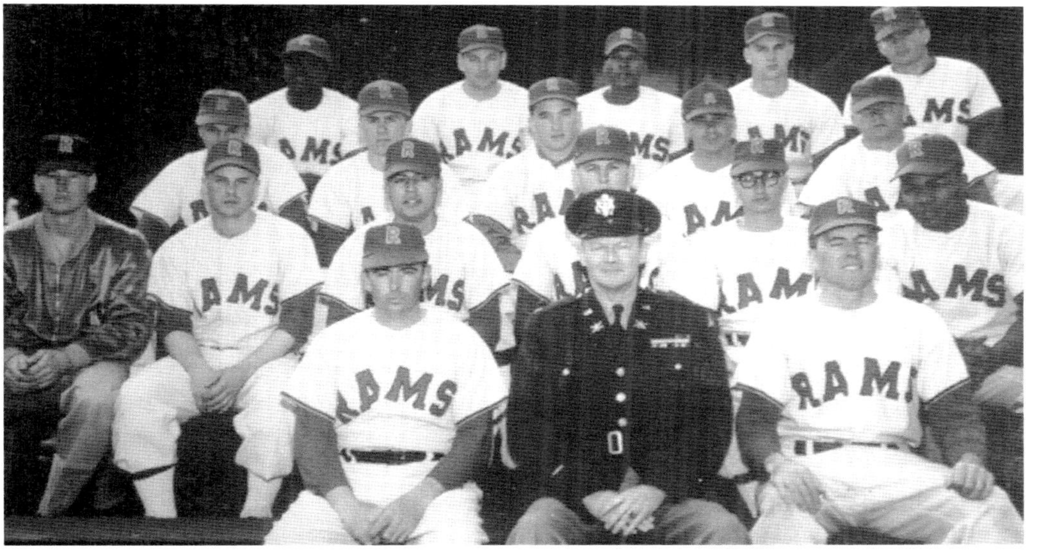

Adolfo R. García (second row, third from left) played football and baseball at Lincoln High School in East Los Angeles during the early 1950s. He played youth ball on the Pico Rivera Golden State Little League travel club as a catcher and made the Peterson Maywood All-Star Team as the only Mexican American. He played military ball in Colorado Springs with the 7th Army, Battery B, 45th Field Artillery Battalion. He was then transferred to Fort Bliss, Texas, with the Operations Intelligence Division. His company was deployed to Germany, where he played catcher and outfielder on the base team. (Courtesy Mark García.)

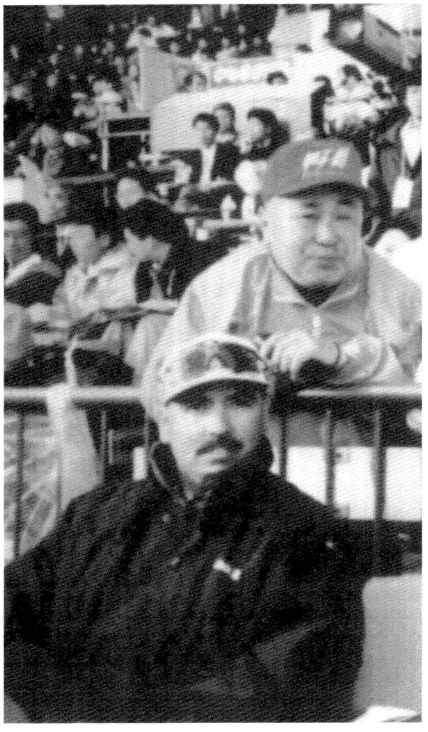

Mark García (bottom) grew up in the northeast part of Los Angeles called El Sereno in the 1960s. He played youth football and basketball at All Saints Elementary school and played for a travel baseball team in the Golden State Baseball League. García played baseball at Bishop Amat High School and Pasadena City College, and played for a development team in Australia. A Dodger scout asked him to try out for a rookie winter ball team coached by Frank Amaya. García also had tryouts with the Cubs, Twins, and the Brewers. He met some of the great Mexican American players and scouts, including Jesse Flores, Reuben and Ernie Rodríguez, Gil Gámez, Dave García, George Zabala, and Al Zunica. Mark García became a Major League scout at a young age for the Brewers, and an administrative assistant in international operations for the Angels, and international scout for the Red Sox. This photograph was taken at the world famous Koshien High School baseball tournament in Osaka, Japan. 50,000 people attend the championship games.

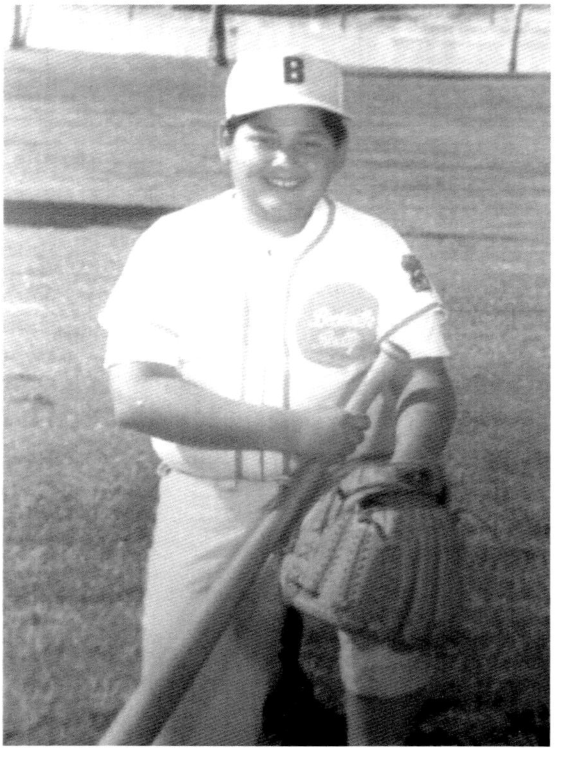

Greg García, son of Adolph and brother of Mark, is seen in his 1974 Santa Anita Little League uniform sponsored by Beckwith Realty in Arcadia, California. Greg grew up in El Sereno, and later, the family moved to Arcadia. Adolph and Mark were outstanding athletes as youths in school and in the community. Greg played two seasons with the El Sereno Golden State Little League travel team, played basketball and football at All Saints Elementary School, and later attended Bishop Amat High School and played football. At Pasadena City College, he majored in business and currently manages his father's business, Adolph Design, in Arcadia. The company manufactures restaurant furniture. (Courtesy Mark García.)

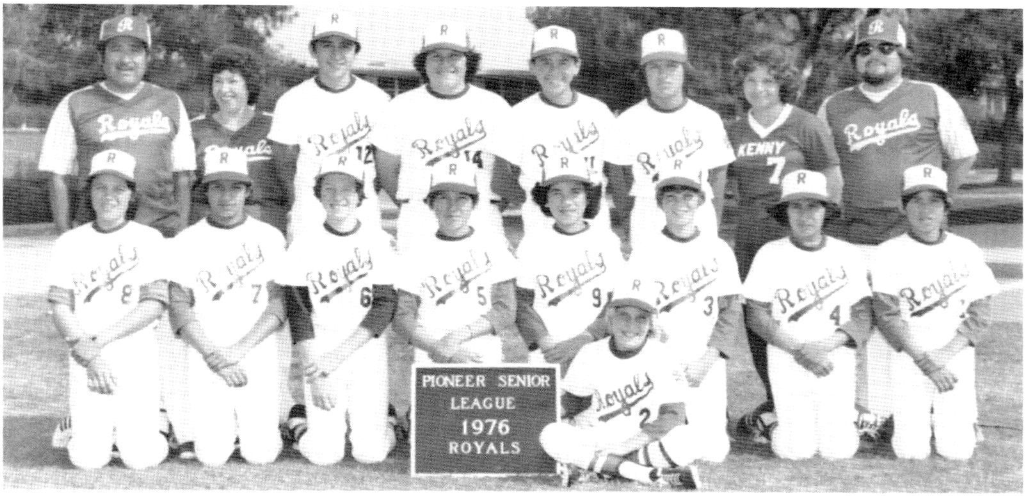

The Pérez family produced four generations of players, coaches, and umpires. Tom Pérez Jr. (second row, far left) stands next to his wife and team mom, Alice, while coaching his sons Nick (No. 5) and Tom III (first row, far right.) Tom Sr. was a player and manager during the 1920s and 1930s. Tom Jr. played in Los Angeles and Mexico. Tom and Alice have five boys who played several sports. Nick played baseball and football at all levels of school and community sports and eventually became an outstanding umpire, including high school championship games at Dodger Stadium. (Courtesy Nick Pérez.)

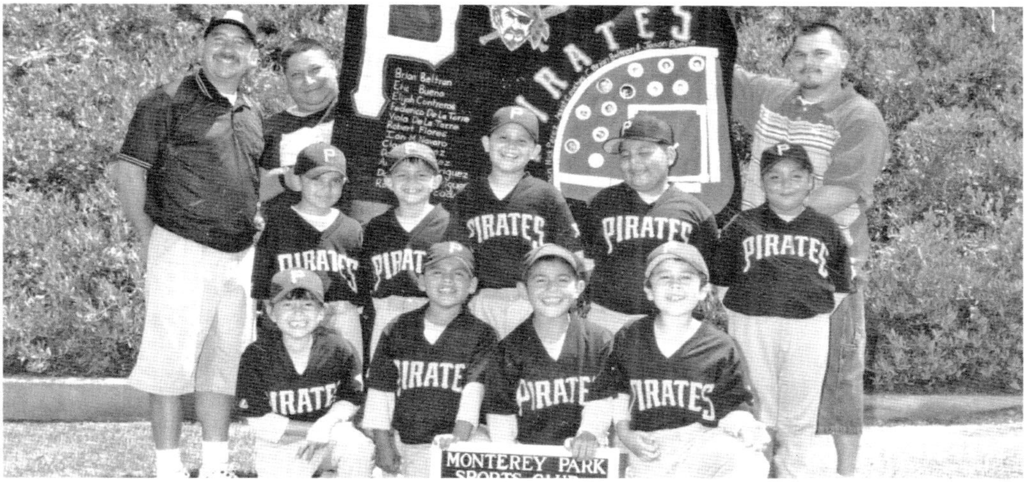

Nick Pérez (third row, left) dedicated himself to youth sports. He is seen here coaching the Monterey Park Pirates in 2004. His daughter Clarissa (first row, left), played all levels of ball including softball at St. Paul High School and currently plays basketball at Antelope Valley University in Lancaster, California. Nick was an outstanding player at the youth level and at Pioneer High School in Whittier, where he played baseball and football. He and his brother Tom played together in East Los Angeles and with the Los Angeles County Men's Baseball League. Tom III served with the 82nd Airborne in Grenada, Iraq, Kuwait, and Afghanistan. He received the Purple Heart. (Courtesy Nick Pérez.)

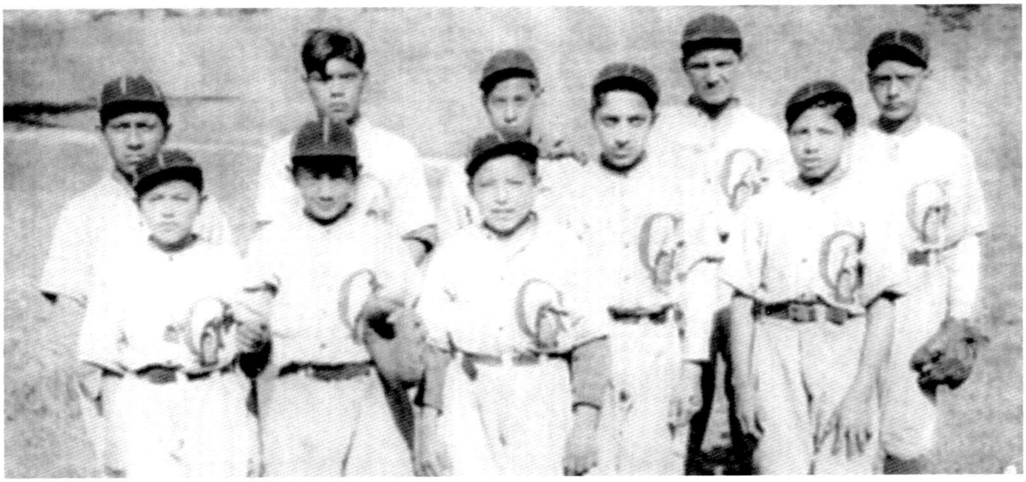

Paul "Waxie" Hernández loved baseball. He is pictured in 1936 (first row, second from left) with his teammates from the Westside in Kansas City, Missouri. The Guadalupe Center, named after the patron saint of Mexico, was started in 1919 by a Catholic women's club, the Agnes Ward Amberg Club, serving the Westside's predominately Mexican population. The center provided health care, recreation, and other services, including sponsoring baseball teams. Only two other players are identified, Simón Montoya (second row, second from left) and Waxie's brother Peter Hernández (second row, third from left). (Courtesy Patsy Hernández Castro.)

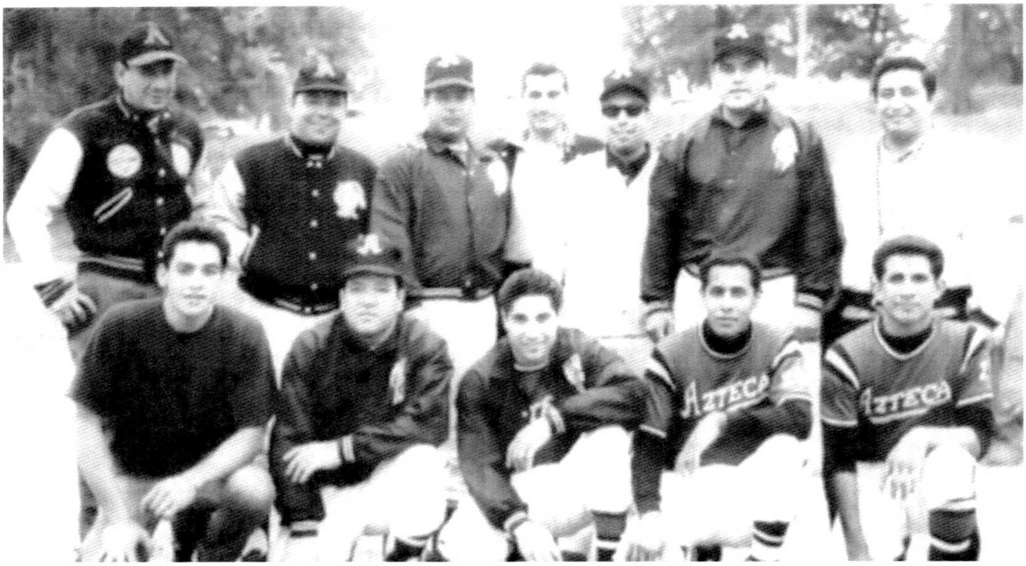

Paul "Waxie" Hernández is shown in 1965 coaching the Azteca softball team, composed of players from both sides of Kansas City. After retiring from playing baseball and fast-pitch softball, Hernández dedicated his life to coaching young people in the games he loved so much. From left to right are (first row) Gilbert Castro, Ramón Reyes, Willie López, Robert Delgado, and Eddie Hernández; (second row) Paul "Waxie" Hernández, Joe Ramírez, Paul Espinoza, Jesse Salas, Albert Guerra, Frank Solís, and Nacho García. (Courtesy Patsy Hernández Castro.)

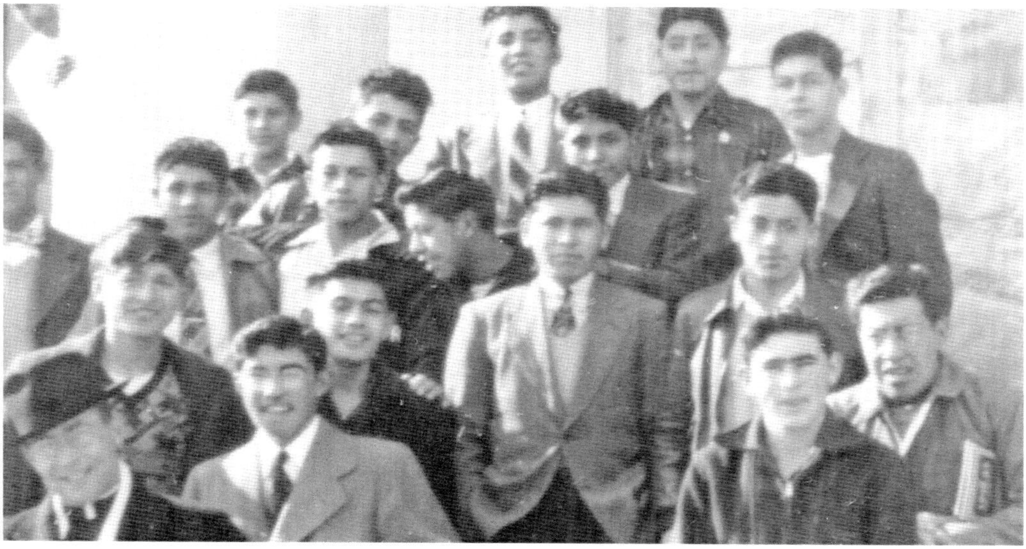

This photograph was taken around 1947 in front of the Southeast Recreational Center in Scottsbluff, Nebraska. From left to right are (first row) Fr. Lawrence Portrey, Eddie Hernández, Bobby Hernández, and Amador Tomás; (second row) Edward Barraza, Héctor Rojas, Bill Salazar, and Joe Rentería; (third row) Willie Payer, Johnny Ramírez, Rodney Rentería, Manuel Tomás, Marciano Briones, and Joe Barranza; (fourth row) Robert Barranza, Johnny Hernández, and Jim ? (Courtesy Palma family.)

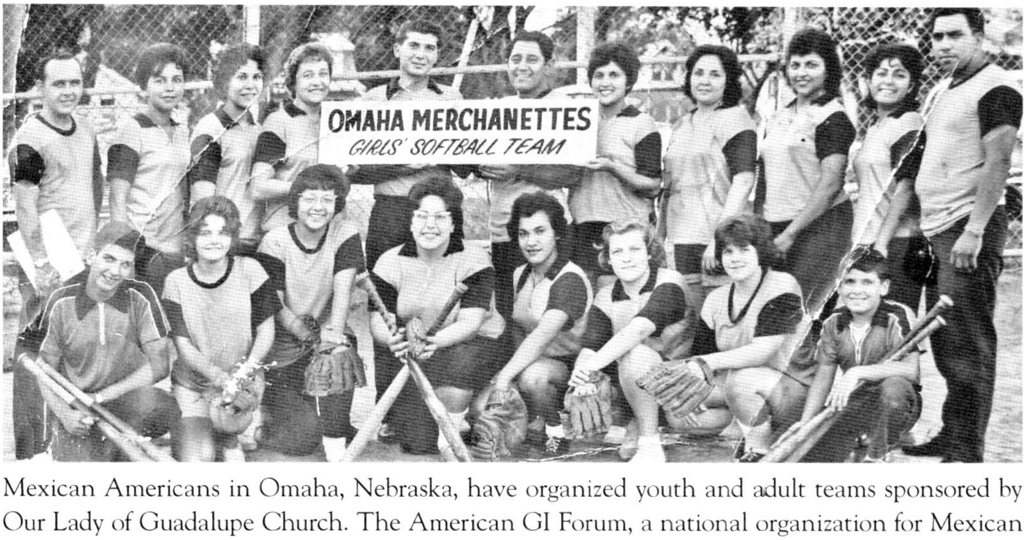

Mexican Americans in Omaha, Nebraska, have organized youth and adult teams sponsored by Our Lady of Guadalupe Church. The American GI Forum, a national organization for Mexican American veterans, sponsored teams as well. These included women's teams sponsored by local restaurants and merchants. Many players were members of the Women's Auxiliary of the GI Forum. Frank Palma (second row, sixth from right) coached many teams. He was a civil rights leader active with several community organizations, including the American GI Forum, League of United Latin American Citizens, Service, Employment, Redevelopment, the Mexican American Commission of Nebraska, and La Sociedad Mutualista of South Omaha. (Courtesy Palma family.)

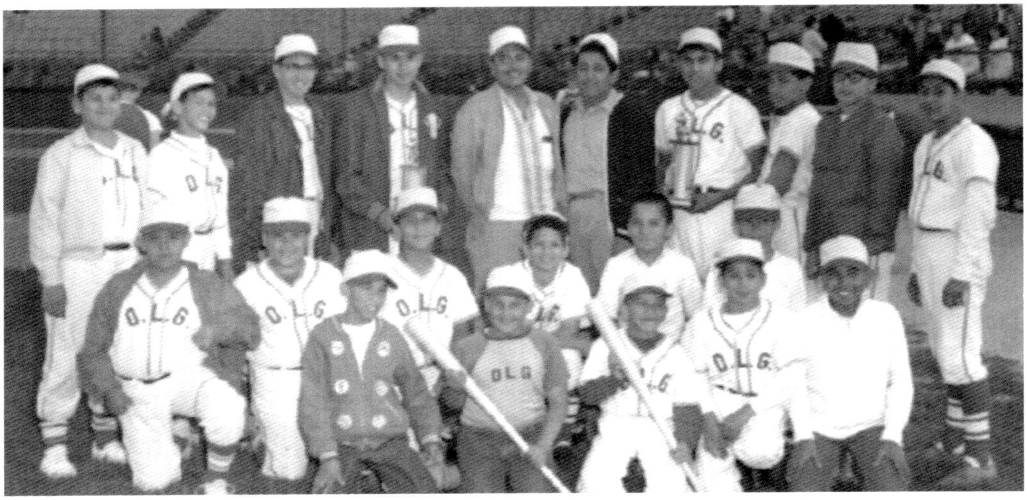

The College World Series has been held in Omaha, Nebraska, every year since the 1940s at Rosenblatt Stadium. The stadium is near the Mexican American community of South Omaha. This photograph was taken in 1963, when Mexican American teams were often denied the right to play in city leagues, and traveled hundreds of miles to play other Mexican American teams. In many ways, these teams were the forerunners of the civil rights movement traveling throughout the Midwest and playing games and staying in hotels and eating in restaurants that Mexicans had not ventured into before. Frank Palma is in second row, fifth from right. (Courtesy Frank Palma and the Mexican American Historical Society of the Midlands.)

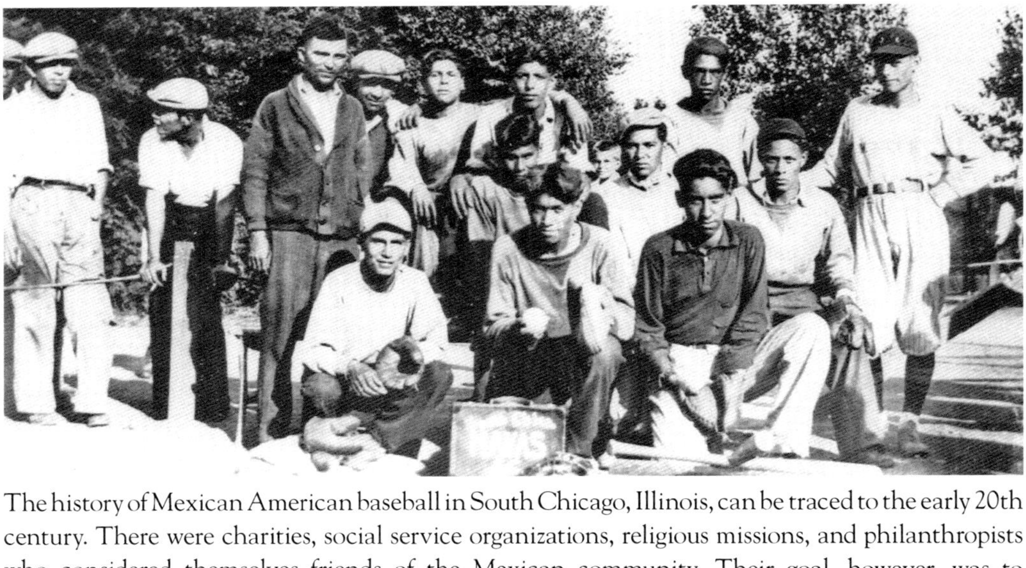

The history of Mexican American baseball in South Chicago, Illinois, can be traced to the early 20th century. There were charities, social service organizations, religious missions, and philanthropists who considered themselves friends of the Mexican community. Their goal, however, was to assimilate Mexicans into the "American" culture at the expense of their culture and identity. One approach was sport. One such organization was Common Ground, run by the Congregational Church. One of the better teams in South Chicago was the Mayas Athletic Club, seen here in the early 1930s. (Courtesy of the Southeast Chicago Project and Michael D. Innis-Jiménez.)

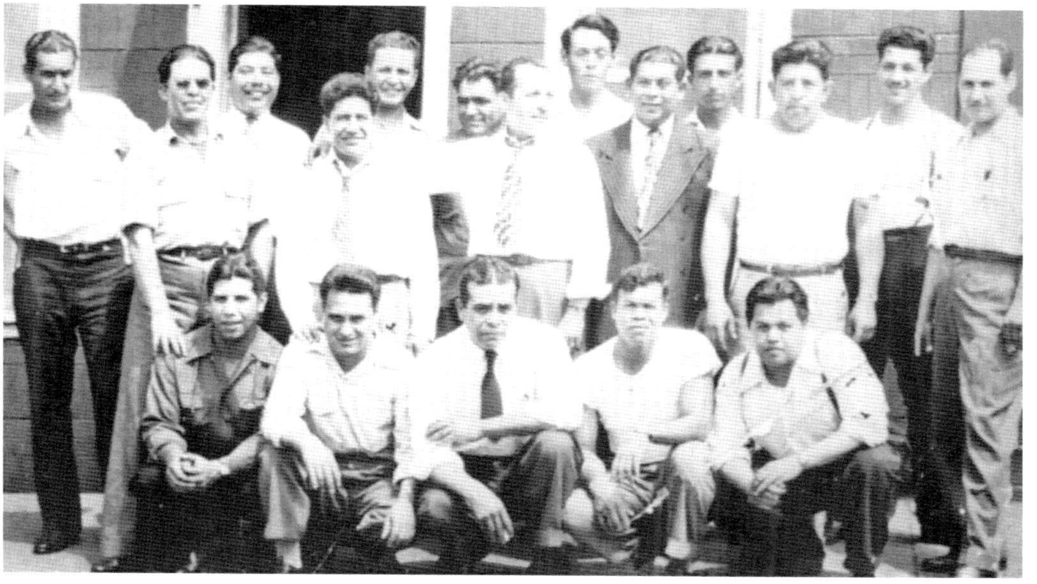

In 1946, the Mexican Community of South Chicago, Illinois, established the Pro Mexico organization that helped promote sports teams. Similar groups were formed to boost recreational activities for Mexican Americans throughout the country. (Courtesy of the Southeast Project.)

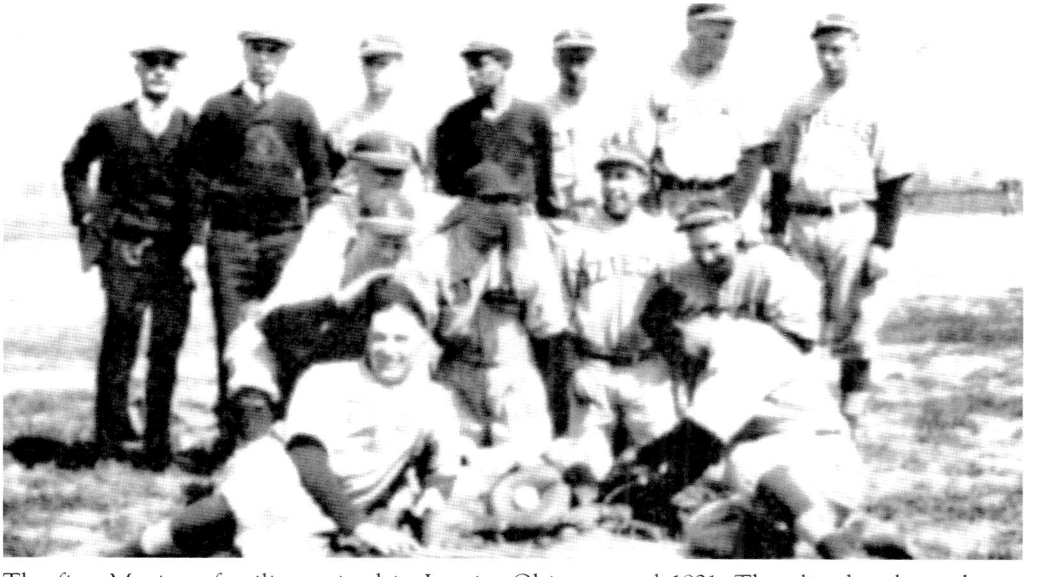

The first Mexican families arrived in Lorain, Ohio, around 1921. They lived in barracks on railroad property until they found suitable housing nearby. Mexicans found work with the railroads and steel mills, and a few entrepreneurs opened small businesses, including grocery stores, restaurants, pool halls, bars, shoe repair stores, and newspapers. Soon, a Mexican business district began to flourish. The Mexican community also formed social, religious, and recreational networks, including baseball teams. There were two teams, the Aztecas (pictured) and Mayas. (Courtesy of Frank Jacinto.)

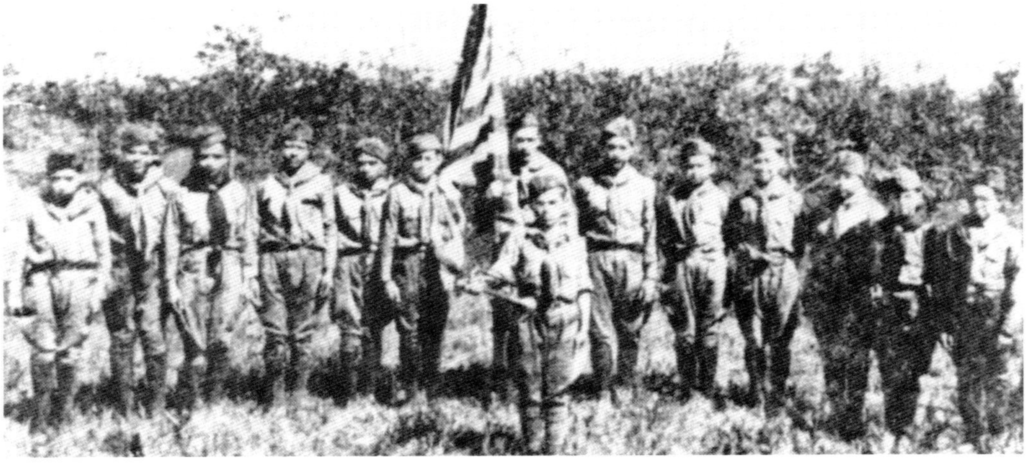

Mexican Boy Scout Troop No. 24 was established in East Chicago, Indiana, in 1931 by the Catholic Boy Scouts Organization. It was a form of assimilation of American ideals, encouraging these young boys to adopt the American way of life and to foster Catholic ideals. Within four months, the boys made outstanding progress, passing their Tenderfoot and Second Class tests. The Kiwanis Club invited Troop 24 to join its baseball league and furnished uniforms and equipment. (Courtesy Las Señoras of Yesteryear.)

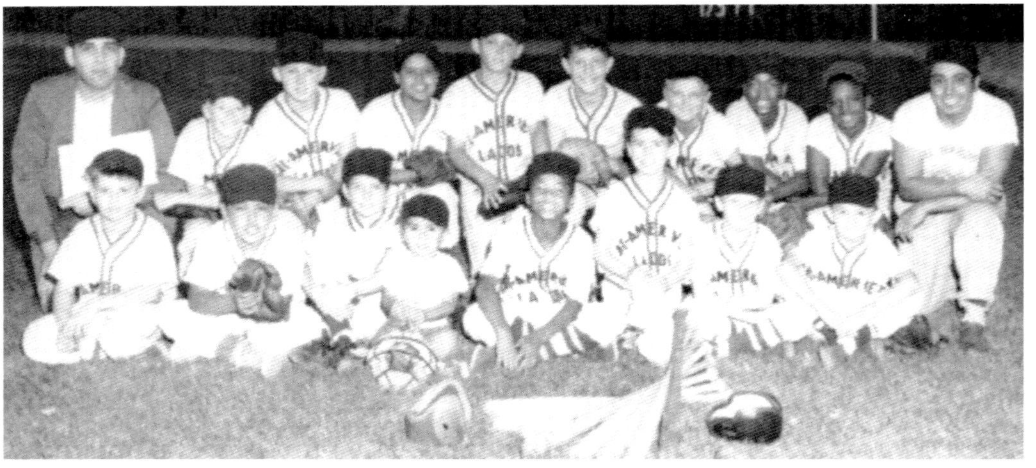

Baseball runs deep in the Mexican Harbor community of East Chicago, Indiana. The first baseball field was located on the corner of 142nd and Euclid Streets. The ballpark was later moved east where a new stadium named El Parque Anahuac seated over 500 fans. One of the earliest teams was formed in 1917. Baseball was very popular in the 1920s, with several teams, including girls' teams. This team, the LADDS, was sponsored by the Latin American Veterans Club. The team took first place in the "B" League and won the 1954 championship. (Courtesy of Las Señoras of Yesteryear.)

8

FIELD OF DREAMS

This is the 12th book in an ongoing series documenting the long, rich history of Mexican American baseball and softball. The vast majority of these photographs have centered on players, teams, and coaches between the 1870s and 1950s. This remarkable collection represents the largest inventory of photographs of Mexican Americans playing ball in the history of the United States. The Latino Baseball History Project, based out of California State University at San Bernardino, oversees the book series. Future books will gradually evolve from this very early period of history to focus on Mexican American baseball and softball teams and players and coaches between the 1960s and 1980s. Nevertheless, future books will continue to include a significant share of photographs from the pre-1960s era.

Many current players represent the second, third, and even fourth generations to wear a glove and swing a bat. Their baseball and softball stories are just as amazing as those of their ancestors who played so long ago. Now their stories must be told, too. Most of them started as batboys and moved into youth ball, high school, college, community, and beyond. They speak in reverent tones of the prior generations of players who impacted their lives. This generation is now in their 50s, 60s, and early 70s. At many community events, the older generation and this newer generation are reconnecting after many years, since the older players actually coached the younger players during the latter 20th century.

Now this generation of players is turning to coaching players from the 1990s to the present. One extraordinary story is that of Al Padilla, who was an outstanding player and coach in East Los Angeles for nearly half a century. Joe Gonzáles coached Padilla at Roosevelt High School in the 1940s. Gonzáles himself had been an outstanding player at Roosevelt in the early 1930s and was coached by Charles "Coney" Galindo. Padilla personally knew Galindo, and now Padilla knows the current high school baseball manager, Ray Ruíz. This means that Padilla has known every baseball coach at Roosevelt High School from 1932 to 2017—85 years! But Padilla is not unique. There are countless versions of Padillas throughout Mexican American communities from California to New York who have witnessed first hand generations of players become coaches who coached players who themselves later became coaches. This never-ending cycle continues just like so many other Mexican American traditions, like Day of the Dead, *quinceñeras*, Pan de Rosca, Ash Wednesday, and making tamales.

The photographs in this chapter provide only a glimpse of the interconnecting meaning, repercussions, and bonds between older and newer generations of Mexican American players with their coaches and managers.

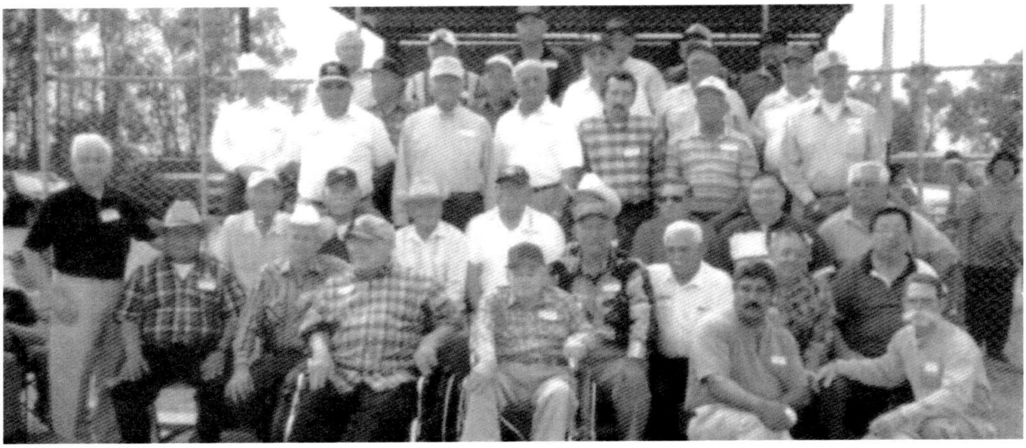

On April 16, 2001, The Field of Dreams dedication and reunion was held on the King Ranch. Former King Ranch Cowboys, 7-Ups, and Lions teams, as well as Laureles-Chapman Ranch Cowboys teams were invited to a formal dedication of Assault Field and a banquet at the King Ranch Museum in Kingsville. From left to right are (first row) Cipriano García, Fransico Quintanilla, Reynaldo Borrego Sr. and Stephen "Tio" Kleberg; (second row) Alonzo Delgado, Francisco Gutíerrez, Alberto Treviño, Gilbert Rodríguez, José Arredondo, Gilbert Mendietta, and Rico Castillo; (third row) Miguel Ochoa, Andrés Soto, Gilbert Treviño, Jesús García, Cipriano Escobedo, Balde Quintanilla, Rene Villarreal, and Moisés Aguilar; (fourth row) José Mendietta, Chino García, Mario Delgado, Óscar Quintanilla, Gustavo Garza, and Gonzalo González; (fifth row) I.Q. Vidaurri, Tules Sánchez, Alberto Cavazos, Henry Bazan, unidentified, and Arnoldo Mendietta; (sixth row) Fernando Rodríguez, Jesús García Jr., Chino Rodríguez, Chito Mendietta, Raúl Buentello, and Coche Buentello. (Courtesy Lupita Borrego.)

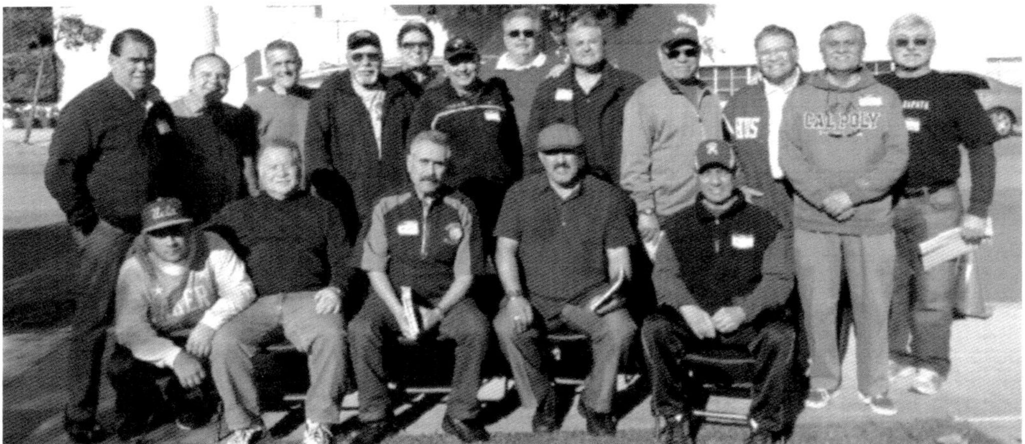

This photograph was taken at the December 17, 2016, event sponsored by the Alhambra Historical Society. From left to right are (first row) Joaquín Arenas, Jack Arenas, Ray Lara, Frankie Sandoval, and Al De La Rosa; (second row) Ray Loya, Monte Pérez, unidentified, Pete Barrios, Joe Ronquillo, Mark García, Rudy Martínez, Nicky Escamilla, Frank De La Rosa, Al Padilla, Richard A. Santillán, and Alex Guzmán. Many of these individuals were outstanding players at Roosevelt, Garfield, Wilson, and Lincoln High Schools in East Los Angeles and at ELAC. (Courtesy Teresa M. Santillán.)

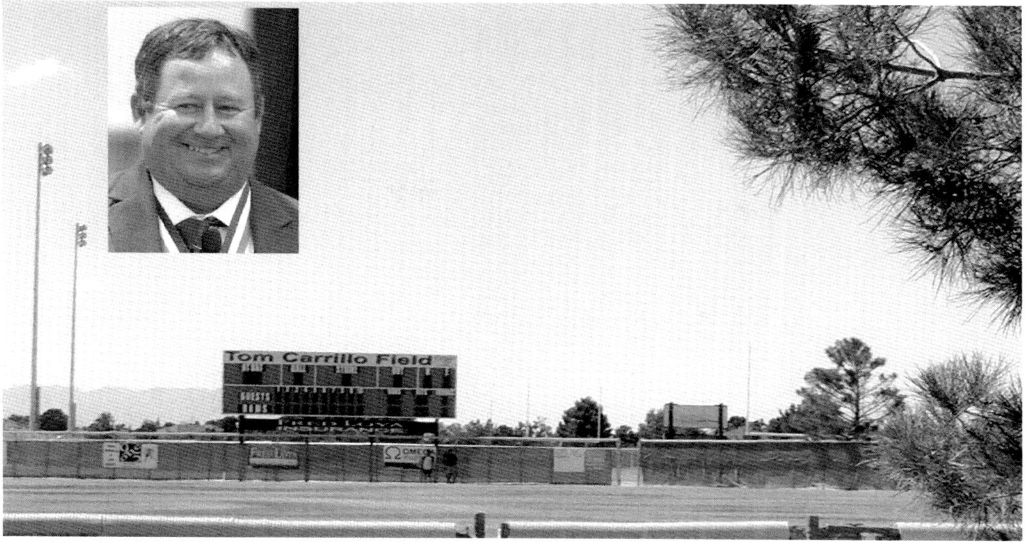

The baseball field at Montwood High School in East El Paso was renamed Tom Carrillo Field in a ceremony on March 3, 2015. Carrillo (inset) was the head coach at Montwood from the school's founding in 1990 through 2012. His career record was 409 wins and 221 losses, and he reached the playoffs 13 times in his 23 years as coach. In 2012, Carrillo's final season, the Rams were ranked fourth in the state of Texas and tenth in the nation, reaching the Sweet 16 of the Texas high school 5A playoffs. Before beginning his coaching career, Carrillo was a star outfielder at Andress High School and Ranger Junior College. He served as president of the El Paso Baseball Hall of Fame in 2015–2016. (Courtesy Eric Enders.)

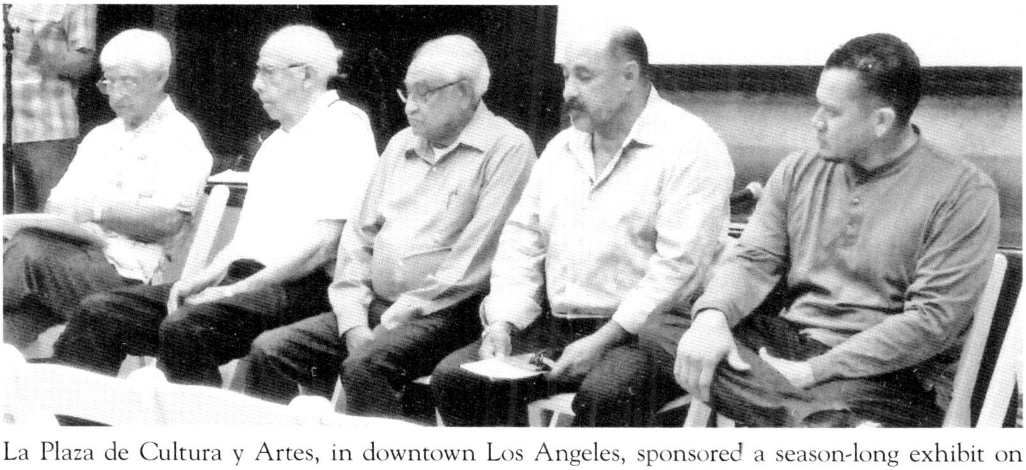

La Plaza de Cultura y Artes, in downtown Los Angeles, sponsored a season-long exhibit on Mexican American baseball and softball in greater Southern California in 2016. The exhibit included several presentations on women players, military baseball, Major-League baseball, playing in Mexico, and sharing scholarly research. This distinguished panel spoke about their playing days in Mexico. Panelists from left to right are Bob Lagunas, Armando Pérez, Tom Pérez, Frankie Sandoval, and Ray Ruíz. Lagunas spoke about his father, Robert, who played in Mexico in the 1920s. (Courtesy Richard A. Santillán.)

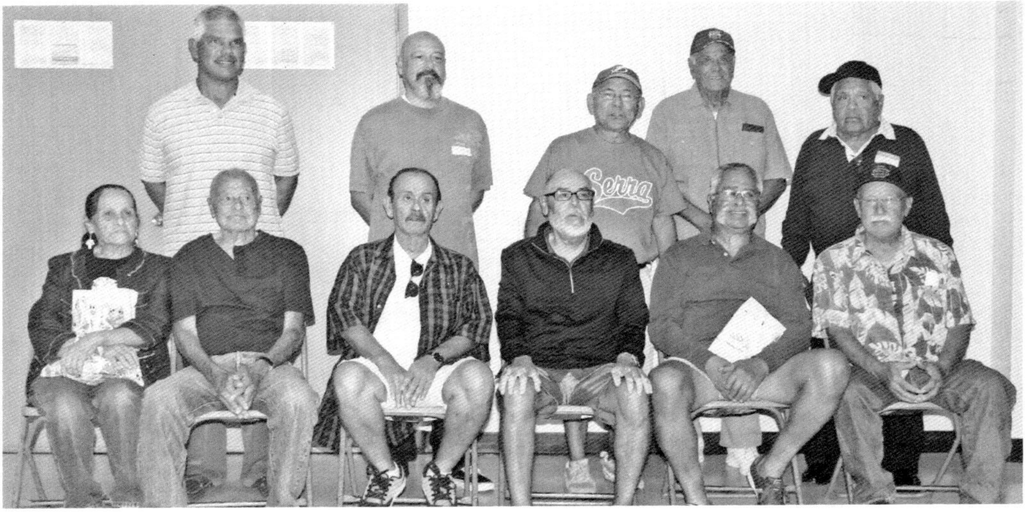

Santa Monica, California, has a long and distinguished history of Mexican American baseball and softball. Brother and sister Ray Serra and Alicia Serra Stevens contributed a chapter to a book documenting this extraordinary history. On October 23, 2016, a book-signing event at St. Anne's Church attracted many former players and coaches. From left to right are (first row) Alice Romo Regalado, Sammy Romo Sr., Manuel Serra, Raymond Romo, Anthony Romero, and Rudy Romo; (second row) Rick Prieto, Ray Romo Jr., Raymond Serra Jr., Frank Casillas, and José Verduzco. (Courtesy Alicia Serra Stevens and Ray Serra Jr.)

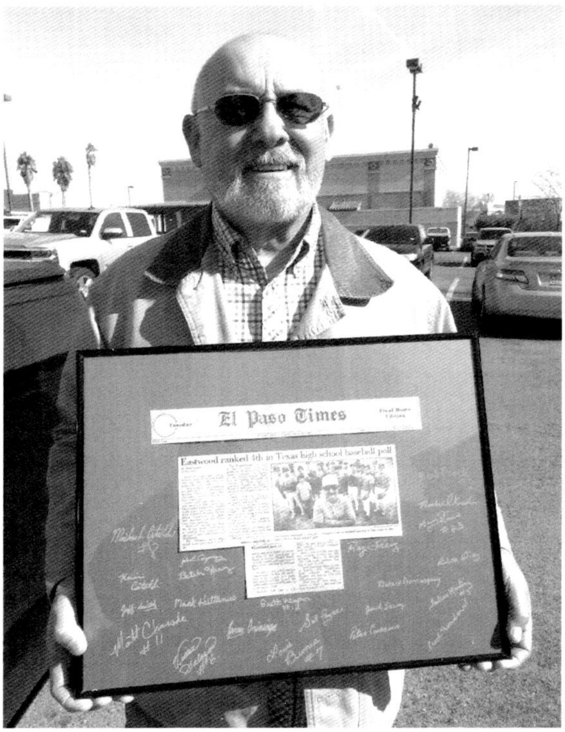

Longtime Eastwood High School coach Ray Sáenz is pictured holding a framed memento from his best team, the Eastwood Troopers squad that was ranked fourth in the state of Texas in 1987. Eastwood won the 2-5A district title that year behind the pitching tandem of left-hander Butch Henry and right-hander Frank Castillo, who were also the team's leading batters with averages of .575 and .430 respectively. During Sáenz's 16 years as Eastwood's coach (1979–1994), he led the Troopers to an overall record of 283-136, winning three district titles and four bi-district championships. He was named *El Paso Times* coach of the year in 1980 and 1981, and later worked as a scout for the Atlanta Braves and Colorado Rockies. (Courtesy Eric Enders.)

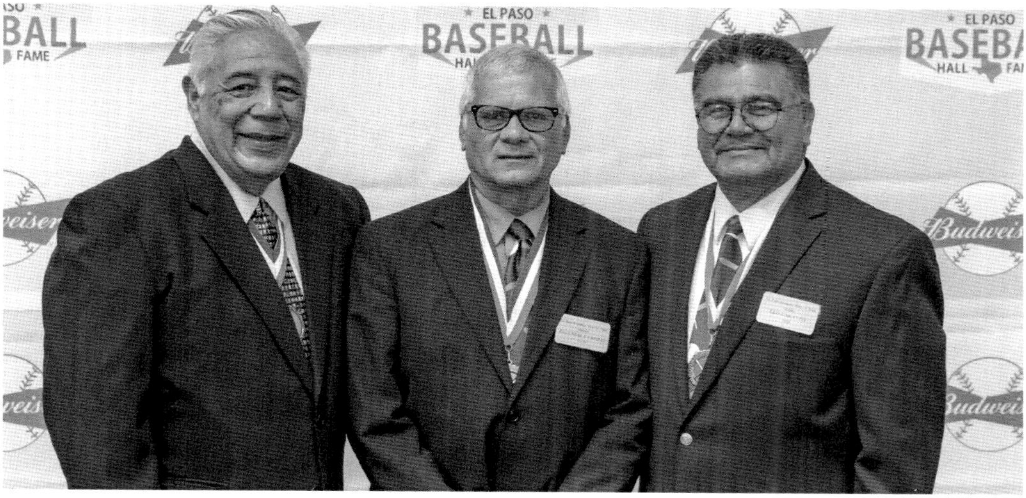

Three leaders of the El Paso Baseball Hall of Fame pose at the organization's 2016 induction banquet. From left to right are Bob Aguirre, president; Raúl Real y Vásquez, treasurer; and Leo Caraveo, vice president. Aguirre was an all-district shortstop at Jefferson High School before becoming a four-year starter for Texas Western College in the 1960s. Real y Vásquez was a teammate of Aguirre's at both Jefferson High and Texas Western, posting a 29-4 career record as a high school pitcher. Caraveo played on Ysleta High School's 1965 district championship team. In addition to serving on the board of the El Paso Baseball Hall of Fame, all three have been inducted themselves for their playing and coaching careers. (Courtesy El Paso Baseball Hall of Fame.)

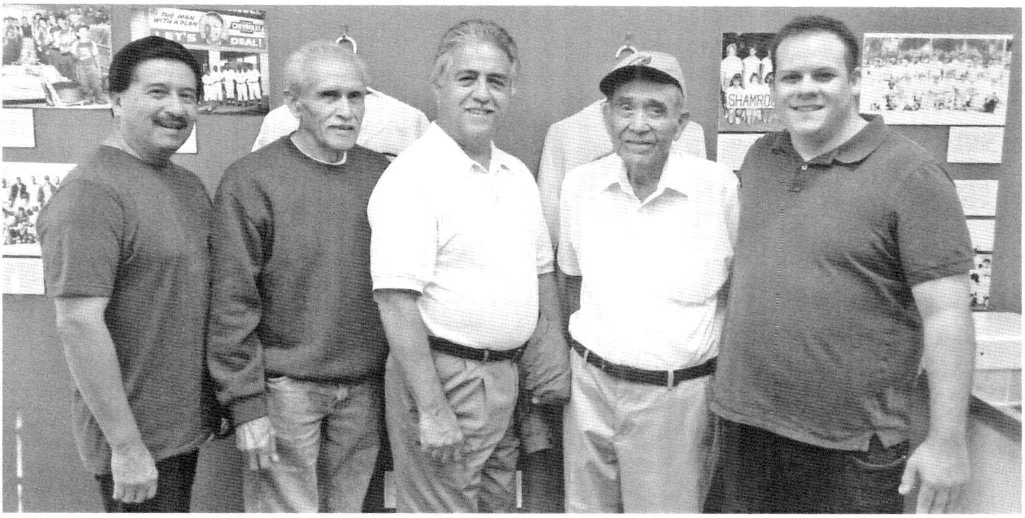

On December 29, 2016, former San Fernando Valley players and authors gathered at the Museum of the San Fernando Valley to view the Mexican American baseball and softball exhibit, which featured photographs and artifacts from the early 20th century. From left to right are Ray Barraza Jr., Ray Barraza Sr., Everto Ruíz, Tony Severa, and Chris Docter. Former players Barraza Sr. and Severa made lasting imprints in baseball and softball history, while Ruíz and Docter wrote *Mexican American Baseball in the San Fernando Valley*. (Courtesy Chris Docter and Richard A. Santillán.)

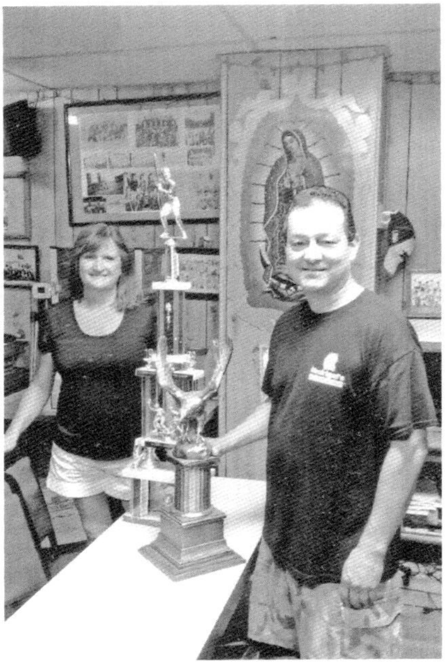

American Legion Post 213 is located in the Argentine neighborhood of Kansas City, Kansas. Mexican American veterans had been denied membership by American Legion Post 111 after World War II. Mexican American veterans nicknamed their new post "The Eagle's Nest." Kerry and Luís Madrigal proudly show off two of several baseball trophies. In the background are several youth and adult team photos dating to the early 1950s. The post developed a regulation fast pitch softball field that became home to the Argentine Eagles. However, over the years, the field became overgrown with weeds and was in disrepair. In 2015, Chris González and his brother Eric, along with others, started work on the field. On May 13, 2017, the renovated field was dedicated and the Mexican American Softball Association started holding games and tournaments again. (Courtesy of Gene Chávez and Richard A. Santillán.)

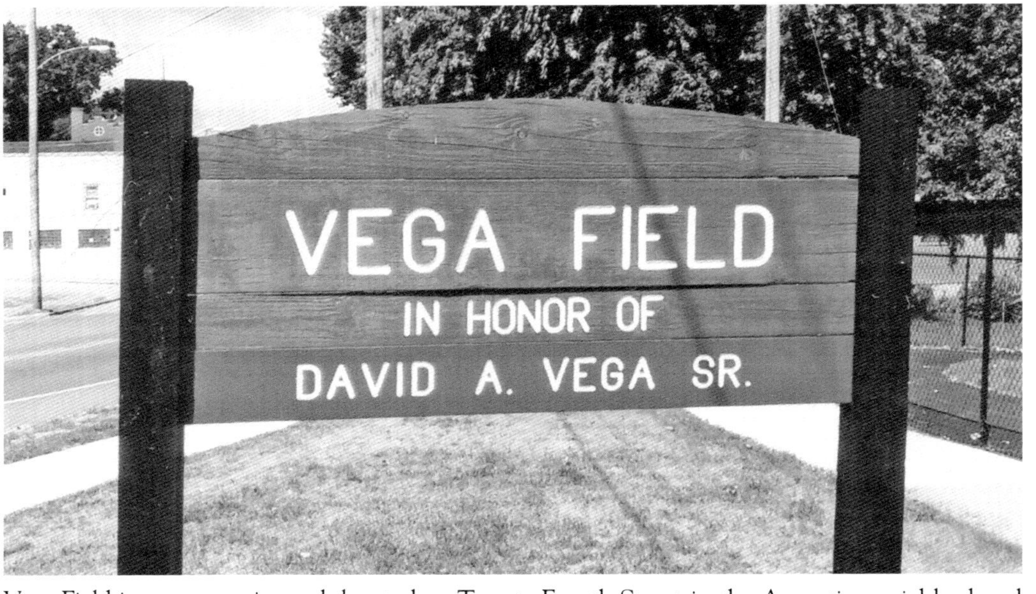

Vega Field is a community park located on Twenty-Fourth Street in the Argentine neighborhood in Kansas. It is a tribute to David A. Vega Sr., a determined community activist. Thousands of Mexican immigrants moved into this area in the 1920s working in the steel mills, railroad yards, and meat-packing plants. Vega's father was one of them. David Vega was born a couple of blocks from where he still lives. He served in World War II. After the war, the baseball league refused to allow his team to join, so he started his own league for black and brown youth. Today, the park has a soccer field, walking track, and children's playground. (Courtesy Gene Chávez and Richard A. Santillán.)

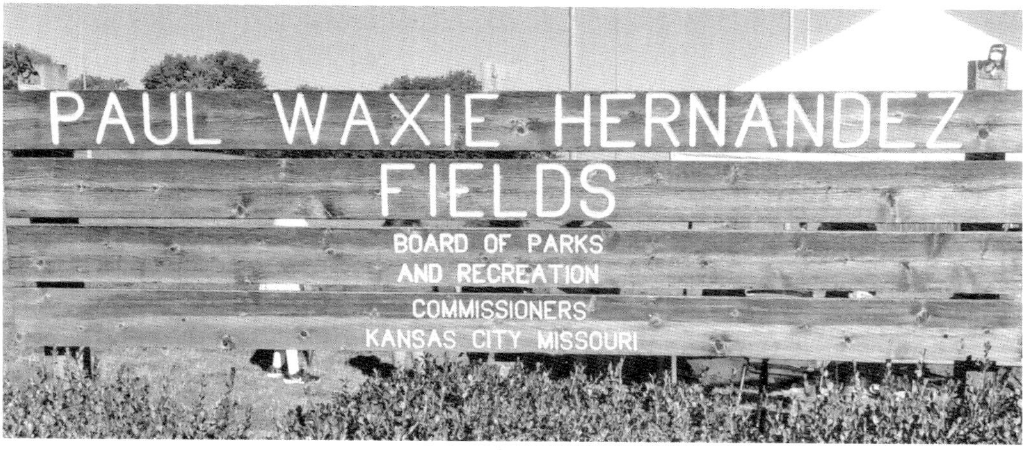

Paul "Waxie" Hernández played baseball and fast-pitch softball well into his 60s. He dedicated the rest of his life to coaching youth from Kansas City, Missouri's Mexican American communities. Many who played the game, and many who are still playing, attribute their love of it to Waxie. Among those he coached were his children Paul Jr., Eddie, Manuel "Rabbit," Rudy Carol, Elizabeth, and Rita. Many of his grandchildren are now playing and keeping the tradition alive. In the 1980s, Kansas City dedicated two softball fields in his honor in Penn Valley Park, in the heart of the Mexican American Westside community. (Courtesy Gene Chávez and Richard A. Santillán.)

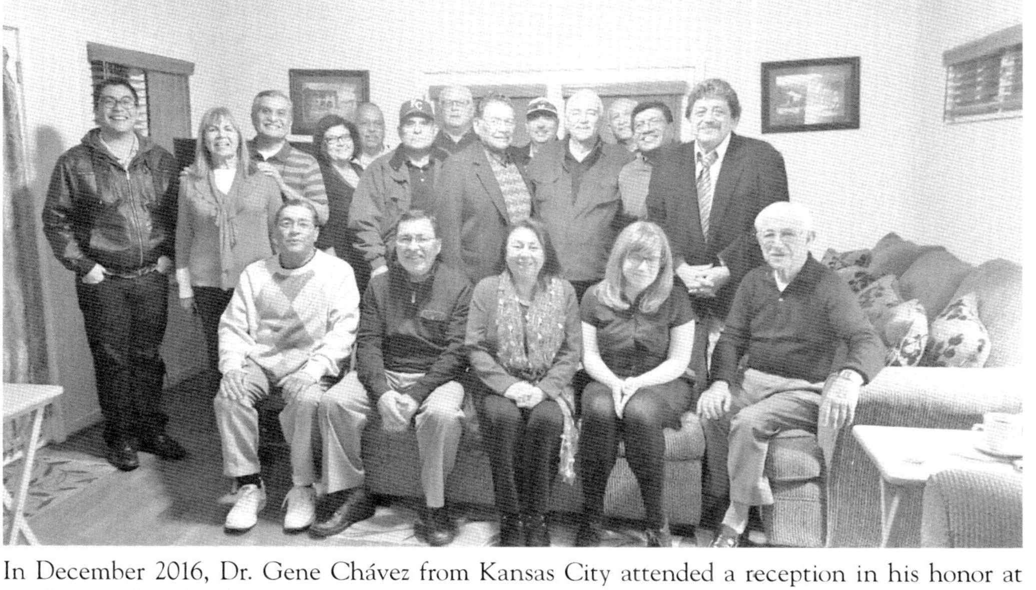

In December 2016, Dr. Gene Chávez from Kansas City attended a reception in his honor at the home of Richard A. and Teresa M. Santillán in Alhambra, near downtown Los Angeles. Richard, Gene, Ben Chapell, and Rod Martínez are working on a book on the history of baseball and softball in the Kansas City area. From left to right are (first row) Victor Pimental, Raúl Cardoza, Irma Flores, Erin Curtis, and Bob Lagunas; (second row) Adrián Mendoza, Teresa and Richard Santillán, Margie and Lauro Montes, Rod Martínez, Richard Lugo, Al Padilla, Gene Chávez, John Echeveste, Pete Flores, and Tomás Benítez. (Courtesy Teresa M. Santillán.)

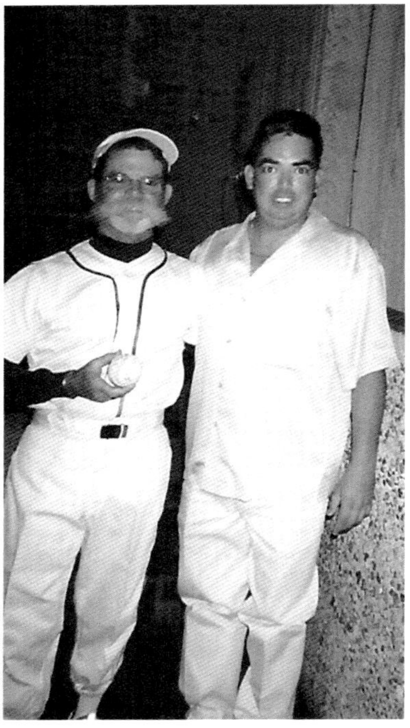

On the left is Stephen "Tio" Kleberg, a direct descendant of Capt. Richard King, the original founder of the King Ranch. Here he is pictured in his original 1961King Ranch Cowboys uniform with author Donavan "Captain D" Lopez at the Henrietta Memorial Center for the team's 2001 reunion. Tio Kleberg has spent his entire career at the world-famous King Ranch of South Texas. From 1971 to 1978, he managed the King Ranch cattle, wildlife, farm, and horse operations. He served as secretary-treasurer of King Ranch from 1974 to 1980 and on the board of directors from 1974 to 1988. From 1979 to 1988, he managed the South Texas agricultural operations. The board was reorganized in 1988, and Kleberg became vice president of agri-business with operations in Texas, Arizona, Florida, and Brazil. In 1998, he became a member of the King Ranch board of directors and continues to serve in that position today. Throughout the area many players, as well as their descendants, continue their involvement with baseball in one way or another. (Courtesy Donavan "Captain D" Lopez)

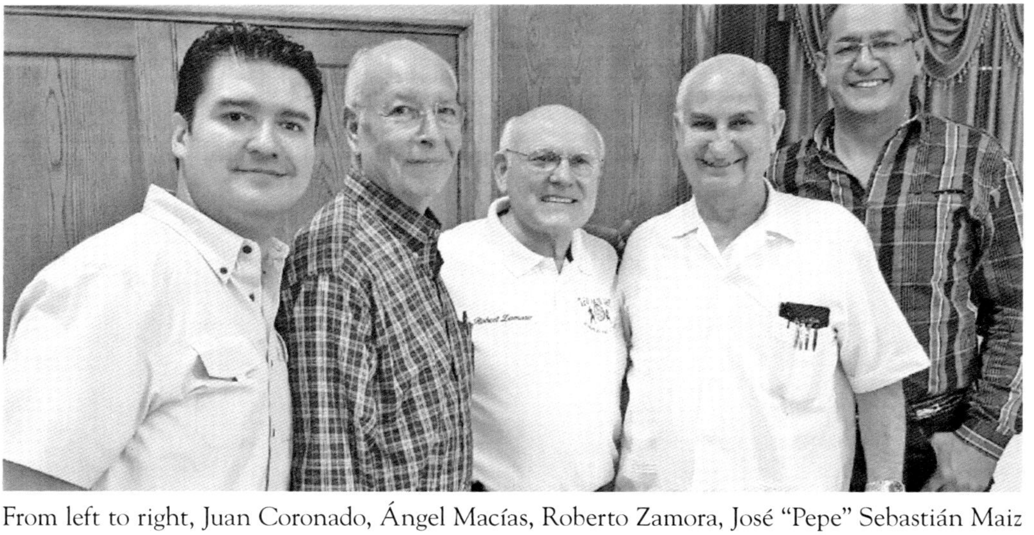

From left to right, Juan Coronado, Ángel Macías, Roberto Zamora, José "Pepe" Sebastián Maiz García, and an unidentified bodyguard are pictured at the 45th Annual Leo Najo Hall of Fame Baseball Induction Ceremony on October 1, 2016. Coronado and Zamora co-authored *Mexican American Baseball in South Texas* and were invited to a book signing in Mission, Texas. Macías and Pepe Maiz played on the 1957 Monterrey Little League championship team. Macías, the ambidextrous pitcher, threw a perfect game to clinch the World Series. Maiz has had success in numerous businesses including as owner of the Sultanes de Monterrey, a professional baseball team in Mexico, and as a politician. Maiz also serves as the national director of Little League Baseball in Mexico. (Courtesy Roberto Zamora and Juan David Coronado.)

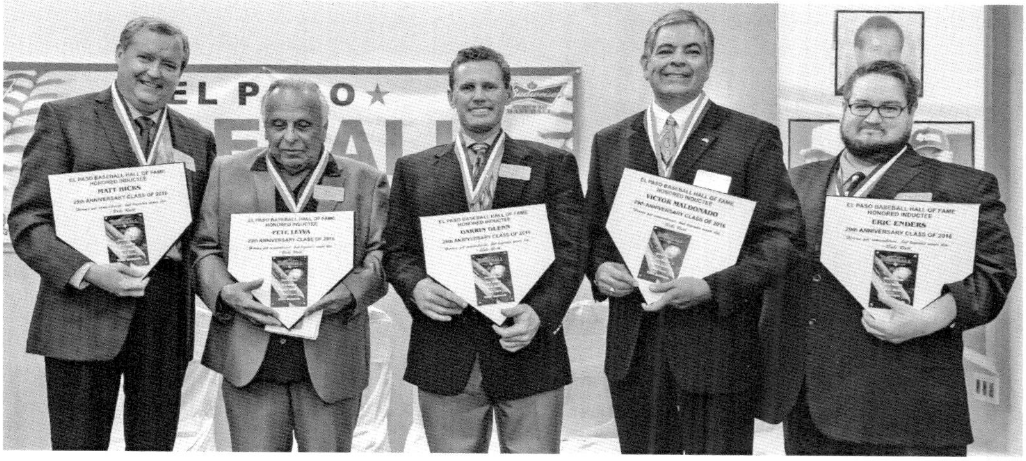

The five newest inductees into the El Paso Baseball Hall of Fame pose at the 2016 banquet. From left to right are Matt Hicks, Ben Leyva, Darrin Glenn, Victor Maldonado, and Eric Enders. Leyva accepted the honor on behalf of his late father, Ben Leyva, the founder of the minor-league El Paso Texans. Maldonado, a federal law enforcement officer, spent decades umpiring high school, college, and minor-league games. Hicks was a longtime broadcaster for the El Paso Diablos, Glenn was an infielder in the San Francisco Giants farm system, and Enders has written more than a dozen books about baseball. (Courtesy El Paso Baseball Hall of Fame.)

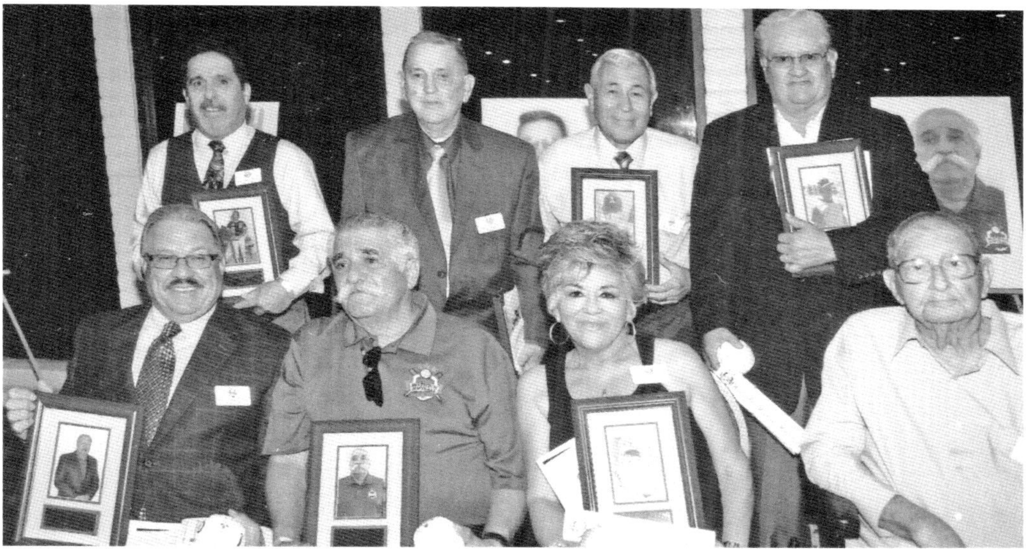

The 2015 inductees into the El Paso Softball Hall of Fame pose at the ceremony. From left to right are (first row) Enrique "Kiki" Bejarano, Jaime Frausto, Nena Olivas, and Enrique "Kiki" Gómez; (second row) Alex Montelongo, Perry Huddleston, Willie Rodríguez, and Ricardo Ramírez. Frausto was a softball legend on both sides of the border, playing in Juárez in the Liga Azteca and in El Paso in the Del Norte Division League, where he pitched eight no-hitters in five years from 1964 to 1968. Olivas accepted the award on behalf of her father, Manuel Olivas, a renowned power hitter and Bowie High School graduate who died in 1994. (Courtesy Bufe Morrison.)

LATINO BASEBALL HISTORY PROJECT ADVISORY BOARD

José M. Alamillo
Eduardo B. Almada T.
Richard Arroyo
Gabriel "Tito" Ávila Jr.
Francisco E. Balderrama
Tomás Benítez
Anna Bermúdez
Juan J. Canchola
Terry A. Cannon
Gene Chávez
David Contreras Jr.
Juan D. Coronado
Raúl J. Córdova
Christopher Docter
Peter Drier
Robert Elias
Eric Enders
Luís F. Fernández
Pete G. Flores
Maria García
Gregory Garrett
Jorge Iber
Rumado Z. Juárez
William Lange
Alfonso Ledesma
Donavan López
Enrique M. López
Jody L. and Gabriel A. López
Susan C. Luévano
Amanda Magdalena
Rod Martínez
Douglas Monroy
Carlos Muñoz Jr.
Eddie Navarro
Victoria C. Norton
Mark A. Ocegueda
Alan O'Connor
Monica Ortez
Al Padilla
Richard Peña
Al Ramos
Samuel O. Regalado
Vicki L. Ruíz
Anthony Salazar
Richard A. Santillán
Teresa M. Santillán
Marcelino Saucedo
Mikaela Selley
Ray P. Serra
Monserrath Segura
Alicia S. Stevens
Joe Talaugon
Joseph Thompson
Carlos Tortolero
Sandra L. Uribe
Elisa Urmston
David Vargas
Alejo L. Vásquez
Angelina F. Veyna
Alfonso Villanueva Jr.
Robert Zamora

BIBLIOGRAPHY

Bevill, Lynn E. *Outlaw Baseball Players in the Copper League: 1925–27.* Thesis. Silver City, NM: Western New Mexico University, 1988.

Corpus Christi Caller-Times.

Cypher, John. *Bob Kleberg and the King Ranch: A World Wide of Seas.* Austin, TX: University of Texas Press, 1996.

El Paso Times, The.

Flores, Pete G. *An Authorized Biography: And Then There Were Seven: The Untold Story . . . Bowie High School 1949 Texas State Baseball Champions.* 2012.

Fye, Sandra. *Historic Photos of El Paso.* Nashville, TN: Turner Publishing, 2008.

Goodwyn, Frank. *Life on the King Ranch.* New York, NY: Crowell, 1951.

Herrera, Ken. *And Then There Were Seven: The Untold Story . . . Bowie High School 1949 Texas State Baseball Champions.* Black Dog Studios, 2012.

Hunter, Cecilia Aros and Leslie Gene Hunter, eds. *Historic Kingsville, Texas: A Guide to the Original Town Site.* Kingsville, TX: Kingsville Historical Development Board, 1994.

Iber, Jorge. *Mike Torres: A Baseball Biography.* Jefferson, NC: McFarland & Company, 2016.

Ingram, Bob. *Baseball: From Browns to Diablos.* El Paso, TX: Paul Brothers Publishing, 1991.

Kingsville Record and Bishop News.

Kleberg County Historical Commission. *Kleberg County, Texas.* Kingsville, TX: Kleberg County Historical Commission, 1976.

Lea, Tom. *The King Ranch.* Boston, MA: Little, Brown, 1957.

López, Donavan. *Practice! Practice! Practice! The History of the King Ranch Cowboys Baseball Team.* Kingsville, TX: Captain D Publishing, 1998.

———. *The Compromise: The History of the Texas A&I University Los Paisanos Athletic Club.* Kingsville, TX: Captain D Publishing, 2005.

Metz, Leon C. *An Illustrated History of El Paso.* Woodland Hills, CA: Windsor Publications, 1980.

Obojski, Robert. *Bush League: A History of Minor League Baseball.* New York, NY: Macmillan Publishing Company, 1975.

Romo, David Dorado. *Ringside Seat to a Revolution: An Underground Cultural History of El Paso and Juárez 1893–1923.* El Paso, TX: Cinco Puntos Press, 2005.

Sánchez, Ray. *El Paso's Greatest Sports Heroes I Have Known.* El Paso, TX: Mesa Publishing, 1989.

Santillán, Richard A., et al. *Mexican American Baseball in the Alamo Region.* Charleston, SC: Arcadia Publishing, 2015.

———. *Mexican American Baseball in South Texas.* Charleston, SC: Arcadia Publishing, 2016.

———. *Mexican American Baseball in Houston and Southeast Texas.* Charleston, SC: Arcadia Publishing, 2017.

Wolff, Alexander. "The Barrio Boys." *Sports Illustrated,* June 27, 2011.